"Felix White's beautifully, elegantly and passionately written book
reminds me why I love cricket so much.
And reading, come to that."
Stephen Fry

"Blisteringly frank, brilliantly funny and profoundly thoughtful."
Radio Times

"Sparklingly sums up how an all-consuming passion can punctuate
and enhance just about every aspect of life."
Daily Telegraph

"This is a tender, hilarious and perceptive coming-of-age tale
to make both your heart and sides ache. Felix White has delivered
a phenomenal writing debut."
Pete Paphides, author of Broken Greek

"Felix White's honest and slightly nutty memoir has a lovely
loop to it. I was often surprised and moved by his passionate
understanding of cricket as comfort, consolation
and rock and roll remedy."
Toby Jones, actor

"The love of cricket is both communal and individual.
Felix has a wonderful knack of evoking both in a book full of life,
joy and resilience."
Gideon Haigh, author of On Warne

It's Always Summer Somewhere

It's Always **Summer** Somewhere

A matter of life & cricket

Felix White

First published in Great Britain in 2021 by Cassell,
an imprint of Octopus Publishing Group Ltd
Carmelite House
50 Victoria Embankment
London EC4Y 0DZ
www.octopusbooks.co.uk

An Hachette UK Company
www.hachette.co.uk

First published in paperback in 2022

ISBN 9 781 78840 365 8

A CIP catalogue record for this book is available from the British Library.

Printed and bound in the United Kingdom

10 9 8 7 6 5 4 3 2 1

This FSC® label means that materials used for the product
have been responsibly sourced.

Contents

Part 2

AUTHOR'S NOTE

I t's nine months after *It's Always Summer Somewhere* was first published, and I am sitting in A&E at King's College Hospital in South-East London.

Only two hours earlier, I was at the Oval nets just down the road, faithfully queueing at the end of my mark, twirling a heavily-doctored-with cricket ball in my left hand as if I were clicking my fingers, wearing an incredibly over-sized Beatles t-shirt I bought on an American tour once. As you will learn in the pages of this book, the Oval is a significant place for me. I have been going to the same nets there in an extremely uncommitted, half-hearted and daydreamy way for thirty years. It must show a little, as a friend of mine genuinely asked me the other day whether I get tingles every time I drive past it (I don't – I drive past the Oval about twice a day, so that would mean an unrealistic amount of tingles). But, with its indoor practice space being the only one available and the same one that Test and County cricketers use, it has had a habit in each of those three decades of occasionally lulling me into the realms of deep fantasy. The optimistic – when their guard is down – are encouraged to sense there might just be a moment when, through the sheer physical alchemy of this shared space, they might suddenly become capable of more than they are.

I haven't been necessarily lulled into that state of mind this week, but I have been relieved by the feeling of the ball come out of my hand, watching it float with no malice whatsoever towards the batters at the other end. It's been a while since I've done it and it feels familiar, safe and for some reason woolly and blissful in a mundane way. The last "spinner" has had their go. It's me again. I'm into the process. The sleight of hand. The few ambitious clicks of the ball, as if it will actually spin this time. The turning up of the shoulder of the t-shirt, then the exposed arm signalling left for no apparent reason whatsoever before it takes the ball from the other hand, making way for the hop, skip, jump I have faithfully (and wildly unsuccessfully) acted out for all this time. It's just that on this occasion, I don't even get to the jump. I just get to the hop, sk–. There are two sudden, harsh noises. It feels like someone has kicked me very hard in the back of the leg. I look behind and no-one is anywhere near me. The next time I put pressure on my right leg, I can't walk.

And as I am waiting in A&E (I hobbled there and it took ages), gently developing nodding terms with all the others hunched over or being sick into buckets or idling away the time for no reason visible to me yet, I am finally called in to be seen. It takes a long time to walk over to the doctor's office, what with my new limp that introduced itself mid-skip, so there is time for another patient-in-waiting to look up and, after a flickering moment of recognition, say to me: "Did you get that bowling your lovely, loopy stuff?"

I've been grateful for many things since writing this book. The many conversations on unprocessed grief with people that have read bits of themselves in the story. The opportunities I've had to speak to all the people who have been close at different times in my life and finding an "It was all quite good actually, wasn't it?" closure with each of them. The surreal privilege of reaching out and contacting each of the cricketers that have shaped my life in some way. The indulgence of compartmentalising a whole adulthood making music. The strangers that have found a way to tell me – in complete sworn secrecy – that they privately wish loss upon their teams too but have never dared say it. It was worthwhile for all those reasons tenfold, but it would have been worth it for the A&E recognition alone.

For that one moment, as we acknowledge each other and I tell him that yes, I did actually get it bowling lovely, loopy stuff, I put myself in the mind of the other patients that briefly observe our interaction. They don't know that he has read my book or what it's about. I imagine them considering that maybe I *am* a professional cricketer, and he is simply enquiring about an injury because, well, that's what I'm famous for. Then I picture an eight-year-old me, watching this in a vision of the future from somewhere and thinking, "Yes, I *did* make it. I knew it."

It was a torn calf muscle, by the way. Apparently, it happens at this age, when you don't stretch.

Felix
February 2022

All the Right Notes, But Not
Necessarily in the Right Order

I t gets in there. It gets in there in ways I tell it to, and it gets in there in ways I do not. I might be crossing the street blurry-eyed in the morning and – stopping for a bus to pass just in front of me – I experience myself not as a pedestrian waiting at an intersection, but as a brave opening bat, swerving inside a bouncer amid a barrage of high-quality fast bowling. Later the same day I am idling in the aisles of a supermarket and pick up a banana but, before dropping it into the basket among the rest of the groceries, I find I am using it as an imaginary bat, flicking an imaginary ball through imaginary mid-wicket for an imaginary quick single.

As I walk home, I am watching my own feet over the pavement slabs and, stepping slightly beyond a crack that separates one from the other, I curse myself for breaching the line and bowling a no ball. Unforgivable at this level, I tell myself, looking up at the sky and noticing London is its unmistakable grey under low-hanging clouds. The ball might swing this morning, I duly note. When I'm home, a glass falls from a shelf and I react with inspired instinct to catch it, juggling it for a second before safely snaffling it at the second attempt. There is a pause as I look at it in my hands, for a second braced for the impact of my celebrating teammates as they run to imaginarily submerge me. Then, as the evening draws in, I find myself batting again, playing more expansive shots now with a tube of toothpaste – by this point I am well set and batting fluidly – and have introduced the sound of a leather ball hitting a bat to the fantasy, articulating a "cluck" at the precise moment the imaginary ball would have hit the imaginary bat and imaginarily sailed for an imaginary four. As my head hits the pillow, another day in the world of the banal navigated, I reel through some looming to-do list for the next morning but find I am not imagining it as a list at all, but as the vital second morning of an imaginary Test match. If I can get through *that,* I say to myself, it will get easier throughout the day. It always does.

Cricket can be in anything and anything can be in cricket. It plunges into the subconscious; a deep, complex map of evolving ritual, strange beauty, Darwinian projections, the completely pointless and the wildly meaningful: sudden action bookended by lengthy nothingness, ready to surface and explain my world back at me – even if the explanation, on occasion, is simply that everything is absolutely fucked.

Satisfying answer or otherwise, it has been my roadmap for growing up. There were untold other things that could have latched themselves into my psyche and acted as an accompaniment to the series of joys, successes, complications and losses one must attempt to process in life. Indeed, there often have been. For me, it's just that the enduring one has happened to be cricket. It was only in eventually unpacking it all, in the pages of this book, that I had to finally concede to myself that maybe *all* those feelings weren't really about cricket after all.

PART 1

Why Cricket?

B uried inside a family album, among old school books and discarded teddy bears, there is a picture of me as a six-year-old. I'm perched on the front of a sofa (so reminiscent that I can smell and feel it just by the rug thrown over it), with my legs at full stretch yet not quite reaching the floor. I'm focusing on something with a curious half-daze. If you squint to dwell on the photograph, giving your eyes a second to acclimatise to the faded black-and-white image, you can make out the title of the book, held tightly in my hands. It simply says, in very big letters: CRICKET.

Being now in the slipstream of life where friends and family are bringing up children, I recognise the handing of a book to a child as an exercise in forging a brief respite from the duck-like existence (kicking manically underwater, totally calm above) that is young parenthood. I don't imagine that giving me a book about cricket was inspired by anything other than the same motivation, me being the eldest of three boys. In this case, however, I'm taking the bait as something far more serious than a distraction tactic. This wasn't a cricket book at all. It was a hard sell into another dimension and, consequently, a decision for me to make. It's my blue pill/red pill crossroads. I am inside the wardrobe about to push through the winter coats and into Narnia. I'm looking into the *NeverEnding Story*, as yet unaware that it is my own tale I am about to read. I have come to think of that image, captured among mounds of less momentous familial photography of the time, as a sliding-doors moment in my life. The decision must have been made there and then. Cricket it was going to be.

Typically for cricket, the odds were not stacked in its favour. My dad, Andrew, from the Isle of Wight and of no cricketing disposition, was aged 36 at the time, my age as I write. From a Christian and working-class background, the middle of five siblings, he was in the vortex of the most chaotic and productive spell in his life, juggling his three children – me, Hugo and Will – with what he would describe as a left-field career in construction, architecture and urban design. A speculative move across the water to London, against the traditions of his surroundings, was now many years behind him. Being the sole family archivist, he is the odds-on favourite to have taken the photo. Importantly in this case, too, six years previously he had privately wished for me to be a girl. He was not enamoured at the prospect of having to engage in the sideline shouting activities at sporting events that having a son cuts the odds on so dramatically. That context adds a small yet vital tension to the photo, as if he is whispering, "Red pill, red pill, red pill" as he clicks the Minolta Hi-Matic which now sits on the shelf at mine.

My mother, Lana, was born in Lebanon – her Palestinian mother, Abla, and English father, Harry, meeting when work took him to design and install telecom lines there – before she was moved to England for a childhood in convent boarding schools, feeding carrots to photos of Jeff Astle and David Cassidy under her desk. She met my father in a social circle of unattached and disparate souls in their twenties that London tends to produce. She was a book editor by then. Her younger brother, Paul, was so bruised by his own boarding-school cricketing experience of being bowled first ball following a record highest opening partnership that he would mention it well into his forties. It didn't do anything special off the pitch, he would say, he just missed it. It was a genuine source of curiosity for me that, every Christmas, he would find a moment to shoehorn this dismissal into conversation. It was as if he was attempting to exorcise a humiliation he could never rid himself of, one year trying it on for size as slapstick, the next with an earnestness worthy of empathic ears. If it did indeed land on such, there was a deeper, more pointed memory that would follow – dropping a catch as the school wicketkeeper. It was shin height and he caught it, but as the slip cordon went up to celebrate, it fell out of his gloves. As he went to retrieve the ball, he overheard his teammate spit, "Oh, fucking hell, Odell." He could never unhear it. I had never heard it in the first place and yet, somehow, I felt as if I couldn't unhear it either.

In any case, my parents continued chasing an endless thread of noticing what piqued an interest in me, gauging whether it was healthy and/or appropriate and then, where possible, encouraging it. More books arrived, each as potent as the last in their own cricket-themed silencing techniques. I can still read them page by page in my mind's eye. The first was a literary sledgehammer, casting an incision in anything I had known up until then: *Postman Pat Plays for Greendale*.

The cover, ominously, pictured Pat looking obviously distressed and mid-flight underneath a ball circling him from great height. Losing the toss and fielding, the opposition, Pencaster, scored 250 first up (I am not proud to admit that I fact-checked this against my memory and, distressingly, I was right). Assuming it was an overcast English summer, I reckon that was roughly par. Exactly par it proved to be, as Greendale, during an innings in which every single documented ball ended up either smashing glass, in a river, lost or in manure, won with a wicket to spare in an absolute nail-biter.

The illustrated book (there were about 50 words in the entire thing) presented oddly cheery images of batsmen ducking for cover as Pat aimed for their throats. He had already taken wickets earlier in the day with completely unnecessary and frankly narcissistic sledges like "Here comes another special delivery" before running in to bowl. It was pretty hostile stuff. The last man in to bat, too, Pat won the game, for some reason batting without gloves but with a helmet. Already a hero of mine for his conscientious community-based work, this being long before I knew of Botham's Ashes in 1981, it solidified him in my mind as the first true great of the game. Soon you could add to that list Brian Brain, whose far more grown-up book than what I could fathom, *Another Day, Another Match*, featured a cover image of four old men looking over a county cricket game. It was a view, deeply foreign then, that in time I would become overfamiliar with myself. The book gave me the sole takeaway, via the occasional rapid flick-through for fear of the grave information inside, that cricket happened a lot, went on forever and mainly everybody involved was bored by it. Still, warning signs aside, the wormhole was open and these instruction manuals propelled me – cautiously, but undeniably – further down it.

Ensuring my two bibles were glued to my side from this moment forward, I was yet to really see a game of cricket at all. There was every chance that the sport could have been slowly dispensed with among the fire engines, dinosaurs and rubber hammers with which it then competed. That summer, though, the fates conspired to drag me further towards the inevitable. For a child burdened with a more sensitive disposition than usual, acutely aware of imbalance at every juncture and striving to police playtime equilibrium before going home to gender-neutral toys, I was already knowingly – if quietly – contradicted, struggling with a part of myself that still wanted to seek out some sort of battle.

It's still laser-sharp in my recall. The shop window of Arding & Hobbs, in Clapham Junction, that early summer of 1990. The proudly dressed-up batter in all its gladiatorial glory. En route to the big Asda, ten minutes down the road, for the fortnightly shop, I turned my head slowly 180 degrees to fixate on the display as we marched past, and I immediately began to formulate how I might be one day dressed exactly like that mannequin. Clocking that we would be returning the same way we had come in order to get home from the supermarket, I resolved to buy some more time with the display later that afternoon. I ensured it became non-negotiable when we did return, simply turning and stopping mid-High Street, letting my hand go limp in Lana's until she released it, and staring back through the window. She must have waited for me, because I wasn't ushered through the general chaos of moving pedestrian traffic.

*

As far as I am aware, in that imperceptible moment, it is me, aged six, and the kit in the window. With time taking on a strangely elongated format, I look up from eye level, noticing each facet and how each is more cartoonish than even my books have led me to believe. Clunky, spiked sports shoes. Tick. Pads bizarrely reminiscent of astronaut get-up. Tick. I tilt my head back further, each accessory confirming an instinct that minutes before had been far less nameable. Thigh pad. Makes sense. Chest guard. Bit odd, but fine. Arm guard. Brilliant. Bat held aloft. Sword. Gloves. Tick, tick, tick. Slowly, now really arching my head as far as it can go, staring almost totally skywards to view the top third of the already elevated mannequin's attire, I view the last piece. A grille-less helmet. It isn't exactly clear where it offers any protection – as if you might have to deliberately go to ram the ball with your cranium, like a cow, in order for the hard lid to do its job. Most importantly, though, for the target audience of one in this impromptu sales pitch, it simply presents itself as a more palatable piece of streetwear than a Roman centurion's helmet. Cricketers were going onto a metaphorical battlefield, I understood this from Pat's sledging, and yet I still required an extenuating circumstance to indulge this reluctant urge of being involved in some sort of combat, without actually being shot at. With an urge for competition pushing its way through my body in the hope of finding some air, the mannequin resembles, for a moment before I am finally ushered on, gloriously attainable and acceptable army surplus.

*

Armed with this vision of a (static polystyrene) cricketer to aid my literary references, very gently acquiring cricket gear deemed generally wearable in public, the perfect storm unfolding within me began to find some hospitable conditions. Every other week, we were driven to our grandparents, on my mother's side, in Purley to spend our Sundays. The journey to the outskirts of London took roughly an hour – enough time for an album and a half. These were important musical field trips. Once we were squeezed into the back

8

of the car, the tape would go on. There were three perma-nently in there, loose in the glove box. Nudging each other back and forth to acquire half an inch more space as the proprietor of the back of the seat (the loser would have to slightly lean forward for the duration), me and the brothers sat and listened.

Firstly, there was *The Best of Van Morrison*. Without any visual aid, we were forced to hear this at once wild and slick voice and conjure up a face and shape. I imagined one that was years later to strike me as exactly that of Rick Astley. In "Here Comes the Night", recorded by his first band Them but compiled onto the collection, Van was experiencing such epic feelings of hurt at seeing his ex-girlfriend in the arms of someone else that he was driven to publicly offload the unthinkable scenario inside a visceral beast of rhythm and blues. As he wailed the song's title, strung out and desperate, I would lean forwards, losing the comfier place on the seat, and sigh. It sounded so terrible that, to a child thirsty for life experience of any description, it was acutely desirable. I could only dream of being able to go through something as terrible as that one day myself.

After earth-shattering heartbreak and aspirational pain, the allure of the gang was piqued through The Beatles' *Live at the BBC* sessions. In it, racing through a collection of standards, an early incarnation of The Beatles experi-encing the thrill of Beatlemania, yet nowhere near the ad nauseum that forced them to retreat from it, you could hear them giggle between songs. John Lennon, dripping with the dismissive charm with which he would navigate much of his public life, when asked to introduce himself by a palpably older, Queen's English host, cracked, "Hi, I'm John. I play the guitar and I sometimes play the fool." The infectious appeal, somehow preserved on that tape and transmitted straight into my pores 30 years later, was that we were listening to a group for whom a set of rules applied to them alone. An impenetrable force ensured that however coldly they were interrogated, admittedly not particularly during this session, the unit never broke their schtick, their flippant take on anything forever unharmed. The idea that packs of people could protect each other from the pressures of the outside world by simply not taking anything seriously at all nestled itself, gently if unflinchingly, into my impressionable if uncomfortable soul, leaning forward in the seats so far I could feel the seatbelt squeeze. The between-songs interviews on the tape did not reveal that John and Paul McCartney had both lost their mothers at a young age and had found each other just in time, prioritising their days since with determined resolve to make music of their own.

When the live sessions ended, side B grinding to its click in the car – which would momentarily jolt awake one of the sleeping passengers – I'd usually ask for more Beatles. The only "more Beatles" option landed us five years later to the bruised *White Album*. It being a studio album and not a recorded radio session, there was no chat, of course; instead there were songs so adjacent that they pulled each other apart, scrapping for ground across a double album where it was hard to work out where you were within it and how long was left at any one time. There were songs that sounded like nursery rhymes, disturbingly dark ones, and other rock'n'roll numbers like the standards of years previously but with life's twisted experience stitched into them. "Revolution 9", the penultimate song, was an endless loop of deranged noise amid chatter and a man, not unlike the one interviewing them all those years earlier, repeating "Number nine" again and again. A scream lasted uncomfortably long enough for it to become applause. Random words in conversation were panned chaotically either side of the speakers. A nightwatchman was talked about. I felt as if I were being tuned in and out of a station that refused to come into discernible being, a trip that threatened never to end and yet when it did Ringo suddenly turned up to sing us all goodnight in lullaby form to conclude the record. It was like being filled with a month's worth of sweets and sat in front of *The Shining*, then told to go to sleep immediately. Was this what happened to units when they were pulled apart over the unavoidable path of collective effort and time? In any case, with nothing but a tape and the back of my parents' heads for company as these thrilling, terrifying other worlds were beamed through, Van and The Beatles had planted a seed which needed a view in which to flourish.

When we arrived, minds sufficiently scrambled by the music we'd ingested, the house of my grandparents, an unusual couple in their cultural blend of Arabic Palestinian and English, was always a source of hysterical excitement. An old suburban detached house, it was removed from London as we knew it and dimly enough lit inside to make it feel like a journey back in time. The garden heightened this sense of adventure, sprawling out to points where it was unclear whether it had ended and the wilderness had begun. A fallen tree from a storm in the early 1980s, for example, lay slain and abused as a climbing frame for its afterlife. Our grandpa, Harry, would answer the door without exception by saying, "No, no, no milk today, thank you" and closing the door back on us. Despite knowing the gag as if watching a rerun, we would never find it anything but uncontrollably funny. We knew that in a couple of hours he would pronounce roast potatoes "roast pa-too-tees" and we would find that, too, uncontrollably funny. He had found a reinvigorated purpose in the latter stages of his life in finding ways to say yes and yes alone to his grandchildren and then actioning the premise even if it seemed impossible. He was our king of invention, our mad professor of economic childlike fantasy and our practitioner of play.

The garden was a walking exhibit of this. A tyre from a tractor was hung from a tree, suspended vertically, undoubtedly with extreme danger, by ever-thinning rope to make "the twirly whirly". The concept of the twirly whirly was quite simple. You sat on the tyre and Harry spun you round until you either felt sick or actually were sick. It was fairly route-one thrill-seeking. There was a tree house, too, with actual floors, boarded up with nails popping out at child's eye level and real electric light switches patched in at high voltage. He had somehow, also probably at great danger, managed to drag electricity across the soaked grass from the main house to the new one, fast becoming an example of why you shouldn't follow a child's every request. It was ravaged in a raid one evening when the police used it to leverage a view of a local burglar vaulting through the back gardens of Purley. The boards had unsurprisingly failed to take their weight and, in the wake of the brief viewing experiment, the temporary benefactors of the vantage point failed to do anything but vacate the broken tree house they'd made no use of. Undoubtedly disguising some frustration at years of amateur DIY being destroyed, Harry ploughed on to the next

Me and my coach.

invention. It was no bother: he always had another project to deliver. Sensing the cricketing enthusiasm building in me, evident in the incremental amassing of books I was bringing and the cricket gear I was being given permission to wear in daily life, he embarked on his biggest test yet and appointed himself my personal cricket coach.

If he was going to be a cricket coach, he was going to need a cricket pitch. My grandma, Abla, was a proud Palestinian, of Christian faith and staunchly non-cricket. Her interest had ended in the younger days of romance, when they had tried to blend their interests into one another and she had agreed to play in a game with Harry. She had been told, romantically, that she was going to be the wicketkeeper. A ball – I'm using my imagination here, as this was not her exact explanation – reared up from a length on a pitch starting to produce variable bounce and smashed her in the face. She walked around with a black eye for two weeks and, safe to say, that was where they left it. I don't think it was related to this specific incident, more a general accumulation between the 50 years that had passed and whatever the falling-out happened to be that day, but the most common place to find her was inside the house rolling her eyes at her husband, muttering something in Arabic. When she'd had enough, she would lean out of the kitchen window, overlooking the garden, shout "*Yala! Yala!*" and usher us in. Peppering my days with peripheral conversations with other adults on the plight of the Palestinians, she was the kind of woman who would look me square in the eyes, a six-year-old child, and pledge that we had an "understanding" together. I wasn't sure what this understanding meant or was, but it was nonetheless reassuring to have one; plus I knew if I nodded to indicate I was on the *exact* same wavelength, I'd be allowed free rein of the freezer, a horizontal slab the size of a bath, where you had to wrench yourself up and into it, feet dangling and arms reaching into the frozen paradise, to find one of the never-ending supplies of choc ices. She had the grace to notice the cricket mission and – no doubt mindful that I had taken the blue pill, was through Narnia and couldn't go back even if I tried – she fielded our canvassing for a pitch to be "built".

The building of the cricket pitch required two things: a lawn-mower, to differentiate the pitch from the grass where the wild looked to be encroaching, and stumps. I wasn't in the board meeting when Harry pitched this to Abla; I only heard latterly, to a swell of memorable relief, that a favourable compromise had been reached. The pitch was approved as long as the grass remained relatively long and, most importantly, the stumps were painted green. This was a garden, not a cricket pitch, and the theory was that if they were green, they would blend into the background and not present an eyesore for Abla when she gazed out onto her garden, already encroached upon by tyres and slides and broken climbing frames. Green stumps it was. If anything, that made their presence feel even more bizarre. They looked like green stumps in a post-apocalyptic assault course.

With a pitch laid out and the beginning stages of building my technique underway (a series of "drills" that often required me to throw tennis balls underarm at Harry, him blocking them, re-marking his guard, then instructing me to repeat), the ever-rising passion was finally enforced, and at last sealed, with some now vital contextual help. Cricket was on terres-trial television then as a matter of course, like a net cast out and waiting for a niche pocket of obsessives to swim towards it; all I had to do was turn it on and it was there waiting for me. Test match cricket. And there *they* were waiting for me, too. The England cricket team right at the beginning of the 1990s. A group of men looking serious about what seemed to be very little going on. Visibly overweight men. Slight, strangely gaunt men. Gigantic men with little towels tucked into their trou-sers, and shoes with the ends cut out so their white-socked big toes poked through. Flawed, scruffy, each in their own way charismatic men who were given eight hours a day of prime-time television for standing around in ill-fitting white clothes. What's more, these men of every conceivable shape of young manhood, looking perennially concerned, were technically athletes. It was a source of gargantuan comfort. I could feel my expression, the curious half-daze, return. This time it concealed something slightly more tangible and memorable: giddy excitement first and, as a subtle aftertaste, belonging. "You can leave me here from now on," I said in an imaginary conversation with the world. "I'm going to be OK one foot away from this screen where they keep promising me the next passage of play is going to be the really important one."

I had found some bizarre Venn diagram where the music I had heard somehow correlated to the cricketers I saw. When I turned on the television to find cricket, and saw in the top left-hand corner of the screen, as the bowler ran in, a line of four people crouching on delivery, then relaxing, kicking divots into the ground, inspecting the back of their hands and whispering in-jokes, before repeating, as far as I was concerned I was watching The Beatles. What were they giggling about together?

The Fab Four.

Thorpe, Hick, Hussain, Russell.

What was the source of this suspended youth? I had found the Fab Four. They were Graham Thorpe, Graeme Hick, Nasser Hussain and Jack Russell: The Beatles live at the BBC. There, personified, were the faces to that sound, the gang I wanted to be in but had no access route to. I felt as if there was no place more worth belonging to than a slip cordon.

The thing about this England team, which was infinitely clear and permeated through everything they did, was that they lost a lot. They were starting pretty much a decade of losing. Like a perfect tragedy, it was as if, on some undetected level beneath the surface, they already knew it too. It was written on all of their faces and forced itself into their body language, forever worried and arched. I thought of Van Morrison singing "Here Comes the Night". The aspirational pain that I searched for was here, on this screen, in the sleepless torment they were all so obviously going through. Australia would close a day 400 without loss having lost the toss (this is an exaggeration, if slight) and as the bowed players left, I'd imagine them turning in the night, singing in Van's tortured tones before the sun, cruelly rising again, forced them to show their faces for another public whipping. It wasn't a version of Rick Astley that song belonged to at all, it was the Fab Four at slip plus Phil DeFreitas, Chris Lewis, Mark Ramprakash et al. The pain and the injustice seeped through the television and into me – I didn't even get a chance to recognise it happening. Before I knew it, there they were: a touchpoint for hurt, betrayal, harsh fate, catastrophe and disaster. There were handfuls of flashpoint images, now seared into my mind in quick roll-call succession. Michael Atherton knocking a bin over with his bat when he thought he was out of view of the cameras. Alan Mullally catching the ball the wrong side of the stumps and interrupting a certain match-changing run-out in Australia. Adam Hollioake being bowled leaving a ball from Shane Warne that pitched on middle stump and continued on to hit middle stump. Graham Thorpe dropping the ball at slip and then kicking it, out of anger, for more runs. Music's beautiful pain visualised. My commitment was to be here, to this obviously doomed cause, because that's where life's juice obviously was. It combined to produce something new rising in me. It was a feeling that was to become familiar over time, one I would silently be able to re-access again and again.

When we left the house in Purley, Harry would walk to the end of the bushy driveway and, left arm aloft, wave us into the distance. We would sit contorted in our seats, waving back, until all we could see was a tiny flicker on the horizon, arms still waving us home. Occasionally he would forget that his right hand was holding his trousers tight to his waist and, just as we began to disappear, he'd throw it up to the air too. We'd be left with the faint vision of his trousers falling down to his ankles as he continued waving us into the distance regardless,

17

looking forward to the no milk and the roast pa-too-tees and the cricket drills that would be there in two weeks' time.

One Easter, many years before it became my cricket-coaching spiritual home, my parents were halfway through the same drive home from the grandparents when Lana's vision began to blur. She had grown tired with regularity over a gentle period of time; a foggy, unnatural tiredness that had been explained away until then as a consequence of having three young children. It was uncommon for her to complain about anything at all. Yet still, while we slept in the back, she remarked, somewhat heavily, "I really can't see very well." It caused a small pool of worry in Andrew. We were dropped at home, left with a neighbour to sleep and they headed to St George's hospital. Sent promptly to the optical department, she was handed an eye chart; it became clear, very quickly, that she could hardly see at all. It was optic neuritis, the neurologist said. And with that came the first mention of the two letters, unknown and abstract then, obstinate and immovable since: "It's a classic sign of MS."

Her eyesight recovered and relapsed that summer while she waited to be sent to the neurologists some months later. On her return, in a mesh of unremembered words and strangely formal information, she was diagnosed officially with multiple sclerosis. It was an illness that could vary wildly from one person to another, they were told. There was no cure, they were told next. There were some other bits about the science. They walked out of the room, back into a world that looked exactly the same, but felt suddenly like one that merely resembled the one they had known before walking in. Their shared hope was that she would maybe have poor eyesight and be tired from time to time. That would be hard, but it would be fine. She was still a perfectly capable mother, looking after her three children throughout the days, encouraging drawing on walls and improvisational dancing to Prince records and free-form reinterpretations of the haka. For a moment, it felt like something that might just leave, a mere inconvenience. Then, she began to feel inexplicably cold. The tiredness returned. It left, then returned again. She needed more frequent help in the house. More of the statements like the first, small admission in the car would begin to litter day-to-day conversation. Her ankle didn't work. She couldn't use her foot properly. And then, most damagingly, came the liberties that society began to take. The optic neuritis was causing strobing in her eyes so, while she was driving, the road that she was looking at would sometimes move up and down and momentarily disappear. She went to a disability driving instructor, who told her she could never drive again and took her licence from her.

Walking us to school still, Lana's leg, very subtly, had started to drag behind her as she went. Unnoticeable at first, it became pronounced enough that she came accompanied with a walking stick. It was an issue, the walking stick. She didn't want one. She didn't need one. At first, she walked with it tucked under her arm, serving no purpose, as her leg lightly dragged behind her. Slowly, through another fog of denial then reluctant acceptance, it lowered until it propped her up, serving its primary function. In these early days of protracted illness, as we grew up alongside it, my parents threw themselves into the research. How could there be no cure anywhere? There must be a cure somewhere. There were a lot of suggestions and a lot of theories. Holistic. Medicinal. Cerebral. They gathered information, scattered hope in the form of all these speculative therapies and, armed with a list of bullet-pointed questions, Lana booked herself into endless doctors' consultations. She would return more confused and more frustrated than she had left.

After a few visits, she asked Andrew to come with her. She wasn't getting anywhere, she said, she couldn't penetrate the language the doctors used and needed someone else to help her pick apart what was being said. He came. The consultant, to Andrew's shock, was simply, repeatedly, saying, "I'm sorry,

Young parenthood.

but there's nothing that can be done." Lana would hear it and immediately put her head back to her list to ask another question gathered from that week's field trip of wishful thinking. He would respond to the next question with the same answer. She'd ask another. The same answer. The entire consultation followed this shape and so, it turned out, had the previous visits. Her list again reaching its conclusion, the neurologist left them finally with something that Andrew could hear for Lana, "Look, there is no cure. If we thought there was a cure, we'd be doing it, even if it meant rubbing tea leaves. There's nothing." And with that, him absorbing the information that she could not, they made a decision between them. Rather than be unable to give their children the time they needed and continue searching for a cure that did not exist, they would instead spend their lives living each moment, being parents first and hoping that the incremental invasion they were promised but not guaranteed would be kinder than it had been to some.

As a child dreaming up versions of fanatical suffering through music and visions of adult responsibility via cricket, I haven't noticed that her handwriting in the phone diary has started to become illegible. The warning signs have just eventually, without any specific moment of arrival, phased into reality. One day, being driven home by a nanny, more inconspicuously consistent in their presence but culturally nourishing enough that we can all now do the dance to "Boom! Shake the Room" by DJ Jazzy Jeff and The Fresh Prince, we come to a sudden halt. She is there, by the side of the road, inexplicably collapsed on the ground, her legs bent underneath her in a sort of V-shape. She smiles as the nanny jumps out of the car, scoops down to lift her and drop her into the passenger's seat. Her legs, she doesn't explain then, still laughing as if to present the (slightly confusing) storyline of "Silly me, I fell over", have given way and won't move. Police, she doesn't explain to us then either, have walked past and assumed her to either be begging or drunk and left her, despite her asking for help, on the floor in the background. She smiled still. It was nothing to worry about.

It was true. There was no cure for MS. It's hard to recollect any surge of desperation that must have run through her as her body slowly failed her. I remember nothing. I don't even remember numbness. It did get worse all the time. But I already knew this from cricket. The game had by then communicated to me in no uncertain terms that everything, after all the effort and the worry and the stress, was absolutely not going to be all right in the end. On some level, I think I respected being told the truth.

2

Lovely, Loopy Stuff

Wednesday finally came. I sheepishly looked across and surveyed the shapes and sizes queued up alongside me in the school assembly hall. We were herded up like a bunch of missing parts.

I was new at Honeywell Primary, as Lana's declining health, still not particularly noticeable to me, had meant moving to a more manageable house on the same road as the school. Number 12 Honeywell Road had initially been an upstairs and downstairs flat. Earlier that year I'd watched Andrew take to the boarded-up division between the two with a hammer, knocking it through in a wake of fog and dust to leave one set of stairs. In a couple of years, the same set of stairs would have a chairlift built into it.

I was still finding my place inside the seemingly rigid societal structures of my new school, which covered a catchment area of Wandsworth that ranged wildly from the kids in council houses and estates to the detached, double-glazed middle-class homes (almost literally) next door, when cricket was reeled off as an option for a "free time" midweek activity. It sprung an optimistic comfort in me. I had waited a week for it to come round. Cool was not yet currency, but still it was unerringly plain as I glanced inconspicuously across this line that those applying were not a collection even the most imaginative could consider the most popular in school. A handful, mostly with double-barrelled surnames, were in full gear including sunglasses which, they told the teachers, were definitely necessary inside "because they were prescription". Others, and this made for the majority, looked as if they just assumed that whatever they were about to do would be less taxing than the other two options offered for a Wednesday afternoon. Cricket, as voiced unilaterally by my new accomplice and best friend Billy Hunt, dressed in a vest to fashion some kind of likeness for whites, "was just standing around, right?" Billy also claimed that The Jam's song of his name was written about him, despite having been released six years before his birth. I hadn't yet done this groundwork. I was just struck by how not green the stumps were. They were blue. The balls were orange. "Kwik cricket" was to be my initiation to the communal game.

Cricket had so many options. I really wasn't sure what part of it I was going to attempt to be when I wasn't sitting watching it on a screen. I certainly didn't imagine myself as one of the lineage of fast bowlers propelling themselves up to the crease and bowling at people's heads (the West Indies tour in progress at the time had given me Devon Malcolm, Angus Fraser, Courtney Walsh and Curtly Ambrose to join Postman Pat). The moment of reckoning, though, was fast approaching. Bernard, a parent who had volunteered his time to rustle up some cricket interest at the South London primary, took to his task by lobbing squidgy orange balls around in a thinly veiled guise of order – yet plainly at random – asking the recipient to bowl at batters at the other end. Eventually, he threw me one. "Felix, you know how to bowl?" I thought I did. I mean, Harry *said* I did, but he wasn't much of a gauge of anything, to be honest. His blind commitment to generous praise had by now turned all his positive enforcement into suspicious white noise. My face suddenly flushed. A blockage was thrust into my throat, as if two invisible hands had been placed around my neck from the inside. For the first time I sensed the burden of being watched. This, I thought, must be the unquantifiable pressure the commentators described on the television that separated Test cricket from the domestic form.

*

I run in towards the stumps. Executing an action as close as possible to what I remember having seen, while trying to not simply throw the ball (as a few before me undeniably had), I let go. The best way to describe the ball's flight is, well, exactly that. It takes flight. It goes airborne. Its path is very high and very slow. It comes down like a paper aeroplane, so uncertain of its destination and so detached from my vague intentions that I watch it as if in awe of some ungodly creation. Demoralised, it lands a few feet away from my opponent at the other end, who does the customary thing for a seven-year-old in a game of Kwik cricket: he chases after the ball as it comes limping to a standstill, swats at it a couple of times, missing each, before trapping it with his foot and smashing it again. The third time, he connects. The ball bounces off the walls of the school hall while the double-barrelled brigade and their "what are those things in the ground for?" counterparts become an indefinable heaving mass, swarming to collect it as the batter runs loops around the plastic blue stumps. I stand, disconnected from the chaos and totally motionless, staring into my upturned palms. The thing I had control of in those very hands just moments ago is suddenly careering around the assembly hall like an orange balloon, causing the early stages of a primal riot. I haven't dared imagine my first competitive contribution, but if I had, it wouldn't have been like this. I arrive home that evening deducing that maybe cricket divides its inhabitants into two different houses: some people live to play and others live to watch. The kids in the indoor sunglasses definitely seem to be the former, and I definitely feel like the latter.

*

Up until that evening, the telephone had not intersected with my life with any real purpose. It would ring occasionally, and sometimes one of my brothers would stealthily pick up the receiver in the other room to listen in secretly on a conversation (though that would only really gather popularity some years later when we started getting girlfriends or multiple detentions that warranted calls home), but that would be it. On this evening in 1991, though, Andrew put the phone down and walked into the other room while I was still in the process of airbrushing the orange ball I'd just launched from my memory. "I've just had a phone call from a man called Bernard," he said. I nodded. I knew a Bernard. "He asked me whether I knew my son was a talented left-arm spinner?" A left-arm spinner? What was a left-arm spinner? It didn't really matter. If Bernard thought that was what I was, that's what I was, and a *talented* one too.

The last part of the phone call was an invitation for a practice at his club the same weekend. So, collecting all the war clothes he had bought me, and no doubt quietly smarting that this was exactly the reason he had silently wished for a girl all those years ago, Andrew drove me down and I joined in my first proper net session in South London. The silence en route was two-pronged. I was full of nervous anticipation. He was no doubt stewing on the fact that if he was attached to me, and I was attached to cricket, he might forever be attached to it too.

It was awful, the noise. The sound of cricket balls being hit and reverberating around a hall. The metallic clang of the stumps being struck and then pinging back. They congealed to form an abrasive sonic boom that made me feel as if I'd walked into some kind of boxing gym meets firing range. Maybe cricket *was* like being shot at? None of the industrial clattering felt as if it had a tangible incident attached to it, either, each clang reaching you a second after the ball was hit, the sound bouncing back around off the walls. It was enough to make you instinctively duck for cover. I curtailed the desire to for long enough to be herded into another line, this time with slightly less familiar counterparts (Billy hadn't shown enough enthusiasm to receive the same phone call), and for Bernard to throw me a ball again. This time it was red, very hard, with a soft frayed seam and rough marks all over it. It was the first time I'd held one.

*

Bernard, whose relatively fleeting contribution to my life is beginning to gather oddly seismic worth, takes me to one side. "Go on, Felix, bowl me some of that lovely, loopy stuff," he says. I feel an immense gushing of pride within me. God, that really makes sense. That is who I am. I bowl lovely, loopy stuff. Without any frame of reference for this lovely, loopy stuff, and in order not to fragment this portal of his opinion on my bowling (based on one ball in Kwik cricket), I run in again. Loopy is easy, that is self-explanatory. Lovely is a more complex idea to action. It must be in the run-up. I attempt a kind of unmenacing gallop. The loveliest gallop I can muster. Lovely must mean the opposite of all the other kids who are running in from the very back of the sports hall, a few feet to my left, sweating and loose-limbed. Trotting in like some young boy's depiction of a graceful calf, I launch the ball, as loopy as I can, of course, into the air. The ball lands in a similar place to where it had ended up last week in the sports hall, only this time the batter, probably due to the fact the nets don't allow it, does not run after it. He lets it hit the net. I turn around and Bernard is smiling. It isn't clear whether the smile says, "Jesus Christ, this child is gifted" or (with hindsight the undoubted truth) that he is smirking about the dedication with which I've taken to his instruction. Either way, I am a lovely, loopy spinner. It feels totally fantastic.

*

The problem with cricket, you will find, is that if one aspect of it does indeed feel totally fantastic to you, no matter how lovely or loopy, there are another couple of disciplines that probably don't. Firstly, fielding is terrible. The ball is hard and the ball hurts. Billy had been right in part: you absolutely are expected to stand around doing nothing for large chunks of the time. It's just that, with no real warning, occasionally someone will hit that thing very hard at you while everyone turns to stare. Everything in my sensitive disposition told me to get out of the way and to do so immediately. So, when the nets were cleared for fielding drills and I was beginning to feel deeply sold short that cricket *definitely was* about getting lined up to be shot, get out of the way I did. There was no game worth participating in, let alone winning, for this.

That wasn't even half of it. The batting. Ugh. Batting. I'd done some dreaming since my Kwik cricket debut regarding, if I was a talented left-arm spinner, what my batting might entail. Even my imagination wasn't asking for much. In my head, I was the player I'd seen on TV who would watch the ball kiss the surface, see it beat the outside of my bat, purse my lips before wryly laughing to myself and nodding back at the bowler. I might even say something like "Too good for me, mate" and chuckle before dismissing it from my mind for the next delivery. That was where I hoped to find myself, as the obsolete partner who glued the story together while the gunslinger harvested the strike at the other end. In reality, told to pad up with the communal kit (nothing like the mannequin's attire), when anyone at all ran in to bowl, no matter how fast I knew them to be or not, I felt my heart rate increase alarmingly. Both of my legs, without instruction from my brain, began walking me backwards (towards where square leg would be), leaving me having to lunge miles back in the direction of the ball that would be comparatively

28

straight when it did eventually get there. This was not just traumatic and humiliating but quite a serious technical issue. Feeling the squeeze of embarrassment as the ball thudded into the nets at the back, I would salvage the situation by lunging back into roughly the right area and effecting a leave, like I'd seen on TV, holding my bat aloft in a picture of zen-like judgement.

Some years later I'd find the same trait betraying me in football. If the ball was launched into the air, I would make sure I wasn't anywhere near close enough to head it as it circled us, very gently backing further and further away as everyone looked up into the sky. Then, when the ball had begun its descent to land and I was certain it was out of plausible reach, I'd begin my gallant sprint back towards it as if I were Tony Adams on a mission to nut the ball at all costs. I fell heroically short every time. I squared it with my conscience that, in the face of my very rational fear of the ball, the *illusion* of bravery was enough. The simultaneous desire to be good at the game I loved more than anything alongside the lack of courage to even participate meant that almost every second of cricket, in reality, was a complete living nightmare.

That summer of 1991 had nearly passed and while England had admirably kept one of the great West Indian sides roughly at bay for the duration of a Test series, there had been little to lodge itself in my memory until the final game. All summer, there had been a lot of conversation about England's new left-arm spinner, yet he'd been nowhere to be seen. Phil Tufnell, an apparently prodigious talent with a reputation for being hard to handle, had made his debut in Melbourne's famous Boxing Day Test in front of 90,000 people the previous winter. While I slept unawares, the swashbuckling Australian Dean Jones had charged down the MCG pitch and hit Tufnell's second ball back at him and into his ankle. If it didn't wake me, it did wake him. Making a decent (on-field at least) account of himself in the exchanges that followed and taking his first

Test wicket in the next Test in Sydney, he was finally to make his home debut at The Oval.

England, to salvage the series, were embarking on the oft futile task of bowling at Richie Richardson et al., all cricketers who had such a trademark gait at the crease that you felt as if you were watching a boxer. The West Indies batted for two hours unharmed as I watched and waited. There was still no Tufnell. The commentators had observed that he "wasn't afraid to give the ball some air" and that he "beat players in the flight more than anything". This sounded thrillingly familiar. As the camera cut back and forth to the man in question on the boundary, looking stranded in a mindset exactly between mischievous and concerned, I was hoping that I would soon be dealt some clues about what life as a left-arm spinner entailed. When he was eventually summoned to bowl and handed the ball, his graphic came up on the screen as he marked his run-up.

Phil Tufnell. Age 25. Slow Left Arm.

The colour of the font of the time, a pastel light blue, offsets a boyish focus from his wispy short blond hair, which makes him look as if he might have been borrowed from the set of *Grange Hill*. Ripping the ball between his fingers as the umpire holds his left arm aloft, he waits. I wait some more. He then conceals the ball, like a jester giving the impression that what he is about to bowl can be magically transformed into any shape whatsoever before he arrives at the crease. He begins his run-up from behind the umpire, too, as if the batter's first sight of him will be out of a puff of smoke. It starts with a skip, before he veers acutely to his left, pumping his knees as if in imitation of the Ministry of Silly Walks, then leaping totally side on, arms wound, and releasing the ball back at an arched angle to his right. Once the ball is in flight, he pivots his whole body through and summons a kind of a click and a stamp as if the final and most important part of the trick is after the fact entirely. It is spellbinding magic. The ball – well, it is loopy. It lands in a rough patch of the pitch, spitting a bit and straightening. The left-handed Clayton Lambert, a less household-name part of the mythical West Indian batting order, yet still rattling along on 39 not out, lights up and spoons it straight into the air. Mark Ramprakash is underneath it. Momentarily the screen feels as if it has frozen, "Ramps" waiting for the ball to fall just as Postman Pat had been. He catches it. Tufnell has a wicket with the first ball I have ever seen him bowl.

Tufnell, who enjoyed plenty of airtime that day, when not bowling could be found boundary bound, trying to conceal himself giggling under his cap. England won. It was the first time they had held the West Indies to a series draw since 1973.

My mind was made up. From this moment on there could only be one reference point. Lovely and loopy was Tuffers manifest. He wasn't like everybody else. He spent his time either devilishly concocting something out of nothing or being banished to field on the boundary. If slip cordons were The Beatles, he was like a pre-breaking point Syd Barrett with a subtle Nick Drake-ish melancholy layered among the mischief. A befuddled and underused genius, he was a strange lone presence, an odd anomaly whom teammates and opponents alike were unsure whether to treat with mystical awe or alien suspicion. Regardless, there was an angle for me, a pathway open for purveyors of the lovely, loopy stuff, and it was one I intended to chase down.

The news, in terms of associational comforts, was to get better still. Even for a seven-year-old with no body-language training, Tufnell looked to share my absolute distaste for fielding. He spent his off-duty time in the field noticeably kicking his feet around at fine leg. The problem with that position in particular is, as I was to find a few years later, it comes at a risk. You are spared the jeopardy of the regular dog work of fielding, but for that respite, occasionally a pull shot will fly in your direction. The issue with that shot, a batsman negotiating a short ball to try and smash it out of the ground, is that when it's heading towards you, it has usually been hit quite hard. There is a moment in which everyone can pause, notice you are underneath it, brace themselves for the humiliation you are about to bring on yourself and wait for the disaster to unfold. This happened to Tuffers a lot. It was almost as if batting teams located where he was fielding and found him at will. The camera would pan back and forth as he palpably willed the ball not to appear in his vicinity. When the ball, still often travelling skywards, had set its course, watching Tufnell settle underneath it was like watching someone move through the stages of grief. There was denial. There was anger. There was bargaining. There was depression. Then, finally, acceptance. The only issue was, he seemed to reach acceptance far later than the rest of England. It wasn't that he wouldn't get there. He would usually reach the ball. It was just that he never looked like catching it. He rarely did. A second empathic light bulb went off in my head. Tufnell not only couldn't catch or throw but showed absolutely no signs of wanting to.

Then there was his batting. Tufnell batted as if it was an existential affliction. As whichever terrifying fast bowler of that time, and there were many, ran in, you could detect the urge of his back legs to move him out of the way of the ball. I felt the tingling as if it was my own, desperate to run away towards square leg. When the ball had passed his stumps, he would lunge back towards it as if to make out that hadn't been his instinct. Bowled often, usually without score, the fielding team acknowledged it as a matter of course, without emotion. Caught on the unfortunate end of a short-ball barrage by Australian quick Craig McDermott in the same recent series, Tufnell had a ball whizz past his flailing bat at head height. Without it touching anything, he made a judgement call, considering his contribution done, and feigned a huge blow on his thumb. "I think you've broken my thumb," he shouted, before walking off. Graham Gooch, his captain, needless to say, wasn't particularly impressed when he arrived back in the dressing room to replays of a ball missing his bat (and thumb) by yards and the umpire not moving. Tufnell had made an executive decision and given himself out. In a Test match. I thought of myself, too, slowly backing away from the ball in the air, and considered Tufnell to clearly be nothing but sound of mind.

In all these three parts of his game, Tuffers somehow succinctly communicated the everyday struggle of having a body at all. My affinity with him would gently spiral over the next decade of my free-falling affection for the game he played. He'd be kicked out of Test teams for smoking weed in toilets. He'd bowl out Australia. He'd drop many more balls.

Tufnell in waiting.

He'd bottle many more fast-bowling inspections. Tufnell smoked, drank, was scared of a cricket ball and still, on occasion, single-handedly won Test matches for England. Despite it all, his skills were required when all else had failed. Fear and unbelonging: the traits I was beginning to find uncomfortable and burdensome in myself were filed into some purposeful, aspirational order through him. Plus, there was more. His nickname was The Cat. I was Felix. Felix the *Cat*. There were too many parallels here to be mere coincidence. Tufnell was paving the way. I had set my path as the next slow left-arm spinner for England. One day I would receive my cap and thank Bernard, then The Cat, formally. After all, I really couldn't have done it without them.

3

Phil Tufnell and the Hop,
Skip, Jump

P hil Tufnell is in his garden during a mid-April when
England is bathed in a perplexed, still heat. It being
morning, the birds have primary occupancy of the
outside and, singing not so much as if released as relieved,
I can hear them faintly down the line while, more overtly,
Tuffers lights up and sucks on a cigarette. Discussing his first
Test match and bowling left-arm spin is not the "passing of
the torch" moment that I had envisaged all those years ago.
There is no cap or official handover or press conference in
which I can thank him for the inspiration as I move on to
discuss my own achievements as an England international.

"Most spinners are a bit strange. We're a little bit fruity
and a little bit funky." He's not referring to "we" as in myself
and him, sadly, but a wider "we": a kind of subgenre tied
together by oddity. "We get hit for four and have to look
back at the batter and go, 'Right, you're gonna get it now,
I'm going to bowl it eeeeven slower.'" Though it's close to
29 years later, it's not difficult to imagine him as the same
young man hiding the ball at the top of his mark, caught
between mischief and apprehension, masquerading as a
magician. It's almost as if, to this day, he's surviving by the
same means. "You've got to get that aggression through
somehow. Otherwise the bloke will go, 'Hold on, he's just

35

bowling fucking slow.' Most spinners are survivors. You've got to have that instinct. No-one taught me it. It was just a hop, a skip and a jump to get myself going and I was away. I'm doing it now as we speak."

Suddenly struck that I could have been imitating him while missing the most important and vital hidden aspect of bowling slowly – aggression – I take him back to his English debut. He doesn't have to reach for the memory. "I remember it vividly. 2-1 down. Beautiful day at The Oval. Lovely sunny day." I imagine him looking up at the sky in his garden, exactly the same brightness as the one he is remembering. "It's always been one of my favourite spots. The crowd is fantastic there. You know, it's more..." – he pauses as if he's rubbing his hands together now, searching for a physical memory of the feeling – "...raucous." I don't need to jog his memory for his first ball that day either. "Clayton Lambert," he laughs, trying the name out again a second time, like stepping back into an elasticated time warp he's created for himself. "Cllaaayttoooonnn Laaammmberrt." As I and the rest of the nation settled on Tufnell through our television screens, taking his hat off, marking his run-up, it turns out that a key subplot to his introduction was undetectable to anyone who wasn't physically there.

"The thing with Clayton was, he'd sing while he batted." This being before the time of stump mics, thus only music to the ears of the close fielders, Tufnell continues to pull back the curtain on the psychedelia of the happenings in the middle. Lambert had taken one look at him and was gleefully rehearsing his intentions. "I'm trying to talk all seriously to Goochy and he's stood over there practising the biggest mow over cow corner you will ever see. He was really going for it." Tufnell was more acclimatised to county batsmen silently rehearsing a block, the kind that I had watched Harry play to me on repeat, as he walked up. He gulps as if about to bowl the ball again. "I've sort of gone, crikey, you know, let's just try and get this down the other end then, shall we?" The rest of the story plays out in his mind's eye, faithful to the televised document. "Clayton didn't stop singing, he's just gone (Tufnell sings) 'Underneath the coconut tr...' and when I've bowled, he plays exactly the shot he's been practising, first up!" He cackles again, still in a kind of stunned respect for Clayton's ambitions. "Thankfully he didn't connect with it, we'd have still been looking for that. I think Ramps caught it, didn't he?" I confirm it to have been Mark Ramprakash. Clearly buoyed that time has not weakened the recollection of his first wicket in Test cricket on home soil, he rolls on. "I took 6-3 or something after that, didn't I?" The 29 years have made the magic spell just one run more economical, which compared with most cricketing folkloric exaggerations is an extremely forgivable one.

Tufnell's own cricketing heroes happened to belong to the very same country he was faced with. He reels off the names as if they were rock stars or presidents or the England footballers of '66. "Haynes. Greenidge. Holding. Croft. But Viv. Viv was the one." Viv Richards, amid a Tufnell hot streak, joined proceedings a little later, batting in his last ever Test match. "I used to watch him when I was in short trousers thinking, wow, that's a real man. He was a hero of mine."

I feel the pinch of the surreal that I'm talking to my own childhood hero as he relives himself at 25 having his own flashback. The very presence of Viv, even with his career about to close, Tuffers explains, was enough to transport international sportsmen back into short trousers. "He was an intimidating man, Viv. He used to grunt and snort on his way to the wicket." Tufnell reproduces a series of snorts as if in total recall. His teammates, the seniors bruised by their decade-long beatings at the hands of the great man, and the fresher faces out of compulsory hushed respect, shut up when Viv arrived. There was no singing. There was no clapping or encouraging from the fielders. Just Viv, taking guard, snorting. Tufnell, negotiating a few deliveries unharmed, flighted one outside off stump. "Viv has tried to come down the wicket and hit me into Southall. It was a bit of a theme developing with them." Tufnell begins to commentate on the ball, suddenly living it back in moving filmic memory. "It's a beauty. It's bounced, turned, spun a little bit." He makes bounced, turned and spun feel like three different acts all together, again like a magician with a few wrist flicks of panache to encourage a trance. Viv outside-edges the ball. Alec Stewart catches it. Tufnell is suddenly caught between elation and anxiety. Merv Kitchen is the umpire at his end. "The problem with Merv as an umpire was, he was famously deaf. As Alec's caught it, I've gone, 'Stump him, stump him, he might not have heard it!'" Alec Stewart whipped the bails off, and John Holder, the umpire at the non-striker's end, gave it out stumped. Kitchen, despite Tufnell's lack of faith, had heard the nick too. "Both umpires were stood there with their fingers up! Viv Richards out twice with one ball! It probably remained my greatest wicket." He stops and breaks schtick for a second and says, as if being able finally to absorb what the moment meant, "Wow, that was so special."

To speak with The Cat is to be lulled back into a place in which events happen for, to and around him and by proxy might to you, too. "I've been there half a dozen times. It's a lovely old spot to be. The zone, they call it," he says, before he ad-libs a guitar solo, a very fast one. "You're not thinking about where your fingers are, are you? It's just coming out of you. It's a mental place to be, you know." I do sort of know, in my own way, I say. "I could have run up backwards and flipped it over my head that day. It was just happening. You have to just be grateful and enjoy it." That would explain the giggling, then.

An element of slapstick and genuine danger laces itself through much of Tufnell's recollection of the '90s, the on-field and off-field blurring into a stretch of never-ending stories.

He heartily relives fielding humiliations and Australian wicketkeeper Ian Healy asking him whether he can "borrow his brain, I'm building an idiot" which suddenly trigger near-death experiences that he goes on to detail. "I knew this bloke who had a double-decker boat," Tufnell says, dragging a cigarette again as if to load the story with a "the sea was angry that day, my friends" eminence. "I don't think he necessarily knew too much about the laws of the ocean, shall we say." As he set off, with Devon Malcolm and some other vital squad members, a "boom" went off in the harbour. "We were like, 'Oh, I wonder what that is? Never mind, pass us a beer.'" The noise was warning of a treacherous storm incoming, an aquatic signal that no-one should leave land under any circumstances. "The next thing you know, we're in this massive..." and he's briefly lost for words, as I imagine him painting the picture from Sebastian Junger's *The Perfect Storm* with his hands. He finds the closest phrase he can muster: "...massive squall." Life jackets on, accepting their fates, the England squad members quietly started saying their goodbyes. "The one thing he did know, this bloke, is that when you see the wave coming that's bigger than the boat, you turn sideways into it and ride it." Ride it they did and Tufnell finishes another dance with disaster with suitable flourish. "There was the odd shark, too." There is a pause as if he is nodding again to himself, knowing his audience is captive. "Hammerheads." Finally, he adds, as if from experience, "They'll give you a big suck as well as a bite." I like the idea of the England cricket team battling the wildlife and general environment as well as the cricket teams, and encourage him to go further. "How can I put this? There were loads of, shall we say, unplanned days off. Let's go and see the crocodiles, you know?" Weirdly, I kind of do, as he's basically begun recounting a tour of Australia I once had. "It was great fun. I loved it all." He pauses. "Even if it might cost you the odd marriage."

I have come for all the stories, most of which, of course, I have already heard, but there's one more thing I need to know, which has been sitting in my throat throughout. Taking a deep breath, and telling him he doesn't have to answer this at all if he doesn't want to, I stumble and go on to reference a section of his autobiography *What Now?*. I had read the book in my teens, in the middle of my continued search for lovely, loopy excellence, the cover being Tufnell smoking with bloodshot eyes. Even having read it twice back then, joining dots and clues in his non-conformist cricketing how-to guide, it only struck me just the morning before calling Tufnell, having rooted through old boxes to find the much-loved copy, what might have resonated to me in it. In his teens, before cricket has become his life and within a book stuffed full of the kind of anecdotes I've just absorbed, there is a small section of momentary ballast:

Dad had gone to work and I was at home with her. I remember she called me into her room. I took her into the loo and back, but when I tried to lift her from the wheelchair back on to the bed, I couldn't lift her; I couldn't get her out of her wheelchair. So she said: 'It's all right, darling.' You know, 'Just leave me, leave me.' So I went and sat in my room and time passed and I remember watching Tottenham on the box. Later I heard my old man come home and the next thing I knew it was dark and there were lights flashing outside our house. I looked out of the window and saw an ambulance, with Mum being taken into it. I went to bed and didn't see Dad again until the next day, when I came back after Sunday football. He was there in the house and he just said: 'Your mum's dead now.' And that was that.

I don't re-read this passage to him, but I clumsily find a way to ask, had his mum not died in the same circumstances, does he imagine he would have lived the same colourful life? There is by some distance the longest pause there has been in our lightning, time-warping conversation. I'm about to say, "Don't worry about it," sensing its poignancy and his discomfort, cursing my nerve at having asked at all, when he answers. "I think it made me a little bit loose, you know what I mean?" I do. "It made me a bit of an angry young man."

Finally, I ask if that anger found a productive home in the way he bowled, slowly but with aggression. He considers it, before responding as if the passage in his book is an elastic band that has been stretched and pinged back to sit him just next to the moment again: "Yeah, perhaps it did a little bit."

Phil Tufnell bowls – "Most spinners are survivors."

4

The Nasty Boys

I wouldn't get the opportunity for real like-for-like time with Tuffers again until the summer of 1993 and, if my projections on my new hero needed a counterbalance to catapult my cricketing imagination, I was soon to be in luck. The Australians were on their way to England for the Ashes. It didn't matter to me then, nor seemingly has it mattered to anyone else ever, that this rivalry, which had something to do with the burning of some bails over a century ago, held priority over all other world cricket despite never being anything other than a two-sided contest. All the important people on the TV, on whom I was bestowing the utmost agency, were at constant pains to express how serious this was: it was absolutely no joke and certainly not fun. Perfect. England had lost the two previous series and were looking, if anything, far less organised than ever before. Even in the build-up I felt as if I was being welcomed into a story that everyone was already broken by yet somehow chained to, and that a pre-written script was about to play out across the length of an English summer.

Every broadcast I was "lucky" enough to glimpse at the end of a news bulletin or each Ashes-related mention that I caught momentarily in the footnote of a newspaper, despite the austere warnings, did little but plant the smallest seed of "but what if?" in my head. Though small, it was a stubborn little motif that refused to be quieted by an Australian clean sweep of the one-day series, 3-0. It was a "what if?" that rang in my ears alongside the usual rotating standards in the car on the continuing journeys to my grandparents every other weekend. A new focus of the trip had sprung up of late on the intersection in Purley, just as London became leafy. A woman in her mid-thirties, with hair as if she had just removed a dinner-lady net from it, would position herself on the corner of the road with a ghetto blaster. Attending to her day as if it were a public duty, she grinned – a wide, blissed-out, vacant grin – and danced while waving. It was like a halfway checkpoint for waving, with Harry 15 minutes behind us, potentially still waving us off in the background, possibly without having noticed his trousers were round his ankles. Unless her timetable exactly coincided with our visits, it appeared she did this all day. For the entirety of 1993. As we passed, the soundtrack becoming whatever indetermi-nate part of *The White Album* we had landed on, I looked to the front and to my parents for guidance. It was a nugget of curious pride to me that Andrew, often reserved, quiet and keen to leave any loud or social situation, would lend her his unreserved support. "Wonderful," he'd nod. "So free." It did feel as if she knew something we didn't, as if she had signed out of life's responsibilities and living had never felt simpler. I was torn for a personal world view between the stern men on television bracing the nation for a beating and this woman smiling and waving regardless. I liked to think of myself as pitched exactly in the middle.

Not only did we know that at the end of the outward journey there was the customary "no milk today" routine followed by cricket lessons, choc ices, roast pa-too-tees and twirly-whirly rides (preferably not in that order, though, for the risk of liquefied choc ice and potatoes flying out of your mouth and onto a spinning tyre), but there was a new incentive. WWF Wrestling had begun to take hold of my daydreaming and yank itself, in all its spandex glory, into focus for my attention. It was only on Sky television. We didn't have Sky (a small, telling, South London middle-class giveaway). Harry and Abla, though, did – solely so they could follow the fortunes of Spanish tennis player Arantxa Sánchez Vicario, a woman who had won their hearts because "she was like a tiger".*

Wrestling was very simple. There were good guys and bad guys. The difference was clearly marked for your benefit and they were, of course, faking the fighting itself. The twirly whirly and green stumps blurred into the periphery as I dazed into another appealing vortex where, like the cricketers with war clothes that weren't actually going to war, I could watch a man in a leotard smash a steel chair over another and be safe in the knowledge that there was no real harm being done to anyone.

When we returned home, there was no Sky. No Sky meant no wrestling. No wrestling meant a void. This void could only be filled by wrestling, music and/or cricket and, not being sure how to operate the record player, there was only one place to get my hit: Blockbuster Video. When every tele-vised event ever was not available a click away, Blockbuster video rental was a young person's chamber of dreams. I knew the local shelves by heart. It was quite a big store, tucked into the entrance of Clapham Junction Station. The first third of it was useless to me. Thrillers, comedies, drama, television. They served no purpose in my world. I rushed past them. The far corner on the right-hand side was where the good stuff was. Cricket and wrestling. The wrestling section proudly displayed almost every year of WWF events since its incep-tion. Survivor Series. Royal Rumble. SummerSlam. These were all gargantuan events, of undoubted historical impor-tance, but there was one whose very name held a pathos that reduced anyone to a kind of furrowed respect: WrestleMania.

---

* She was.

It had a mystifying worthiness that I knew in only one other event across the world: the Ashes. No-one could explain exactly why, but it was the most important event. That was an unquestionable fact, and I was *not* going to be the first one to question it. In March 1993, my visit to Blockbuster coincided with a fatalistic reorganisation of the shelves that left WrestleMania VII exactly at my eye level when I turned into the aisle. It was sitting slightly in front of the other videos, which appeared to give it a comparative three-dimensional quality. Andrew asked if I'd decided yet what I wanted. I had.

My good-guy affinity had already been won over in Purley via Sky by the tag team The Hart Foundation. Bret "Hitman" Hart, a vision of any boy's aspirations, wore ludicrously cheap reflective sunglasses indoors (much as the double-barrelled brigade had in my first cricket practice). He and his real-life brother-in-law Jim "The Anvil" Neidhart, dressed in comparatively conservative pink leotards and were the tag-team champions (of the WORLD). They were walking incarnations of everything that was good and defended their titles at WrestleMania VII against The Nasty Boys. The Nasty Boys were absolutely abhorrent. Brian Knobbs and Jerry Sags, in mohicans and spray-painted black uniforms, would low-blow opponents when the referee had his back turned, pull them by their hair (even when he was looking) and spit into the crowd. The match was a simple, quantifiable contest between good and evil. It rattled along at a fluid pace, with 15 minutes of the usual balletic fare where the momentum would shift dramatically from one team's favour to the other's. The Hart Foundation were far The Nasty Boys' superiors and had the thing won fair and square, executing their finisher ("the Hart Attack") with their graceful nice-guy schtick. Anvil pinned Sags for the win. All it required was a simple one, two, three count from the referee. And yet, to my distress, the referee was nowhere to be seen.

I never questioned the frequency with which referees would

46

have their back turned in significant moments of wrestling matches – it was almost as absurd as having a deaf Test-match umpire. Earl Hebner, as safe a pair of hands as there was, the Merv Kitchen of his industry, was missing. With his attention turned elsewhere and the fight being momentarily unattended, Knobbs jumped in and smashed a biker's helmet against the back of Anvil's skull. Hebner turned round. Suddenly, it was Anvil who was covered. Wait, no. That's not... But you haven't seen what happened. One, two, three. It was all over. I could barely look out of sudden, sickened pain. As The Hitman ran back, helpless, only in time to see The Nasty Boys crawl away cackling and howling with their titles, something inside me changed. This was a deep injustice, could nobody see that? When we went to give the video back the next week, Andrew asked if I'd like another for the week. I would. WrestleMania VII again, please. For reasons beyond my understanding, I needed to experience the whole ordeal again.

As all the signs had indeed indicated, the Ashes were to play out like the WrestleMania VII video: my small and stubborn "what if?" failing to overturn the result, each time it was exactly the same. What was worse, too, was that, captained by Allan Border, the Australian cricket team were an interminable vision of every WWF bad guy that lurked inside those videos in Blockbuster. Unable to define a difference between the two, I responded to them as if they were an immoral nuisance to peace and harmony. When lined up in their baggy green hats, Border, Taylor, Waugh, Waugh, Boon, Hughes in the field crouched around the bat looked like a disturbing meeting of evil masterminds that blurred between the real and the fictional. It was as if, should the camera keep panning around the field, it would eventually show Margaret Thatcher, Shredder, Darth Vader, The Bloodbottler and The Nasty Boys, all of them having done a deal with the devil that endowed them with buckets for hands that refused to drop any catches whatsoever. Not only that, and I don't know where they kept it or why it was so disturbing to me, but gum was constantly available to them. They knew cameras were watching their every move and yet they allowed the residue of white saliva to gather on the side of their mouths as they chewed. And as they chewed, they did so with their mouths wide open, smiling as if they had won a tag title behind Earl Hebner's back and were reliving it in perpetuity.

Brian Knobbs and Jerry Sags – The Nasty Boys.

5

What If?

I didn't see the ball of the century in real time. I was at school daydreaming of my next opportunity to lob an orange ball skywards very slowly. I saw it that evening, after the fact, on the actual news. It flashed up in the opening trails. All scheduled planning disturbed by a *force majeure*. We interrupt this broadcast for some important news. Stop what you are doing. Something terrible has happened.

The footage, even just a day after the fact, has a strange feeling of a tape a hundred years old and yet as raw as the second it happened; within it an odd magic of evoking some timeless transcendence. Old Trafford is grey. The televised sound induces a distant hum underneath the action, as if it is already a vacated battlefield. Shane Keith Warne, a young ball of arrogance in waiting, stands at his mark with flared whites, a blond buzz cut and unnecessary sunblock on his nose and lower lip. He is a face unfamiliar to the already braced English cricket fans. At the other end, to receive his first ball, is our goatee-bearded stalwart, Mike Gatting. Even in the moments before the ball is bowled, the two appear to belong in distinctly different eras, green-screened as if to portray modernity vs the way the game used to be played. Warne saunters up to the crease. It isn't like Tuffers, a run-up of a thousand quirks and rhythms boiled into a hop, skip and jump. This has a stirring simplicity to it. He just walks. In a swift and sudden propulsion of action, he lets the ball go, releasing it out of the back of his hand. The ball floats in the air, simultaneously looping and swooping sharply to its right. It pitches six inches outside of leg stump. Gatting, with a motion of cautious fatigue, half plays at it. The ball grips the surface and spins viciously back the way it has swooped, in an instant leaving Gatting standing there in his frozen prod as if simply to usher the ball through. Next, the clatter of the stumps. Then, as if part of the motion itself, the immediate reaction in a series of televised camera cuts. Ian Healy, no doubt beginning to be spoiled for choice on brains he'd like to build an idiot with, cartwheeling his arms in celebration. Then a shaking umpire Dickie Bird.* Richie Benaud, who had a habit of commentating as if an omniscient presence from the future and the past, telling us, "Gatting has absolutely no idea what happened to it." The camera cuts to Gatting, walking back and turning his head back to the scene, genuinely bemused, finding himself playing the victim in a play he wanted no part of, as Richie concludes, "...he still doesn't know." The entire sequence, not longer than five or six seconds, is a concoction of shock and absolute inevitability that comes to summarise the past five years and suggest the following twelve.

The "ball of the century" somehow hung heavily over Tuffers, too. It was one thing to *suggest* that the ball might do three things at once, but Warne could actually enact it. The devilish magic with which The Cat whipped the ball in multi-purpose freneticism was somehow suddenly made to feel workmanlike against Warne's. Warne would go on to take 33 more chillingly destructive wickets in the series.

It wasn't just the "ball of the century". The first two Ashes Tests in 1993 came loaded like a starter pack of concise moments of cricketing pain. Graham Gooch, whom I was gathering a grasp of via his game *Graham Gooch World*

---

* It was cold.

Class Cricket (every batsman looked exactly like Gooch – Caucasian with a big, thick, manly moustache – no matter which country or batter you were playing as), was given out handled ball at Old Trafford. I didn't know handled ball was a thing. Gooch himself didn't seem to until it was too late. In the second Test, his opening partner, a young Michael Atherton, was run out for 99, Gatting sending him back when approaching his third. Atherton, it turned out, was wearing the wrong shoes, half spikes and half trainers, and as Gatting gestured to run and then sent him back, he slipped, ending on his knees as Ian Healy took the bails off. The commentary cruelly depicted every second of the unfolding calamity: "Runs. 98...99...Will they go for the third? He's fallen, he's slipped down. Oh...tragedy..." There was nothing more to be said. It was a tragedy.

When Gooch, less of a computer-game character with every day of the series, implied the defeatism of some players after the second, crushing, loss at Lord's, Phil Tufnell and Chris Lewis were not seen again. Even to a nine-year-old, it didn't feel particularly cryptic. Don't rely on people being around, I told myself. Even if you really, really like them.

There were many others that summer, briefly on the television all day toiling and then dropped with immediate effect. Almost all of them were called either Martin or Mark. Mark Ilott, his whites hanging off him as if he were a clothes peg, his shirt loose and flowing beyond his midriff, long sleeves pulled up and held in his cuffs. Then gone. Martin Bicknell. Gone. Mark Lathwell. Gone. Martin McCague. Gone. Had nobody noticed? I hoped they were OK. England fielded 24 players in the course of the series, introducing cricketers that I would become unfathomably attached to, then brutally whipping them from view, depositing them back in county cricket to see out their careers, but more pertinently placing them in my imagination in a Battersea Dogs Home for Lost Cricketers, where all these

Marks and Martins were caged, stuck in time, cursed to be forever looking for a home.

The final exchanges of the drawn-out summer had some bigger news attached to them. Graham Gooch gave way and Michael Atherton was to replace him as captain. It was the first time I had seen anyone appointed captain of England. Atherton's side were a new cast that I was on the beginning of life's treacherous path alongside: a classically head-banded Graham Thorpe scoring a hundred on debut, the gentle, looming presence of Graeme Hick, Alec Stewart twirling his bat, pulling his shirt collar up and fixing his pads before every delivery, Nasser Hussain determinedly taking everything twice as seriously as anyone else, Devon Malcolm running towards the crease as if he had been thrown down the stairs before unfurling an action of unstructured, visceral beauty, Angus Fraser looking oddly tired before he'd even started to bowl. These were the faces with which I was going to live out the next ten years – not so much *with*, but through. They won the final Test at The Oval. It had been 2,430 days, 11 hours and 49 minutes since the last win against Australia (I had been just two years old). There was a lightness in this consolation that meant, despite finishing the series 4-1 in deficit, they moved into the winter with a genuine if beautifully doomed hope, my "what if?" miraculously being given an excuse to live on.

This "what if?" was contextualised neatly too by something of a synchronicity in all English sport. Firstly, the footballers. In the penultimate and most vital qualifying game for the World Cup in 1994, England failed to beat Holland in controversial circumstances, leaving the country in a sort of collective belittled shock. Meanwhile, Damon Hill had become a driver in British Formula 1 team Williams. Formula 1 was a terrestrial television mainstay on the BBC and Hill's season had played out in front of the country as a disturbingly solid supporting role to the Ashes plot and footballing failure. Hill's father Graham, an archetypal old-school racing-car driver of huge repute, had died in 1975 in a plane crash through thick fog when Damon was 15.

*

It is hard not to pitch Damon as Bruce Wayne in my mind: a gentle, wounded soul on a retribution mission in a remorseless world. He has suffered a series of unthinkable technical disasters this season which have continually retired his car when he is in winning positions. In Germany, halfway through the season, he leads the Grand Prix by seven seconds from Alain Prost. I sit there energised by the commotion being stirred up in Murray Walker, the voice of Formula 1. Walker, who took Hill under his wing after the death of his dad, counts down almost every corner, speaking as if he believes Damon will be listening. "There are only eight miles between Damon Hill and victory, he can afford to take it relatively easily, to back off the amount that you need to, to make sure everything is OK..." On cue, Hill's Williams begins to shake and, unthinkably, his left tyre just bursts. "I cannot believe it!" Walker corrects himself, before pausing and gasping in horror himself. "Urgh... There's Prost going through... for the second race in a row, Damon Hill has had appalling luck." My dad and I have watched this in silence. When he turns round to look at me, I am sobbing. There is nothing he can do to fix it, he doesn't have to say. There is nothing anyone can do. I already know this from Michael Atherton's run-out and WrestleMania VII. It is better written than the tag-title victory, more painful and precise than the Ashes and more profoundly unjust than the footballers in Holland. In the final image of Hill, sitting in his car, shaking his head, it could just as well have been any of Bret Hart or Bruce Wayne or David Platt or Michael Atherton, under the helmet. All of them thinking, "What if?"

6

Being Yourself

It was a Sunday like any other Sunday. I leaned forward in the back seat and inhaled *The White Album*, past the waving lady and through beyond the outskirts of London, anxious to arrive at my grandparents where I knew there was a Test match waiting. Oddly, on arrival, there was no "no milk today" routine waiting at the door. Sidestepping this disturbance in our grandfather's comic routine, I raced through regardless, navigating the corridors like a well-versed go-kart driver to the television, which had England vs South Africa – their first tour since the lifting of the apartheid ban – waiting. The portal of escapist cricketing joy was unusually soundless. "It's despicable," Harry frowned, marching despondently behind me as I found the remote. "The captain of England…" He choked on his words, through genuine betrayal. "Cheating." I had never seen him like this. It was unthinkable that anything could ever stir any negativity in him. I reached for the remote which, in its usual position on top of the TV on its left-hand side, suddenly took on the appearance of a stick of dynamite, and turned the sound up carefully. Ensuring the volume landed on an even number, which for some reason was important, I slowly faded up the background hum as the camera kept playing back a short, fuzzy clip of Michael Atherton receiving the ball in the field, reaching into his pocket and putting his hands back to the ball again.

I was left to my own devices with this repeated image, innocuous to a non-cricketing eye, as Harry studied it once more with me, tutted again and briskly walked out. From there, the commentators took over, speaking in hushed tones. The footage was inspected as if it were a police investigation of incriminating CCTV. Was Atherton rubbing something illegal onto the ball? Needing a minute with which to digest this information, I muted the screen again, unmuted it, muted it again, unmuted it again, stared slightly through it and eventually turned it off and back on again as if rebooting might allow us all to start over.

As I waited for the television to restart once more, I moved to go outside. The events had stirred some kind of shame in Harry – a hurt he was not prepared to hide for anyone's benefit, let alone his nine-year-old grandson. Andrew, through the sliding doors that led out into the garden still decorated by green stumps, was having a private word. I hid just out of sight and listened. "You know he's a hero to him, have a think about what that does..." Harry interjected as if Michael Atherton was standing next to him and they'd both been pulled in by a headteacher. "But *he's* the England captain. It's disgraceful behaviour." Of course, being the England captain didn't carry much weight with my dad, and putting some dirt on a red ball was of even less consequence. But I felt disturbed. My world distorted. The Nasty Boys, they were cheats. I had video evidence. The Australians were (no evidence but probably). If Michael Atherton was too, then life must be a far more bewildering place than I could have possibly imagined.

Atherton would be fined £2,000 for rubbing dirt he had collected in his pocket onto the ball during the first Test against South Africa. The dirt, supposedly, would help the ball to swing for his bowlers in testing conditions. The collective frothing, it turned out, was not just triggered in Harry that day. Atherton was swarmed by journalists. It was to keep his hands dry, he said. It was important contextually that this happened in a cricket match which, it was becoming apparent, tended to provoke a generally moralistic set of issues wherever and whenever it could.

The sprinkled dirt was in vain. England lost the first Test by 356 runs. It was a huge, and familiar, disparity. When Atherton turned up for the second Test, he seemed to have lived a number of lives in a week and took on the appearance of someone entirely the same but completely changed. Winning a toss he was "hoping to lose" and "batting from memory", having spent a week off the pitch with journalists camped outside his house, he went out to bat. He was, of course, bounced early, receiving the ball full in the grille of his helmet. He shook it off as if it was a punch he had been expecting. Once this was dealt with, alleviated from some kind of schoolyard comeuppance, he took to his job with a reinvigorated focus. He was eventually out for 99, one short of a redemptive hundred. He always seemed one short, yet – this time – he walked off with a different purpose. Suddenly embodying a three-dimensional warts-and-all truth, his shirt half unbuttoned, he swaggered off like a newly electric Dylan controversially leaving the stage at the Manchester Free Trade Hall. I thought of Atherton, as he moved behind the curtain, and imagined him morphing into Bob in *Don't Look Back*, being met by the folk masses outside waiting for a sight of him, only to eyeball one of them while entering the back of his waiting car and remind them, "I saw you booing", before lighting a cigarette and instructing his driver "Let's go."

I had emerged from my wrestling infatuation, not so much out of a lack of love, but because it seemed that maybe it wasn't acceptable to be into it anymore. The adult world, and more presciently "cool", was starting to flex its will on my conscious decisions – and the news from the adult world of what was cool came from two places: sport, mostly cricket, and music, mostly *Top of the Pops,* a British heritage show with a legacy as concrete as *Test Match Special*, broadcasting half an hour of the most successful chart music every Thursday evening. Each act would mime through their hit to a crowd that, as inconspicuously as possible, craned themselves between shots of the presenters so as to be seen on television. When the band started playing, they'd scream at the chorus and cheer, regardless of who it was. The acts varied wildly. It was like a pick'n'mix of what the world had to offer – every week was half an hour of potential you to stitch back into your being after you'd seen it. The first song I decided was a piece of me was the three-piece girl band Eternal, dressed in black and red leather, with their latest single, "Power of a Woman". It was a nailed-down tune.

That Friday, it was all I could discuss at school. Had anyone seen Eternal last night? What a band! Secunder Kermani had. We hatched a plan. On Saturday we'd go and buy "Power of a Woman" on cassette. We were both fairly sure that Our Price, just before Arding & Hobbs (the department store which had presented the cricketing mannequin years earlier), was a straight walk down the High Street past school. I knew that if I ran it past Lana, accompanied everywhere with a functional walking stick by now, in a flippant enough tone, as if it was the kind of thing I did all the time anyway, she would accept it for just that and allow us to go. She did. I was growing to eye level with some of the previously out-of-reach places in the house. I knew where Andrew would leave change for anyone who needed it, stacking up the pound coins, the 20p pieces and huge, chunky 50p coins neatly and precisely in their own piles, the edges of each directly matching the ones below and above. Taking Lana's word as gospel, I borrowed ten pounds total of loose change and we set off.

We were going over the horizon, intrepid explorers on a cultural mission to bring back the music we'd seen and couldn't live without. We bought a tape each, in little paper covers, from Our Price for £1.99. Then, as hatched during school as if it were a covert operation, went to Pizza Hut. The All You Can Eat buffet was £4.99. Eating as much as possible was not just the tag line as far as we concerned, it was a prerequisite. We took it as a compulsory demand to eat as much as we physically could and made journeys to and from the buffet, returning with pizzas stacked high on our plates, then left crusts just as mountainous on the side of our table as the kitchen tried to cope with the demand two nine-year-olds were suddenly putting them under. It was thirsty work. Drinks were not included in the price. The salad bar, however, *was* included and you were allowed, I know because I asked, to have as many cucumber slices as you wanted without extra charge. We emptied the cucumber vat on to our plates and, in between visits back to the pizzas, sucked on the slices, one by one, for maximum hydration. We returned home both culturally nourished and biologically replenished. Andrew, who the afternoon trip was news to, asked where ten pounds from the side had gone. I had already stacked the three pounds change neatly back and, feeling sick from the pizza, saturated by the cucumbers and dizzy from the adventure, I proudly presented him with "Power of a Woman" by Eternal on cassette.

Every week from then, a news bulletin of the adult world was awaiting in *Top of the Pops*. I knew where I had to be at 7pm. So did my brothers and so did the cats, who all flanked me in wing formation as we sat three inches from the television, transfixed. My parents had Bob Dylan, Van Morrison and The Beatles. Waiting on the shelves were Loudon Wainwright records, Cole Porter tapes, deeper Dylan cuts, bluegrass and Cajun compilations, a lifetime of record buying to pass on to their children. I had steeled myself to decline, though, for I had chosen my own path, and that was three women dressed head to toe in leather and their mission statement "Power of a Woman". Who would I choose next week?

Well, next week, I chose Boyzone. Appearing in bright and brilliant white suits, they performed "So Good", their new single, which had just landed inside the top five. They were a mass of limbs, bouncing around each other, their loose sleeves flapping in the artificial wind they were creating through excessive energy; a sugar-rushed concoction of winking and high-fiving and fist-pumping and patting each other on the side. I'd never seen a group of men with such recurrent instincts to touch one another. These were *real* friends. I was in, and like anything I had pledged allegiance to, I was loyal. The next single, "Father and Son", released a month later, was a ballad for which they all sat on stools. Andrew witnessed me awestruck in front of the television as this tender thing of reserved beauty, a daring, mature leap from their previous incarnation only a month earlier, played out in front of me. No doubt reeling from the impossibility that he had somehow raised a cricket-loving Boyzone fan, he waited for *Top of the Pops* to end and then he played me the "original" of the song by Cat Stevens. I listened patiently. It was good to be given the option, I thanked him, but Boyzone's was definitely better.

Pop music continued to distribute pearls of wisdom from another planet with regularity that year. "Gangsta's Paradise" by Coolio featuring LV communicated some kind of affinity in pretty much every boy at Honeywell School. I'm not sure exactly what it was we all connected with. We had certainly not been spending most of our short lives living in a gangsta's paradise, as the song reported. Still, somehow, we decided, we got it. Back home, we were three brothers quite willing, in the safety of the house, to stage immediate performances infused by what we had seen. We learned every word of every song we had ingested – the same way dinners would be a speed contest to be first to eat whatever was left, so too was the committing of what we had seen to memory. Then, with a sense of enormous importance, and armed with the latest compilation tape

Now That's What I Call Music (from later, more sanctioned trips to Our Price), we'd wait for our audience.

*

When our parents have anyone round, we seize our opportunity. A quick rehearsal in the bedroom with matching pyjamas on. Then, preferably at the most unsuspecting moment, when we are supposedly in bed and finally an evening of adult conversation is being had over dinner with their friends, I burst in through the side door to the living room, a stereo on my shoulder, my brothers in tow. I know what we need to do. Get. Their. Attention. Press play. Turn it up. Loud. "So Good", then "Power of a Woman", then "Gangsta's Paradise". Between each song, we do very quick costume changes to become whoever our next performance is. This entails stuffing more or fewer cushions in our pyjamas depending on how big or small we remember the artists to be. There is an element of ambition to our work and we intend it to be quite powerful – including switching of vocal roles and an enthusiasm to match what we'd seen Boyzone execute so determinedly that year. The faces of the dinner guests, meanwhile, are frozen in a sort of stoic acceptance once they realise we intend to perform multiple songs in their entirety. Lana beams gently and then claps. It is an artfully persuasive clap, pitched exactly between encouraging us while communicating that this really shouldn't last all night.

There is nothing that could have prepared us, the three boys and two cats lined treacherously close to the television, pledged to Eternal and Boyzone, for where *Top of the Pops* would next take us. This week, among the usual fare, five men from Manchester appear, with sunglasses (definitely not prescription) and Marks & Spencer shirts and jumpers, four like versions of The Beatles and one almost completely bald, sitting there unplugged and miming on the set. They have instruments in their hands. They all seem to have inherited some kind of predetermined personality. They don't move. The song, "Wonderwall", sounds as if it might have been lifted from somewhere in those tapes in the car. Like The Beatles, or the ball of the century, it was as if they have been around for eternity, like we already know them, and in their hands we are simultaneously safe and completely out of our depth. The brothers, Liam and Noel, sit there, totally in charge of their universe, and we brothers stare back at them, beginning to build our own. Boyzone are dead.

Will on *Top of the Pops*.

(*What's the Story*) *Morning Glory?* became the first long-playing album I owned. It was better than anything I could have ever imagined. Oasis had taken my confusion and searching and turned it into words. They too were going into battle, but rather than with cricket gear, they were armed with gibberish and love songs. The information that they sent to South West London and into my infatuated mind, as I leaned in ready to take note as if they were dictating from their own Bible, however, could at times be quite confusing. Rock'n'roll was the only form of music worth listening to. Got it. I double-checked that the bins where I had dispensed with the Boyzone and Eternal tapes had been taken out. Guitars were the best. Yep. Synthesisers were terrible. I didn't know what one was, but got it, agreed. This was where the mission statement started to blur. Rock'n'roll was about being yourself. Noted. It's just that in the same breath, they seemed to not approve of anyone who was "themselves" and wasn't, well, them. So, rock'n'roll, I imagined, joining up some loose dots, was about being yourself if being yourself was being working class and Manc? Got it.

Fashioning an upbringing from Burnage when you live next to Wandsworth Common is a complicated manoeuvring act. It requires delicate and imaginative reinvention. I had faith that I could achieve it by osmosis if I made sure I was exposed to Oasis at all times of the day. Before I'd sleep I would plan what Oasis song I would listen to first thing the next morning, fast-forwarding the cassette to the exact position, so that I would only need to press play for it to begin. I then fell asleep with Liam and Noel like circling talking heads around my closing eyes, filling my mind with their instruction manual. I learned the interviews, some that were released on tape and actually charted, such was the band's wider popularity, completely by heart. I would now refer to people as "our kid" whenever possible.

There were physical manifestations required, too. Both feet needed to protrude almost at right angles, pointing away from each other. Your legs were bent so, if you stood still, you'd be presenting a diamond shape between them. Then, when you walked, your arms hung, dangling, moving with your stride, with a little more purpose than being totally limp, but just a little. I, very cautiously, began to ingratiate this Manc swagger into my day-to-day. In order to truly be myself, aka be more like Oasis, I shrewdly recognised that this walk needed to be developed over a period of time so to not arouse suspicion. Immediately walking like that would be crass and classless. I tried to incorporate tiny aspects of it into my being slowly and steadily, so that when I had eventually evolved into the fully fledged article, no-one would question my seamless transition. They would simply recognise me as the descendant of the Gallagher brothers that I undeniably was. God, I hoped they bowled lovely, loopy left-arm spin.

It was a saturated sort of rebellion. In morphing into my new sense of self, unlike the principal motivation of most youth movements, I desperately wanted my parents to like Oasis. They *sort of* did, in a kind of loosely accepting way. Liam and Noel, after all, clearly liked some of the music that they liked too, and there was a kind of gratitude on their part towards the conduit which had pulled me away from Boyzone. With the insistence of Oasis, *Top of the Pops* changed from a show in which I waited for music to tell me what was happening, into a show where *I* would tell *it* what was happening to *itself*. It was an exercise of sports-like competition. I would sit and, literally, boo anyone without guitars and cheer anyone with them. That was the criterion: if you had a guitar, you were excellent. I scrawled the charts everywhere over my room, putting the groups with guitars in capitals. By then, I'd been given Oasis's debut album, released a couple of years earlier. *Definitely Maybe* was possibly even better than (*What's the Story*) *Morning Glory?*. It was certainly more direct, strangely wiry and full of even more gibberish and romance than the first. It was a done deal. Screaming nonsense at the top of your lungs was incredibly liberating. I would be screaming it, mostly silently, and where applicable literally, from hereon in.

And with this, the performances for our parents' friends evolved into a more studied, nonchalant art form. There would be no ghetto blaster or manic limb unfurling. There was no changing of acts. We'd just walk through the door in whatever we had that would pass for sunglasses (sunglasses inside were an obvious prerequisite of being yourself), press play and stand there, motionless, as the unsuspecting audience would listen to the entirety of both Oasis albums while, in essence, we stood still and very, very vaguely lip synced, just as we'd seen them do. When the song ended, we would expect applause, which occasionally I would have to prompt, before dismissing it. After all, we were doing this for ourselves, nobody else, and that was what being yourself was.

If being myself was being in Oasis, I still hoped that, by some exceptional circumstances, it allowed for being an England cricketer too. The Surrey players, I heard reassuringly, sold Christmas trees in the off season. Maybe I could do the same, but be in Oasis in the winter, rather than sell trees? The West Indies were to return that summer for a thrillingly taut series between two sides on different trajectories. Atherton's England had begun to find some resolve and Dominic Cork, running in at an irresistibly rebellious angle when he bowled, had caught the cricketing public's imagination. In a series tantalisingly tied, the most piercing moment for fragile souls came in The Oval's customary last gesture of the summer. Alan Wells was 33 and making his debut for England. A long-standing servant of the county game, it was almost a gesture of apology from the powers that be that he hadn't been selected before, when in his prime, while the rest of England had seemingly had a go at batting in the middle order. He walked to the crease an unusual debutant – an old man by the metric of the game, already weathered on his way to the crease, but with a nervousness that betrayed how important the occasion was to him.

*

Curtly Ambrose, on a rampage all summer that will solidify him as one of the great fast bowlers, stands at the end of his mark. We all know the first ball Alan Wells will receive. Wells probably does, too. It is going to be short and at his body somewhere. Cricket, though, has the odd knack of summoning an unavoidable fate in your head before it has happened. Ambrose runs in and, of course, bowls a steep ball at Wells, who, with the flinch of a man who has waited a lifetime for something and yet been taken by surprise when it comes, plays the ball into his thigh pad. The ball loops into the air off the hidden protective equipment, in slow motion, giving me the split-second inclination to check twice whether exactly what I had imagined would happen has actually just happened, and is caught by Sherwin Campbell, stationed at short leg. Wells has spent an entire career building for this moment, and it is already gone. As he walks off, he finds the moving camera walking with him back to the pavilion and mouths "Sorry" into the lens. At least, I am sure he does. I look around to find the living room empty. Maybe he had said sorry to *me*? I think of the number of people who have sacrificed everything in their lives, only to have Curtly Ambrose bowl them an unplayable first ball.

*

Cricket and Oasis weren't just totem poles of worship upon which my new value system so precariously hung; I needed to get towards them and into their worlds. When Liam looked squarely into the camera in the live video *There and Then*, luring it towards him, I wanted it so much to be *me* he was dragging towards him that I sometimes allowed myself to believe it was, just as I had hoped Alan Wells *had* actually said sorry into that camera. I had something to tell them back. I wanted Oasis to know that they'd made something so magical that they needn't worry about anything ever again. And I wanted to tell Alan Wells he had no need to be sorry.

7

Alan Wells and the Apology

Alan Wells, near on 24 years after his only Test match and now the head of cricket at Bede's School on the south coast, is possibly more deeply entwined with the game than ever. His eldest son, Luke, is a professional cricketer and after a short break from it has picked up a bat, hanging around the house, for the first time in months. It was an indescribable relief to Luke, Alan tells me, it being the longest he could ever remember without doing so. "A bat, to us, is like an umbilical cord, sometimes it's as if we are attached to it."

Alan's own inseparable connection to his bat and to cricket began from as early as he can remember. Growing up in a council house in Newhaven, there was cricket always on the television, which he would absorb and then race out to the alleyway with his elder brother to recreate what he'd just seen. "There's nothing like being inspired by what you see on the television," he reminisces. "I remember watching Tony Greig as a kid. His upright stance, batting with a cap on to Lillee and Thomson,* flipping them over the slips. How inspirational is that?" Very, I say, before he continues, "It was just in the blood, I guess." His first ever competitive game was at the age of 12. "My two brothers and my dad were in the same team. They were one short on a Sunday. I was so

---

* Australian greats and year-zero Nasty Boy fast bowlers.

desperate to play." He persuaded them he should be involved and, wired with adrenaline and gratitude when he got the nod, he packed everybody's bag for the day. When he got to the ground, he realised he hadn't packed his own. Batting at number 11, not given a bowl, he was sent to field on the boundary, by the trees. Halfway into the innings, they had to put a white floppy hat on him, just so they could make him out from the overgrowth behind him.

Camouflage is a decent metaphor in general for how Alan describes growing up with the game. Colin, his elder brother, was, by all accounts, a trailblazer of a cricketer locally. "Whenever I was introduced to anybody they'd say, 'And this is *Colin Wells's younger brother*, Alan.' To be introduced as Alan Wells was a major ambition of mine." As their careers developed in the professional game, Alan, being the youngest sibling serving him decent preparation for professional cricket, became captain of Sussex. It didn't occur to him until a hot streak of batting form, standing upright and fearless like Greig before him, that he might ever play for England. "I always looked at the players in the England team and thought, flipping heck, they are just...brilliant." Even in form, and with a reputation on the county circuit as one of the most prodigious batters around, he struggled to imagine himself as an England cricketer. It wasn't until David Smith, a tall left-handed batter, came from Surrey to Sussex that Wells's mind was tweaked. Smith had opened the batting for England. Wells recalls, "He told me, there's one final barrier you have to get over." What's that? Wells asked. "You have to genuinely believe, when you are walking out to bat, that you are the best cricketer out there. Everybody else knows it, but you need to know it too..."

Feeling that this attitude wasn't something he could immediately pluck from within himself, Wells saw a psychologist, who recommended that he develop some kind of signal for himself which acknowledged he'd just played a good shot.

"It's weird how these things happen, but you remember Pete Sampras?" Sampras, the dominant male tennis player of the 1990s, was on television all the time. "Sampras used to, just as he served, pull the top of his shirt a couple of times, as part of his routine." I remember it clearly, I tell him, as if he was briefly letting the shirt breathe. "Exactly. I don't know why, but I decided that's what I'd do." Every time Wells hit a good shot, he lifted his shirt twice, just to recognise in himself that he knew what he had done was worthy of praise. Nobody else would have ever known. It really worked. "It was like an out-of-body experience, when it was going well. Like I didn't even need to participate in it." It's a beautiful vision I have for a second, of Wells watching himself flick his shirt, in acknowledgement of another boundary, and I daydream about what my trigger might be after hitting a boundary in professional cricket – less a subtle flick of a shirt and more possibly screaming, "I am a golden god" back at the bowler – but just as I am slipping into it, he stops me short. "But, you know what cricket is like, it doesn't let you stay there forever. It evens things up..."

With that, we are into his Test debut. Like Tufnell, there is no need to search or ask anything else. "I remember it very clearly. It was going through my brain on occasions, when I let it, you know, what's my first ball going to be?" Wells scrolled through his imagination, yorker, bouncer, a good length, before jerking himself back to reality. "I thought to myself, well, it doesn't matter what it is. *Just be ready.* I remember walking out to bat. I was enjoying the moment and I was actually quite relaxed. I was repeating to myself, 'You've been waiting a long time for this, just be ready.'"

Wells turned around and looked at the slips, who looked miles back and, of course, Curtly Ambrose at the end of his mark, about to run in. "I took a deep breath, took my guard, did my normal routine. Then he started charging in and I'm going to myself, 'Just be ready, be ready, watch the ball.' I swear to God, my eyes must have been out on stalks because as soon as he let the ball go, I saw it as clear as anything." He was expecting the ball to be fast, obviously. "Literally as he let it go, I thought, 'That's not *that* fast.' I saw it so clearly. I picked the length quite well and I went back to play it and..." – there's a pregnant pause, as if he's reliving it – "...it just got steep on me. I got an inside edge, onto the top of my thigh pad. As the ball was ballooning up I thought, 'Oh my God, I cannot believe this.'" Wells had never done it in his life before or since. "I thought, 'I've been waiting 15 years for this, and it's over?'" The reality of what had just occurred was so disturbing that he questioned for a second whether it really had. "I genuinely felt like saying, 'Curtly, bowl me the same ball now and it won't get me out, I promise.'" He kept the words in his mouth, and began to leave. "I realised, I can either slink off into the changing room with my head down and my helmet on as though it never happened, or I can be proud still. I decided I wanted to say, to the crowds and all the people on telly, 'I want you to look at me, because I'm still here.' Then I started trying to find a camera around the ground, because I knew how devastated my late wife and my sons watching would be. I thought they'd be feeling worse than I did, because it's horrible watching someone you love fail like that. I found the cameras and said the word 'sorry' to them."

I can't believe he has confirmed it. He *did* say sorry. I tell him that I saw it, and that I felt like he might be interacting with me and I thought that I might have hallucinated it, putting it down to boyish psychedelic visions of climbing through the television. He is laughing now, time having rubbed the sting away. "Yeah. That was real. I wanted the world to see me and to show I'd survived."

Wells did survive, if at first in body rather than mind. "If I'm totally honest, I was never the same player." And just before he grew out of one skin and into another, he did at least have his childhood dream chalked off. The day after the

Test, he and his wife were doing the shopping. A man stacking shelves, noticing Alan next to him, stopped. "He said, 'I'm so sorry, but you're Alan Wells, aren't you?'" He was indeed Alan Wells, *the* Alan Wells, and not Colin Wells's younger brother. "He said, 'Oh, mate, I was so sorry you got out first ball the other day, but if it's any consolation, I got out first ball on Saturday as well.'" The shelf stacker had been clean bowled for his club's third XI. "It put it in a lovely perspective," Alan remembers. "He probably felt as bad as I did."

Alan Wells finds the camera – "I want you to look at me, because I'm still here."

8

319

L ana's initial reluctance to use a walking stick,
which had bled into acceptance once it became an
absolute necessity, had turned itself – as with each
signposted moment – into a reluctance towards an electric
wheelchair. This was brought in, she conceded, with a
condition. She would only use it indoors, and she would
control it. There was, however, a small issue with this plan.
A tremor in her hand had developed. Like each invasion of
multiple sclerosis, at first it was a glimmer, an oddity, before
becoming, in the sinking sand of moving time, a part of her
day-to-day. As she sat, at first privately, in the house, on the
wheelchair, she held her tremoring left hand still with her
less tremoring right on the joystick. The tremors colluded
with the recurring optic neuritis to cause her to forget which
way would go which. Pausing for a second to consider at
the end of the hallway, instead of moving forwards into the
hall, she would propel herself backwards, at a rate, into the
doors behind. Andrew at first concealed the dents, painting
over the marks that were accumulating by the day, but in
time grew fond of them and allowed them to become part
of the living, breathing, changing house. And as the illness
forced itself not just through her body but through the house
too, a new stairlift arrived, a cumbersome mechanical track
which occupied most of the staircase to transport her up
and down. It was there, we boys decided, to be used as a

tool for hilarity, as we tried to stand on one leg on it or invented a new high-risk ritual "International Rescue" as one brother hung precariously from the bannisters waiting to be "saved".

While the house gathered bumps and dents and moved with this forced change, I had got used to walking myself to school. It was not a particularly big deal. With Ted the lollipop man always at the stop, there was only one aided road crossing to get there. This morning, Ted wasn't there. I shrugged. I was 11. I could still get across that road. The 319 bus was just passing as I reached the end of the pavement, its indicators blinking to its left. Without regard for the speed it was going (which made it literally impossible for it to turn down the street I imagined it to be indicating down), I walked out, straight in front of it. The next things I remember are in a series of static images. The bus is suddenly very close to me, and I am turning my back. Then there is the gravel, in front of my nose. Then a kind of glossed-out recall of the contingent at the bus stop 100 yards away – beginning to run towards me in slow motion, getting closer with each slide. Then I am looking up and there, through the throng of onlookers, is the bus driver. He is staring just beyond the wheel into a vacant nondescript spot just above my head, his face drained of colour. As I was discharged from hospital with no serious problems, I wished there was some way of telling him.

Perhaps out of relief that the bus had damaged me little more than exaggerating my already minuscule capacity for danger, I managed to use this sudden bus-crash capital to wangle going on a cricket course at The Oval, once a week. The nets, the only ones in the facility, were the same the team would use. The moulding of the everyday and where the greats dwelled was very appealing at The Oval; around any corner, you might bump into Graham Thorpe or Alec Stewart. You never did, but you *might*, and the might was the important thing. The nets came with a viewing area, so parents could watch the practice from above. As I bowled, still as lovely and loopy as I could, I would turn and look directly up, after each delivery, to see if Andrew had seen me. He was watching. Plainly a bit tired. But he was watching.

*

The same club has arranged tickets for everyone to a Surrey one-day game that summer. Disbelieving at the amount of cricket he is being dragged to, Andrew is sitting next to me as the Surrey Lions take on Gloucestershire, my first game at The Oval. Surrey bowl first and, on a day as typically raucous as Tufnell's recall, towards the end of their allotted overs, all the other kids, as if it is some accepted routine, lurch with a uniformed zombie rhythm towards the advertisement boards that divide the stands from the pitch. They crouch behind them. I am not sure what they are doing, but in a primal desire to join the pack, I move with them. I crouch underneath the boards too, peering across the line at all the other kids. For a second, I sense a pang of horrible panic, as if we are soldiers about to jump over the front line. The last ball is bowled and, true to my fear, everyone takes off, over the boards and onto the pitch. The fear not yet subsided, without having made the conscious decision, I am running too, first out of surprise, then in embarrassment and then in abandon, across the patch of rare holy green expanse inhabited only a few seconds previously by all the players. When we reach the other side of this uncharted land, panting and delirious, there is a growing sense of calamity and a chaotic queue. I barge through. Sitting in front of the boards in front of the pavilion, his smile even bigger than it seemed on TV when playing for England, is *the* real-life Chris Lewis. He is patiently signing small bats and big pieces of card with 4 and 6 written on either side – an actual living cricketer in blue and yellow pyjamas, smiling. I am sort of inside his world, so close at least that I can reach out and *almost* touch him.

9

Chris Lewis and the Autographs

"I think what I found," Chris Lewis tells me, thinking back to the cricketer he once was, waiting on that boundary to sign autographs, "was that in that space, there was acceptance." Lewis, it turns out, made a habit of being attentive to kids on the outfield waiting for autographs, while the other cricketers dodged the parade, darting back into the sacred space of the dressing room; he even spent one lunch break at Sussex taking part in a kids' game of cricket. "I must have been in my early twenties, so the lungs were working properly back then. I stayed on the outfield, played with the kids, and then the players came back out and I just kept playing, but with them." What does he remember of that person, I ask. "I remember enjoying that in particular, perhaps because it wasn't a space of judgement. All the kids wanted to do was play cricket. That was easy for me." I tell him about how it tied fantasy and reality together for me for a brief moment, somehow making anything seem possible, and he finds a second to pause to remember the feeling and being able to hand that tiny but powerful gesture down. "That's really made my day," he says. "The important thing is that you remember that and it made some kind of difference. It was a natural gravitation for me, I think."

Lewis moved to London from Guyana as a ten-year-old, with a list of West Indian cricketing heroes such as Lance Gibbs and Clive Lloyd vivid in his imagination. At his comprehensive school in North West London, in a widely diverse community, he became well known for taking a cricket bat to school every morning, where most others took footballs. Although it was tempered by his mother's desire for him to be a doctor, Chris gathered a reputation as an unusually gifted all-rounder, the disciplines of batting, bowling and fielding each informing the last. "When I was batting, it really worked when it was automatic," he recalls. "Sometimes I was playing a shot and I'd genuinely think, how did that happen?" His fast bowling, hostile and aggressive, played off against this instinct: "It made me think, so as a bowler, the goal is to really overload a batter's thought process, to really make them *think*. I found I could make them think quite hard if I bowled bouncers at their head." That should do it.

This combination of abilities eventually led him to become a professional cricketer, playing 80 times for England, including in the famous losing 1992 World Cup final side, a flicker of a memory of mine, where he was bowled first ball by Wasim Akram, in a spell of lightning inswing. The highlights from Melbourne still show Lewis, frozen for a fraction of a second, not believing that it has happened. Like Wells, it wasn't himself he was upset for. "There was such a build-up to that game, I'd spoken to family members and friends, and everyone was setting alarms so they could watch it, whether they were into cricket or not." Lewis, who had opened the bowling that day, heard the immediate clatter of his stumps and thought of home. "I just thought, after all that, everyone I know has tuned in for about 20 seconds of cricket. They'll all be going back to bed straight away." As he walked off, he imagined all the popped anticipation of his friends' homes, televisions being turned straight off and everyone rolling back around to sleep.

In 2008, following a string of "bad decisions that had worse consequences" that left him in a financially desperate situation, Lewis attempted to smuggle £140,000 worth of liquid cocaine back to England from St Lucia. He was sentenced to 13 years, of which he served six. "If you think about time in prison, it goes very slowly," he says. After a prolonged period of soul searching, he slowly began to find inner strength through cricketing memories. "Getting through the process was actually all down to realising that those skills were transferable and that a lot of the things I'd learned, I could apply back into life. I can make a plan, I can focus, I do know how to achieve." Lewis started repeating to himself, "You've done tough things before and you can do this." "If you're a cricketer," he tells me, as if it is never truly in your past, "you see cricket in everything."

His experience since his freedom has been turned into a play, *The Long Walk Back*, and time since has seen him slowly making sense of all the people he has been, from the boy from Guyana to the man on the boundary signing autographs, the Test cricketer, the man arrested at Gatwick Airport, the man passing time in prison and finally the man he is today, never falling out of love with the game. "In a lot of ways, cricket is still that thing for me," he says. "It's my vehicle to explore the world, to meet new people, to make your mistakes and try to make it better again." When he hasn't been able to play, he's ended up picking up the sponge ball in his room, running his hands over it as if it had a seam, to bowl, in the definitive grip that has become part of his muscle memory. "I don't know what Test match I'm practising for, but there you go. Sometimes I'll be picking up fruit and it's a ball. It's like a comfort thing, the same way a smoker might miss that feeling of having a cigarette between their fingers once they stop."

I remember the heartbreak of the news that Lewis had been arrested, distorting the vision of the man I'd seen so calm on that boundary, and am happy to have found a Lewis at relative peace. "When I look back on my life, if I take the fear out, all I have is gratitude for the experiences. Once I didn't feel fear anymore, the lows became really extraordinary learning experiences," he gently affirms. I wonder whether he sees himself in the modern-day cricketers, so full of the dynamism and eclecticism that he embodied. He clearly has thought it through, too: "I think it would be right up my street. The only thing is, with mobile phones and stuff now, I'd be in so much trouble," he laughs. "That cricketer would have still wanted to go out dancing, and last time I checked, the clubs still don't open until 11 these days."

His last televised appearance for England was in 1996 against Pakistan back at The Oval where, in trouble for turning up late after one of those very late nights, he was sent to field at fine leg, where Tuffers would so regularly be hiding, "in the naughty corner". Pakistani batter Asif Mujtaba ran the ball down to the same boundary I had hidden behind, then watched Lewis sign autographs; with the batters attempting two, Lewis flung the ball back perfectly,

Chris Lewis signs autographs – "In that space, there was acceptance."

leaving Alec Stewart nothing to do but receive it and take the bails off. It was an extraordinary piece of cricketing brilliance that would prove to be his last on the Test arena, the powers that be deciding to draw a line under his off-field unpredictability. "As I'm speaking to you," he tells me, "I can feel myself running, picking it up one-handed, throwing it in." It's in my head as I replay it, too, so at odds with the era he played in, exhibiting a different level of cricketing instinct to all the other forlorn English cricketers I'd also grown so fond of. It is, in fact, an image of the modern England one-day team, who wear kit almost identical to that of Lewis's 1992 finalists, as if to invoke their spirit. "They actually sent me the kit, with Lewis on the back," he says. "It was a very nice surprise to be remembered in that way."

10

Gates of Burnage

There is, in middle-class people of my generation – at least in those that I've come across – a period in which we have all tried to find ways that we are not middle class at all, but born of some kind of mild trauma or austerity or, at the least, vague rootsiness. Someone's brother's girlfriend works in a pie and mash shop. Your dad lost all his money once before you were born (but then made it all back). You support Millwall. It goes on. A few years on, as I reached my mid-teens and found myself flanked by friends who silently yet patently held the same sensitivity, it would break out in everyone like contagion. The most popular physical expression for it, given that guitar music sat secondary to drum'n'bass rave culture in South London, was to wear a hood slung over your head at all times, allow your jeans to fall below your bum, keeping them up by tying a belt loosely as they hung precariously over the top of your thighs, and litter the words "bruv", "heavy", "safe" and "mandem" across your sentences as if they were mandatory seasoning for any interaction. All t's pronounced could be a giveaway for your middle-classness and were to be dispensed with immediately. Affected, general pseudonyms were acquired to greet other people: chap, fella, geezer.

This was, no doubt, all very bizarre posturing for my dad to witness. Not being into sport or, for that, any public shows of alpha behaviour of any description made him a strange working class for me to work with – one which I couldn't quite capture or align myself to. His was a more reserved and weary type of working-classness, not the advertised one for which everyone was reaching. My Palestinian blood at least gave me some non-English currency, which I held onto like a grenade, should I need it as protective ammunition. This manoeuvring to defend myself from being middle class, the worst thing you could ever be called by anyone, had started prematurely in the years when Oasis were at their peak, when I had astutely recognised the need to be working class and from Manchester in order to survive.

I looked around at my associated interests and asked myself, *when* I eventually met Liam and Noel – as they guarded their gates to Burnage like bouncers to a club, looking me up and down to see if I fitted the dress code, and then, if so, gazing into my soul to see if that was pure too – would Oasis approve of me? This is where, at these gates of Manc heaven, Oasis confronted cricket in a particularly vicious dressing-down. I suddenly looked back at the game, for which I was once only seeing characters and theatre, as a slapstick encapsulation of all things middle class. Cucumber sandwiches. Tea. Cosiness. Manners. I was repulsed by my previous comfort in the niceness of it. The men, older and softer, with accents that leaned heavily on air or hair or lair, whom I had been so keen to impress, would be cannon fodder for Oasis. There was absolutely no chance that they were getting into Manc heaven. It was not a particularly harmonious landscape to nurture in my imagination. I'd slip into the cricketing mind, full of lovely, loopy spin, doomed commitment and the rigidly uncool, and then be confronted by Oasis in my other being, condemning the entire thing and forcing me to hide cricket from them behind my back. Like two separate friends to whom I had given such different impressions of myself that I dared not introduce them for fear of my cover being blown, I tried to keep them as far from each other as I could. After all, I was unwilling to make a choice between them.

As I pinballed them back and forth in my mind, looking for unlikely loopholes in which I might appease both, Bernard, my cricketing chairman of selectors, whom I had decided Oasis had time for because of his longish brown hair, invited me to join Honor Oak Cricket Club. At weekends, Andrew drove the three of us boys down to the leafier part of South East London, indicated by a perimeter of white fences that shielded deep-set gardens on the front of the road, where we would take part in outdoor club practices and friendly matches. Honor Oak was like a surrealist cricket-breeding factory. There were hundreds of Bernards, all with packed lunches and flasks, and rolling fields sliced into different-sized painted boundaries, each with 22 yards of cricket pitch in the middle. I switched off my Oasis voice for a second and sunk into a hesitant but blessed relief. This relief, enveloped by a hundred Bernards, would accommodate itself in stabi-liser-like beginner games where teams would bat in pairs. A wicket wouldn't mean you were out, but instead the team had five runs deducted, as you and your partner batted your allotted four overs. My brothers, on our first trip, witnessing me walk off the pitch minus 35 not out, decided that playing looked at the very least preferable to watching. When they came back with me the next weekend in their various collated whites, I flinched and loaded unnecessary context onto my every action on the field, as they simply walked out and hit and threw and caught. Without even grasping the rules, they were much better than me immediately. I was the eldest. I cared the most. I was the worst. I knew it and they did too, though none of us dared speak it.

Within weeks, despite the age disparity, we are all on the same team. Dad, an Andrew in a field of Bernards, suddenly looks like a high-achieving Cricket Dad, being the father of a quarter of the team. With Bernard, or one of the senior

Bernards, making this assumption, he is roped in to umpire the games. As both sides take to the field, he ushers me to one corner. He speaks calmly, but with an air of urgency too, as he asks me what a wide is. I stand there, bat in hand, demonstrating where, roughly, the ball needs to be for the umpire to call it a wide. Just for his benefit, we go through some more signals and rules too. LBW, byes, no-ball. From a distance it appears that a son is teaching his father avant-garde dance inconspicuously and in a hurry. As I stand at a wide third slip, a fielding position intentionally somewhere within his eyeline, I keep my eyes fixed on him. First, I flinch as the ball is sent down by the bowler, praying for it not to come towards me, and then I very subtly spread both hands out to my side, a kind of micro-signalling, and nod, like a police detective cautiously actioning a raid. He micro-nods back and then turns, arms outstretched, to signal a wide to the scorers.

*

My primary-school years were coming to an end, with Ted the lollipop man having been dispensed with and a new, more punctual lady, whose name no-one had yet learned, being deployed. The disappearance of Ted had exactly inter-twined with me being hit at the unmanned crossing by the double-decker 319. I didn't need to be told. Ted had been sacked. Every day the new woman shepherded us over the road, I smiled and thanked her but silently thought of Ted, and how I might have cost him his job with my misreading of some indicator lights. While loading myself with guilt, I had used the incident to spin a kind of folklore around myself at school, which had contributed to an eventual, full-scale social acceptance. A victim of a bus crash with an encyclo-pedic knowledge of this week's pop charts is a neat little niche and, having done the hard yards early on with little progress, I was keen to capitalise. As the recipient of the class's belated approval, I chose to use this new power simply to learn things of my classmates. I surveyed them with a poll on who was better, Oasis or Blur. Like a ticket inspector, I walked around from table to table, solemnly handing down my notebook and asking each classmate, without being swayed one way or the other by consensus, to place a tick. At the end of the exercise, I counted the results. Oasis 29. Blur 1. The solitary name in the Blur column belonged to Rhianwen Davies. I looked at the lone tick under her name in the Blur column, then across at her, with her thatched red hair that sat above her shoulders, as she twiddled her pen and stared into middle distance, and was overcome by an uncomfortable, sick confusion.

I harboured the feeling until the celebratory leaving do from the school, an "adventure weekend" in Sayers Croft with a disco at the end. Nobody had ever participated in a real disco before and, picturing the closing scenes of *Grease*, we whipped each other into a frenzied tension during the assault courses and canoe expeditions that built towards this last dance. In doing so, a message came through Billy Hunt, still my best friend, having been passed to him through one of Rhianwen's friends. She was enquiring about my availability at tomorrow night's disco. I was available.

When the moment came, we stood in front of each other, at least two feet apart, feet totally static, and headbanged to "Firestarter" by The Prodigy. I wasn't sure how to do it or what the chemistry would be between us, but I took to the task with a stubborn determination, frantically thrashing my head up and down while the rest of my body remained perfectly still. When the song ended, I looked at her, hair completely dismantled from its usual thickness by the storm we'd created to the song. She looked back momentarily at me before we both ran back to opposite corners of the room. She didn't need to say it. It was over.

Five years previously, on holiday, a girl of my age, Spanish with a ghost-white complexion, rakish figure and long, straight, blonde hair, had lowered herself into the swimming pool. For reasons beyond my choosing, on witnessing this figure enter the water from my peripherals, I began to frantically swim front crawl across the length of the pool. My head down, splashing and kicking and racing as fast as I could, occasionally coming up for air, I waited until she had gone before I finally relaxed again. I had tried for a long time to work out what had come over me that day and, running away from Rhianwen, dizzy and embarrassed, I felt it again: no more certain of what this propulsion had been, but at least recognising its giddying return.

The social circle I had utilised a bus crash to get inside was painfully deconstructed just as it had been consolidated. Primary school was over and everyone was headed in different directions. With my Sayers Croft t-shirt signed by anyone I could find, including Rhianwen, who wished me, unknowingly coldly, to "have a nice life", we were off. For three months previously I had been sent to various school examinations across the stretch of South London. There were state schools to visit and private schools to sit exams for. One of the latter was Alleyn's, in Dulwich, housed by the same white fences that popped up around Honor Oak. I passed the exam with a state-assisted place. This was a source of small but obvious pride to my parents. It wasn't going to be possible to walk around the school when we visited – it would be too tiring for Lana – so we went for a meeting and I sat, blank and speechless, in front of the Lower School Headteacher as he reeled off the school's facilities. I nodded when required, sensing a strange sadness and surging pulse around my throat. As we left, feeling as if I should run somewhere, preferably towards a cricketer, but having to keep in step painfully slowly with Lana, I looked out in the distance at the school's playing fields. There was a boundary, a pavilion and a pitch.

That world looked far bigger than I could ever fathom it to be, like I might be engulfed and swallowed by it and never be able to speak again.

When we got home, I found myself completely unable to articulate which school I wanted to go to. Billy Hunt was going to Emmanuel. I didn't want to leave him. How could I leave Paul Weller's muse? After I had thrown this out there, loosely bookending any comment I made with "I don't know", Andrew asked if I wanted them to make the decision. I said yes. I was sitting upstairs awaiting the verdict when Andrew, excitedly, called me from the bottom. "Felix! You're going to Alleyn's!" I knew my credentials at Oasis's door of acceptance were now smithereens. My brothers, when they both ended up at the more local state school a couple of years later, decided, when an occasion presented itself where the point needed to be made, to call me "posh boy". My cover was blown. *They* knew I wasn't from Manchester.

The summer that separated the two schools was marked by the Ashes series returning to England. Shane Warne had spent the four years since his earth-shattering first Ashes delivery roundly destroying cricket teams all over the world, with Glenn McGrath his forensic fast-bowling counterpart. England had lost the previous Ashes series 4-0, 3-0, 4-1 and 3-1. Despite a mini-series victory against India the previous summer and an overseas victory in New Zealand, Atherton's captaincy had been nearly as bumpy as the period that went before. There was not a great deal to suggest that this series would play out any differently, but inevitably the "what if?" returned as the build-up began. The Surrey team were at the start of a period of domestic dominance at The Oval, and their composite personalities were beginning to populate the England side, too. Most exciting of all were the Hollioake brothers, Adam and Ben.

Adam, a refreshingly fearless and aggressively-minded cricketer, captained the one-day side and, in the short-format series that set up the Test match sustenance over the bulk of the summer, had built a new enthusiasm and energy into England. Two unbeaten half-centuries in the first two games helped England to take an unfathomable and unassailable 2-0 lead in the series before the third, in which England, sensing a spirited voodoo he might have, introduced his younger, more naturally gifted brother Ben Hollioake to the team, batting at number three.

*

We jump in the car to Purley that Sunday, driving past the woman manically waving, into the leafy suburbs, up the driveway, through the "no milk today" routine and into the front room where the cricket is. Australia, bowled out for 269, have taken the early wicket of Atherton and young Ben is at the crease.

He is tall, blessed with an unfussiness and youthful nonchalance when he sets up to bat. Michael Kasprowicz runs into bowl. Ben is off the mark immediately, hitting him straight down the pitch. It is a fluid motion of complete calm and destructive tranquillity. Then he thrashes McGrath through cover. He whips him through mid-wicket. He watches Warne float the ball in front of him, simply stands still and dismisses him back the same way for four. Then he deftly sweeps him. He gets on one knee and smashes him for six. When he is out for 63 off only 48 balls, a strike rate far beyond its time, he has embedded something into the English summer. It is breathtakingly beautiful. I think briefly of Adam, and whether he felt the same twinge of resentment I did that his brother was obviously capable of something he wasn't, before landing on a more settling thought. Ben Hollioake, 19, was so at ease and so cool, his innings such a work of anti-establishment iconoclasm, that maybe even Oasis would have appreciated it.

Though the Hollioakes weren't initially involved in the Test side, the sense of possibility with which they'd infected the English psyche seemed to hang in the air when the Ashes proper began at Edgbaston. The television radiated an unfamiliar positivity on the first morning, and it somehow, as it so often can, crept its way into the cricket itself, as England bowled Australia out for 118. At one stage Australia were 45-6, Andrew Caddick with his big ears, serious disposition and oddly idiosyncratic saunter at the beginning of his run-up, taking five of them. England, remarkably, would only have to bat once, with Nasser Hussain scoring 207 and Graham Thorpe 138. It was genuinely trippy. I'd begun to travel through enough vicarious hardship with the compact partnership of Thorpe and Hussain that when they put their arms around each other to celebrate England's highest fourth-wicket partnership against Australia, it contained all the closeness of the school leaving do I'd just had, a sense of a road travelled together, as if they were leather-jacketed T-Birds embracing in a summer that they knew they'd never beat.

It was, of course, a premature high. Australia levelled the series at Old Trafford after a draw at Lord's and England lost the next two Tests convincingly, Atherton being dismissed by McGrath seven times in total in a summer that resumed its conventional path. Not even the debuts of the Hollioakes at Nottingham, receiving their caps together in an image of each other, and batting next to each other in the order, could reverse the fortunes. Atherton, who had left the season of four years before with a bounding step of what might be, was, in every newspaper throughout the summer it seemed, being asked to step down as captain. Tuffers, who had been picked for every squad and then sent home each time, was eventually selected for the last, consolation Test. In the most memorable Test performance of his career, he almost single-handedly bowled out Australia in their first innings, with his slow (but angry), lovely (but aggressive), loopy stuff, grimacing between deliveries and wrapping up another lost Ashes summer. He took the last wicket, too, of Glenn McGrath, with Australia only 20 short of their modest target of 124. The England players raced off the field in elated release, beaten but with yet another cruel "what if?" intact, somehow, despite another sound thrashing, prouder than ever.

I walked into my new school like every other boy and girl, with a confusing concern about what to expect and a uniform at least three sizes too big for me. Lana was awake as I left, upright in her wheelchair, wishing me good luck, grinning, as her head shuddered left and right. That was the latest symptom. It was as if with every step I took further into the world, her world reclined slightly more. I left with a vision of the England cricket side that summer, losers again, but celebrating all the same, and with Oasis's first two albums and a Walkman stuffed into my bag. The band and the game might not have agreed completely with each other stylistically, but at least I had them both to sink back into.

11

The Currency of Losing

I f you were to pool a group of 11- and 12-year-olds, scoop them together and stand them next to each other, as they did in the first week for a school photo, there are a handful of universal truths you would make in observation. Girls, on the whole, mature quicker than boys, who vary almost incomparably in height and appearance. I was still small, not the smallest, but small, and skinny. The school photo portrays me exactly as I felt: slightly engulfed. Some of the boys had already begun their early ascent into manhood and almost doubled me in either direction. A lot of the girls towered over me, too. In the early exchanges of manic societal jostling, my bus crash no longer of any popularity-contest use, there were a couple of months of frantic exchanges, the loudest often leading packs and then the packs abandoning the gobshite and doubling back on themselves to leave a regular sense of group dizziness and frantic decision-making.

Imagining myself as Tuffers in a world of quick bowlers, I worked out an unspoken schtick with some of the boys in my class, exactly the same age, but twice the height and width.

Dominic Edwards was one. Without any spoken agreement or sense of how it evolved, Dom and I began to stage fights, pitched somewhere between theatre and real fighting. It was an art form of sorts which consisted of many moving parts, a spectacle in which I was always destined to lose, but would do so heroically by jumping theatrically off lockers, hanging off Dom, before he flung me, as if swatting a fly, back onto the lockers or onto a pile of bags. We developed a telepathic understanding in which we were able to execute these patterns of war succinctly in between lessons, so as one teacher left, the class would instinctively gather around the perimeter of the room, like fielders ringing a boundary, and watch me get beaten up by Dom. We'd turn the whole thing round, pieces of strong narrative arc in feigned violence, in a matter of minutes, so everyone could laugh, boo, cheer and then return to their seats in time for the arrival of the next teacher, who would assume we had been sitting completely still for the entirety of the changeover. It was very important for both of our senses of newly carved selves that I should lose these fights. When I did so, beaten and lying slain underneath his foot or a pile of bags or locker rubble, girls would gather round as I lay on the floor, and ask if I was OK. "I'm OK," I would say, coughing unnecessarily to imply a physical bruising underneath the surface. The girls formed a net of infinite female attention, which would last for the rest of the day at least, while the boys would in turn observe them and, as I returned to my feet or my seat, look at me with a confused respect. How did I get all these girls to like me? Just by being beaten up? Faking injury that year became a huge string to my bow and, buoyed by its effectiveness, before long, I was walking into school and affecting a limp. I was rolling down hills and then lying at the bottom a second more than was necessary for a moment of suspense before gallantly rising to my feet. Plainly, and like most 12-year-olds, I needed everyone to like me. I would do what it took in a world where my attributes were often tucked away in subtle little areas.

The issue with this complete swindle was that the fights, in order to retain the same level of gossip collateral throughout each day, needed to escalate in order for my public not to become bored. As a result, I was relieved by the distraction offered when the summer term came around. I'd somehow got myself into the football team, playing at left back, which at under-12 level required little more than staying out of the way, occasionally executing one of my heroic near-headers and sometimes throwing the ball down the line. So, when cricket season came, the resourcefulness through which my feigning constant injury had received attention and the effectiveness with which I hid from criticism at football left me some space for cricketing optimism.

*

The setting up of the nets themselves takes the first hour. Wide netting hangs at the back of the sports hall in pinned green tarmac-like material. Unhooking it is like an army drill undertaken by lemmings, requiring a full squad just to set it up. Dragging the sections back down the hall on the pulley system requires each of us to hold a section, amassing the webbing in one arm and yanking it while all walking simultaneously back to the hall. There are quite a few of us left in its wake, tangled and floored in the nets. Then the pitch itself, an artificial rolled mat, requires four (at least) of us to get on our knees behind it and unravel it in as straight a line as we can. When all this is done, we are lined up against the wall. "Who are the bowlers here, then?" I stick my hand up. Peter "Coach Roach" Edwards, a cricket specialist of whom I am going to become very fond very quickly, saunters down the line, stopping at each of the self-confessed bowlers. What do you bowl? Fast. The next. Fast. Fast. Fast. Everyone, in their own words, chins raised to the ceiling, bowls fast. He eventually reaches me and raises his eyebrows in anticipation of another quick in the ranks. I puff out my chest and announce, "Slow left-arm, sir." Coach Roach stops. He ushers that year's manager, Mr Bucknor, over. "Felix bowls left-arm spin, he says." I pause, as if wondering if I have done something wrong, before nodding again. They have a impromptu private mini-meeting. I can tell then, by the change in their body language, even without having seen me bowl a ball, that I've just got myself into the team.

*

The brilliant, halcyon wonder of playing under-12s cricket and being a spinner was that you really didn't need to spin the ball at all. There was some kind of psychological window in which it was impressive in its very act alone. If you could bowl relatively straight, you were in. That year I had the season of my life. There would be a moment, on receiving the ball, of tiny Oasis-like belonging. I knew that all life was expecting of me was to run up and bowl that ball. All I needed to do, too, was to mark a run-up in as diagonal and short a line as I could feasibly muster, do some eccentric stuff with my hands, which I would re-enact as close as possible to Tufnell, and then lob the ball as high and as straight as possible. Some boy in fatally oversized kit, struggling to see through a helmet four times the size of his head, would always miss it and I would return home with an enormous sense of satisfaction, wickets in the bank. I was guaranteed to be mobbed by my team, bathed in an all-encompassing love and focus. I could really articulate something about myself in the act, too. I wasn't trying to knock people's heads off. I was bowling lovely, loopy left-arm spin. It was unthreatening. It was successful. It was loved. And that was enough. I was invited that year to go to trials for London Schools' Cricket Association. It was the apex of my cricketing life.

My non-cricketing survivalist techniques, however, finally ran out of steam that year on a school trip to the Lake District. It was the kind of innocuous half-fight manoeuvre Dom and I carried out all year without any harm. Overexcited this time and feeling the pressure to accentuate the danger to retain social currency, I'd moved too close to Dom as he gestured to knee me; he connected directly with my left testicle, sending it sickeningly and momentarily back into my stomach. Floored, I looked back up into the sky, hyperventilating, as the rest of the class leaned over me, my eyes bursting with water and, most notably, my twisted, writhing body in actual, real pain. The girls looked less committed in their sympathy, walking backwards from the mess on the floor, their infinite net of attention dissipating before my eyes. I knew then that next year my quest to gain approval from absolutely everyone would need some evolution.

12

40 Minutes of Empathic
Transference

Within the next year, the stairlift was gone. It was a move they had been reluctant to make. The stairlift disappearing was symbolic. She was not going upstairs again. She couldn't even use the wheelchair unaided now, her arms unable to follow any instruction she sent to them, and the walls had received their last indelible marks. She was in too much pain, too distracted by forcing her smile through every time her boys walked into the room to notice. Upstairs was now an unfathomable journey.

I'm sure with some desperation, she is beginning to be unable to give me what I need: conversation, touch, reassurance, advice. She strives to every day, through her now difficult speech, through her eyes and through her general strength of character, but it is going to be impossible to do it anywhere close to how she had imagined 13 years earlier. If I'm not getting it here, I don't ask myself then, where am I going to get it? Armed with all the things she has built so naturally into my being – a general affability, a social ease and an innate empathy – I take these traits, so specific to her and so interwoven in me, and move with them outside, towards indefinable masses of people, a numbing from intimacy washing across my world. I leave home every morning, saying goodbye to her in the room next to the front door, as she lies in bed, her head tilted up to watch me leave, with the cats now permanently positioned either side of her head, as a carer arrives. On leaving the door, taking a deep breath, I run to the bus stop. I am never late. I just always choose to run there, as fast as I can. And with that, I roll myself into school with a new philosophy on how to evolve a subtle popularity.

I had discarded the daily losing of preordained fights, and rebranded my outward world view in this quest for validation. People, it seemed, responded to a couple of things. Firstly, they liked it if you were so interested in something that you could forgo any kind of social grace by just diving into your passion and telling them about it. I had a long list of these passions. Secondly, people liked it if you were genuinely interested in them and, more importantly, if you communicated to them that you understood *exactly* where they were coming from. It was something I felt almost genetically capable of, having spent my early years watching Lana do exactly that and, unknowingly, I chose to engage all these traits she had stitched into my make-up. I'd listen to people speak, encouraging some kind of safe forum for them to vent, and then make some comment, which I had been formulating in my head while they talked about themselves, that was designed solely to make them pause, as if unwittingly meeting a soulmate, look deep into my eyes and say, "Yes... *exactly* that." I had an uncanny knack for this. It didn't matter whether it was teachers or pupils or newsagents. There were untold bonds to be made everywhere. I noticed that if I owned my genuine curiosity and slightly caricatured it, it worked. This is where I found myself at the age of 13. Wrestling had given me sincere commitment to completely ludicrous causes; but with it now discarded, that commitment had attached itself in turn to pop music and then inwards on Oasis, who had sold me definitive tribalism as an artistic prerequisite. Cricket had fed losing into my veins as a form of honourable self-identity. My mum's illness, squeezing the home into a kind of held stillness, meanwhile played out, ever worsening, alongside. It all swirled in my mind restlessly in need of some fortification.

It was an impressionable time to land inside the 1998 England vs South Africa series that fizzed with an unwinding sense of drama. England, of course, were the weaker of the sides, but both contained perfectly flawed yet vital cricketers questing for a sense of validation. South Africa brought a collection of personalities with enough boisterous *joie de vivre*, mixed with a surface-level sensitivity to guarantee their watchability for the duration of a summer. Jonty Rhodes, at the zenith of his form with the bat, a fiendishly dynamic fielder. Paul Adams, their spinner who let the ball go while contorting his body the completely wrong way round, his head looking the other way. Hansie Cronje, the captain and country's saviour, handed an almost humanitarian responsibility by Nelson Mandela. Makhaya Ntini, who had walked to school barefoot and covered his feet in cow dung to keep them warm not much more than a year earlier, running in and bowling fast. Mark Boucher, a very young wicketkeeper with a wide-eyed, roguish glint, and the fast-bowling duo, already entrenched in their decade-long duels against England's batsmen, Allan Donald and Shaun Pollock. Both sets of personnel seemed hell-bent on a kind of immortality that might only come with avoiding humiliation. The two, especially this summer, felt perilously close together. As I began to peer over the ledge of what adult life might ask of me, the cricket was to play out as a brutal collection of coming-of-age folklore.

Even by the usual standards, cricket had begun the summer as a secondary consideration behind football as the "golden generation" headed to France for the '98 World Cup. England – the cricketers – were sent scurrying every which way off screen to Allan Donald's fast bowling, and soundly beaten at Lord's. There was no sense of popped optimism as there had been the previous summer, more a general sense of malaise.

England's footballers were then, to a whiplash of national heartbreak, knocked out of the World Cup in the second round by an Argentinian side who would have sat very neatly in my Nasty Boys one-size-fits-all bad-guys prototype.

The received worthlessness from the disposal of the football team that somehow fed into all things sporting and English had crept into the joys of my bowling, too. I had grown, slightly up and slightly out, and yet my loopy spin stayed frozen in time. Trotting up and launching the ball into the sky, relatively straight, had started to get me found out. Boys had continued to suddenly spurt at completely different times, the odd anomaly occasionally popping up to resemble a man. Those who had reached that size, it seemed, would spend their weekends in the middle order of opposing schools' teams. I'd watch them on Saturday mornings, walking up from the other side of the pitch, chasing each other around, and then turn to *my* schoolmates and we'd gawp, already beaten, before looking for some kind of excuse for the inevitable. "There's no way he's 14, look at the fat one." "The fat one", who probably *was* 14, would usually take a shine to me. He, a kind of archetype reappearing every week, would watch the ball, almost have time to visibly chortle to himself and then, at will, take turns at hitting the ball as far as he could. I would be sent back from an over of public execution to my Tuffers-like spot at fine leg, to hear the batting team, rolling over their cricket bags and restlessly throwing balls at each other, report back, "You know their spinner?" "Yeah?" And they'd all smirk, waiting for the punchline. "He doesn't spin it." I could still hear the laughter echoing around my head before going back to bowl. When I did shuffle back, as I looked back to face my imminent dispatching to wherever else next, I sensed from my peripheral vision my fielders and my so-called friends moving further and further towards the boundary until they lined the perimeter. I hadn't instructed them to do that. They were already looking for the ball in the bushes or under the benches that he hadn't hit it into yet.

Of course, when I wasn't bowling, and stood around in the field with a sudden melancholic unwillingness, I somehow conspired, like Tuffers before me, to suck the ball towards my general vicinity. It would always feel as if it took hours to land and, of course, I'd never get anywhere near. The routine slip catches pre-game, in which our new thick-moustached coach would ask us to stand as close to him as possible and would whack cricket balls at us alarmingly hard, became a kind of archaic public-school form of whipping. I'd drop one. He'd shout, "Come on, Felix, put your bra on." Everyone would laugh. He'd hit it at me harder. I'd drop it even worse. The humiliation of it was absolute. I thought of Van and "Here Comes the Night". I went out to bat a few games later, was bowled first ball and turned to see another teacher celebrating, high-fiving the captain. They'd placed a bet I'd do that. Needless to say, this plummeting of confidence did not arrest itself for my performances with London Schools, which were very brief and very painful and very conclusive. I was not headed for a life as a cricketer.

Maybe as a result, I came to like the fact that the deflation of the football World Cup exit had permeated most of the rest of life for everyone. It convinced us *all* how doomed we were. It was a rhetoric that I was comfortable with; a communal refocusing on everything being fucked. English cricket continued to punctuate that, too. Old Trafford was disturbingly empty for the third Test in which England – 1-0 down, again – spent much of the time not so much playing catch-up as clinging on for dear life. In a not unfamiliar rearguard to save the game, England again depended on Atherton and new captain Alec Stewart who, occupying the crease for six and seven hours respectively, looked to have almost done it, batting in front of what could easily have been deemed a county cricket crowd. Until they got out, of course. Robert Croft, a Welsh spinner who had been preferred to Tuffers that summer, was wicketless all series, but he came out to bat with a determined resolve. He survived for three hours with Darren Gough, who himself was nobly keeping all of his aggressive instincts locked up before failing to negotiate a short ball from Donald. I spent the entire day watching it, unaware of the carers moving in and out and brothers darting around in the background.

*

As Angus Fraser walks out, the last man in, the sparsity of spectators in the ground seems to have morphed into a stark intensity, and with it, bristling with nerves, I feel somehow as if I *am* Angus Fraser, completely unprepared for what is about to happen. Croft begins to block balls and punch the air gently to himself as he does so, each ball he survives being a small event closer to implausible safety, as I wait and watch at the other end. Fraser is stranded at the striker's end, charged with facing Donald for the final over. With Donald powering in at rapid speed, Fraser takes to turning slightly away from the ball as it comes towards him, just as I do while watching, as if even he literally can't watch. Maybe he actually *is* me? Maybe I am controlling him somehow? The ball jars down into the ground, then slightly right of fielders, then somehow anywhere but the stumps. Finally, with one ball left, I implore him to watch the ball. Please, Angus. Just one more time. I'll watch it too, I promise. He does watch it, a lethal inswinging yorker. He and I watch it straight onto his pads. Straight in front of the stumps. The South Africans all go up in appeal. Not out. England have saved the Test match. Fraser has batted for 13 balls and Croft for 190 minutes. It is quite a feeble kind of joy, to be celebrating mere survival, and yet a nugget of proof that some things in life are perhaps less unnegotiable than they first appear.

*

Just before summer that year, Andrew had developed psoria-sis at the back of his head. It was a condition often brought on by stress, he was told. It being hidden from even his own sight, we developed a routine in which he would dictate his work emails or meeting minutes as I wrote them up, teaching myself to touch-type in the process, then I'd help him with the bins and the dishwasher, before he would sit on the sofa in front of the television and I would check the worsening of it. He would ask how bad it was and I would give him my appraisal. Its severity always seemed somehow intrinsically linked with how bad Lana's condition happened to be and I began to find the process informative and deeply satisfy-ing. The situation in the next room, its worsening so hard to understand, was beginning to find ways to show itself not just in the house, but on our bodies, too. He was bringing up three children, working a full-time job and looking after his terminally ill wife. I was grateful for the psoriasis. I knew how bad things were without having to ask.

The house itself had become a thoroughfare of carers in and out and vague chaos and, in response, his disposition for order and space begun to – understandably – increase. I came to think of myself as Angus Fraser or some other slightly clumsy tailender at the non-striker's end, watching my dad absorb pressure as we tried to save another Test, just trying to stay out of the way as much as possible while he negoti-ated the majority of the fast bowling. This kind of tension began to spill out of the house too, where, on one final trip to Blockbuster, a fine for a late video return had made him so upset he'd asked to see the manager and, when the manager arrived, had torn the Blockbuster card in half in front of our eyes. Blockbuster cards were quite rigid plastic. I watched the manager's face, respectfully observing my dad slowly and painfully tearing the card to pieces, while consoling myself that it was OK, I'd gone off wrestling anyway and I'd committed the bulk of the cricket videos to memory by now. Anyway, I had a feeling it was not necessarily all about the Blockbuster's card: Andrew just needed to do what he needed to to save the Test.

If school was becoming a place of life and adventure and a reaching for approval from everywhere I found it, when it broke for the eight-week holidays, I knew there was only one place I needed to be. The Test series. I tuned in every morning at 10.30am where again the background of the living room, the ins and outs of conversation, the back and forth of carers, the cats coming and going through the cat flap adjacent to the television, my brothers' attempts to move me as if they were badgering a human statue at Covent Garden, all warped into a white noise that I was forever tuned out of. It was just me and the television, which took on a vital electricity. What's more, there was suddenly no England in the football World Cup to be contended with and cricket, only a couple of weeks from the empty first days in Manchester, had an opportunity, on terrestrial television, to preserve a feeling of national joy. In Nottingham for the fourth Test, England thrillingly bowled South Africa out cheaply in their second innings to set themselves 247 to win on a slow, flat pitch staying true. With the game poised and England one down, Mike Atherton and Nasser Hussain at the crease, Allan Donald took the ball.

*

With sunblock on and beginning from behind the umpire, Donald runs in with the ball, as if completely possessed. The ball darts just past Athers' outside edge and Donald stares back at him, eyes clamped wide, adrenaline palpably coursing through his body, talking to himself and his opponent. He turns to bowl again. After each delivery, every ball somehow is slightly more intense than the last. Donald stops

and stares, Atherton looks up and stares back, the kind of
return glance that says a lot about Athers: a refusal to back
down, but underneath it a shyness, a mild embarrassment at
being locked in such a theatrical duel. It is as if he has been
cornered by a rabid dog and calculates that there is not much
else to be done but look back, pay him respect and not invoke
any further anger.

The outside world now an inconsequential mush of nothingness, I feel myself, ambitiously, no longer as Angus Fraser but
as Athers himself, locked in a fight, continuing with caution.
Another ball misses my outside edge. Donald stops and talks
to Athers. Donald stops and talks to *me*. The camera, tight
on Atherton's face, shows him staring back, slightly exposed,
mostly unmoved. I assume the same face, before returning
to my mark and preparing for the next ball. Donald bowls a
ferocious ball next, one that jumps, and Athers, turning his
back slightly, punches it straight to Mark Boucher, diving
to his right. It is out. Atherton, though, stands his ground. I
stand my ground too. The umpire doesn't give it out. Donald,
muttering at his most possessed, can do nothing but walk
back to his mark, quivering with anger.

Donald runs in and the ball, this time fuller in length
but no less venomous, spits out of the pitch and Atherton
inside-edges. The ball skews over the stumps, wrong-footing
Boucher, and away for four. Atherton looks relieved, half
shocked, half smiling. I practise the look, half shocked, half
smiling, before preparing myself again. The next Donald
unleashes is his quickest yet, short and at Atherton's body.
He swerves just out of the way. I swerve too. When we both
turn back round, Donald is standing there again, eyes wide,
talking straight at us. We look back, Athers as if negotiating
a wild dog. Two blinks of two sets of eyes. Donald turns,
Atherton finally looks down. I do not. The next is just as
quick, but not quite as short as we expect, and when Athers
realises it is hitting him in the chest, he pulls his bat down on

it, squirting the ball off to point. He looks up, slightly off his feet. I am standing up now, slightly off my feet too. Donald is there again, in front of us. A bloodthirsty nod and a little sideways glance this time. He is relentless, this time round the wicket to create a different angle that feels even more dangerous. Atherton is unmoved. He must simply not blink. I promise him I will not blink either. We will get through this.

Escaping to the other end, Atherton passes the strike to Nasser Hussain. I'm grateful as I'm exhausted. Nasser is beaten immediately, by one almost too quick for him to respond. Then it happens. Donald bowls a perfect bluff for a new batsman expecting the short ball and tempts Hussain into a faintly relieved prod. He nicks it clearly. This time it's out, surely. It flies to Boucher, who receives it in his gloves and then, in the same motion as the team go up around him in celebration, inexplicably spills it. He dives to his right to try to retrieve it. The ball is gone. The ball is grounded. It's the first ball that Boucher has dropped all summer, and it is the one that matters most. Donald, in a primitive explosion of pure anger, is screaming. He's screaming into the lens of the camera. The camera cuts to the body of a young Mark Boucher, face down on the floor. He's at first obstructed from view by the legs of his slip fielders. When the camera finds his face, his green cap is pulled over it. As he reveals himself, both eyebrows are peaked inwards, like a boy who has just been responsible for something indeed irreversible. His captain, Cronje, looks down at him and, as if disciplining a child, simply says, "Get up." Boucher looks very young, even younger, and very changed. He looks, in fact, exactly like I'd imagined my uncle Paul, a bizarre real-time rerunning of the story he used to tell, where I can suddenly see him young, absorbing his captain spitting, "Oh, fucking hell, Odell" at him. During the next over, with Donald contemplating the events at fine leg, he runs over to Boucher between deliveries in a gesture of solidarity, pats him on the back and reassures him. Boucher doesn't look particularly reassured. He looks distraught. Suddenly, I am Boucher too, wishing the world would swallow me up.

It is a very complex 40 minutes of empathic transference. The English batsmen survive the evening, and the next day, as if a storm has passed, weather the same bowlers with comparative ease. With the game gone and England close to victory, Donald bowls Atherton one more bouncer, which he pushes down into the ground, before being slightly rocked on his feet and staring back. It is the last punch. The last Donald has to offer. He doesn't stare or talk back this time, he just turns around. When Atherton hits the winning runs, leaving him short of a hundred again, unbeaten on 98, he is so blocked out in his own world that he nearly misses Alec Stewart's exuberant arm reaching towards him to mark victory while they cross for the last time and crowds flood onto the field in jubilation.

*

Atherton and Donald were two fighters in a team sport that allowed for the spectacle of individualism: Donald inspired enough to summon life from a flat, slow pitch and Atherton inspired enough to survive it. Dovetailing at exactly the right moment in each other's career, they propelled each other into the realm of myth that day, locked into a battle that transcended the game it took place within, like two boxers who could understand each other in a way that no-one else could. It was purpose and connection and, strangely, for all its alpha jostling, it was intimate. The event, too, was as close to a cultural happening as cricket had got in my lifetime. For the first time, the game was being spoken about everywhere as a source of joy and cause for celebration. Atherton had been poised between repetition and instinct, negotiating untold blows. There was more proof still. If you weather it, sometimes it *does* pass.

In a summer when England's golden generation of footballers were supposed to tap-dance themselves to something historical in France, it was an ugly, brooding, half-empty encounter in Nottingham that produced the one bragging right England would have in world sport. By the time the two teams reached Headingley, the series was swept into a cultural focus unimaginable only a month earlier when Angus Fraser/I had walked out to bat to save a Test match. In a final game that seesawed like a microcosm of the series before it, England won on the morning of the last day when, needing two wickets and South Africa 34 runs, people travelled from across the country and queued just to see the only hour of play.

I watched it, three inches from the television set. On celebration of the final wicket, that of Ntini, the television cameras followed the England team into the dressing room, over the shoulder of Alec Stewart as he shook hands with his team. We'd come through a lot this summer, I thought, a summer in which I had found myself inside the heads of various of the personnel in that room. I didn't want to turn the television off or for it to end. I knew, on the other side of the England dressing room I found myself in, as my living room came back into focus, there was a stillness but for the sound of my mum next door, struggling, with as little fuss as possible, to pin her arm to her chest to stop it shaking.

13

Michael Atherton and
When the Body Says No

P honing Michael Atherton to talk about Allan Donald
at Trent Bridge in 1998 is a bit like phoning Paul Weller
to talk about The Jam or Bob Dylan to talk about folk
music. The story has been told, there is nothing to add and
the more the world leans in and contorts the memory further
into swollen myth, the less likely Dylan/Weller/Atherton are
to contribute anything more themselves. It's not until the
phone is actually ringing, as I stare into it in my palm reading
"Mike Atherton", as if to double-check this is where my
life has actually led me, that it occurs to me this is the very
thing that I'm doing myself. The lead voice of cricket in many
ways since his retirement, both with pen and in commentary,
Atherton has proved himself, like Dylan or Weller, something
of a survivor and artist in personal reinvention. His success in
his non-playing life, one gleans, has in part been because of an
unwillingness to have his own myth fed back to him. Indeed,
he reflects on being forced to watch the infamous Donald
duel solely through rain-delay television reruns for which the
moment has become time-filling cannon fodder. "It's almost as
if I'm watching another person, to be honest," he says. "I just
spend it thinking, 'Did I really do that? Am I really out there?'"

Sensing it is too early to coerce Atherton into an existential contemplation – or, for that, inform him that there were

moments when I actually began to believe it wasn't him doing it at all, but me – I land on a far simpler and altogether more prescient question than I had planned. What with it being off-season, does he miss cricket? He springs into a new life, as if relieved that he won't be forced to relive all the moments to which he is occasionally chained. "I *do* miss cricket, actually." He says it in a bright, hopeful tone. It's refreshing to hear, I tell him, as I've come to expect anyone who has played cricket for an extended period of time to express a kind of weariness for the game, either in authenticity or as a face-saving schtick. He laughs. "It sounds an odd thing to say, but not everyone that works in cricket all the time necessarily enjoys watching it. I genuinely do enjoy it, still." From my own experience, I don't tell him, not everyone who watches cricket for leisure, let alone work, actually enjoys it either.

There is, undeniably, a sense of relief about the Atherton of now over the burdened young man, growing up in public, criticised and tested in front of doom-laden grey skies and the lenses of television cameras, while very tall men ran towards him and tried to knock him out. "What is really fortunate now is that I don't take the game home with me. In the past, I'd get out to Glenn McGrath for the nineteenth time and wouldn't be able to sleep." He pauses. "Even when I *would* sleep, it was always there, gnawing away at me. Now, I don't really care whether we've won or lost. I enjoy a good game of cricket and then try and write or talk about it as well as I can."

It's a brief insight into the Atherton that I heard and read about as a player but always struggled to see: the cricketer who, by all accounts, had the messiest corner of the dressing room. "I've never been someone who's been very good at planning what to do. I'm not particularly ambitious," he says. Despite their different traits on the field, it somehow calls Tuffers to mind, a personality who has let cricket come to him rather than choosing it. "I just do what I do as well as I can and hope the cards fall the right way." I'm lulled back into a zone where I might do as well as I can and hope my cards fall the right way and just find myself captaining England.

Trent Bridge, unsurprisingly, in its cauldron of grey, is recalled as not so much dreamlike as nightmarish. "It was so visceral and there was so much sledging that…" Atherton eventually concedes, "I do still remember certain parts of it pretty vividly." I try and mine for some of them, reeling them off in my mind's eye as if it *was* me who remembered facing each delivery. When he is caught behind and not given. "I remember a fleeting moment of thinking to myself, I should walk off." Some inexplicable intuition prevented him from doing so. "I'm slightly embarrassed that I didn't, to be honest. For some reason, I don't know why, I stayed there." Then comes the next ball, the near miss off his own bat and just beyond the stumps, as I picture a wince down the line. "A terrible inside edge," he observes. "I think I might have even heard it graze the leg stump." Then the final, most Shakespearean piece of them all, ironically with himself at the other end: Mark Boucher dropping Nasser Hussain, to Allan Donald's primal rage. "I can see it in my mind still, frame by frame. Boucher, diving across, two-handed. Popping it down. Donald was beyond me, down the pitch, screaming." I describe Boucher as he came across on television, cap over his eyes, at which Atherton's tone lifts again as if in acknowledgement of sporting drama. "That's right!" he continues. "I bet he grew up pretty quickly after that." There was a lot of growing up being done by a lot of people, inside and outside of the ground, that Sunday evening.

During the famous final morning at Headingley two weeks later, in what Atherton has previously described as the "nastiest, most ill-tempered match I was ever involved in", it is total news to me that he wasn't on the pitch to celebrate the victory. He was in hospital. "I suffer from an auto-immune condition that can affect you in various ways. It can attack your eyes or your bowels or your back." He says it in a typically matter-of-fact way that at first disguises the actual information. "I had suffered from ulcerative colitis specifically at the time and, bizarrely, it was the last time I ever had it." It's fascinating timing for a final bout, landing simultaneous to the victorious relief after the years of constant stress and upheaval, the small consolations and false dawns, before finally, then, shepherding his country home for the first time in over a decade.

It coincides strangely with a lot of reading I had been doing in the time leading up to our conversation, totally unrelated to cricket, that had not so much plagued me, but begun to re-explore what I knew about illness. It was only on recommendation from my brother Hugo, in the middle of a wave of enthusiasm for philosopher Gabor Maté, that I read *When the Body Says No*. He didn't explain, as I took to it, that it's a work that theorises that people with diseases in which their bodies essentially attack themselves are often suffering from a build-up of stress or mental pressure, which has found no other place to release itself, so chooses to do it through the body.

Stress is a complicated cascade of physical and biochemical response to powerful emotional stimuli… When emotions are repressed, as Mary had to do in her childhood search for security, this inhibition disarms the body's defences against illness. Repression – dissociating emotions from awareness and relegating them to the unconscious realm – disorganises and confuses our physiological defences so that in some people these defences go awry, becoming the destroyers of health rather than its protectors.

It is a difficult theory to read, one that changes my view of my mother's health and disturbs me enough to completely abort the reading of the book. I ask Atherton whether he's ever picked apart the timeliness of the last bout, as Maté's theory of a body's communication of unprocessed stress and trauma tumbles out of my mouth. Did this last wave indicate some kind of mental relief? "It's a good point. There are a lot of studies that suggest that stress makes things like that worse. I do have exactly what you are describing, where the body attacks itself." Athers's balanced contemplation is somehow calming, as I can almost hear him shrug. "It's dodgy genes. My dad had it and it stopped him being a footballer. Maybe stress makes it worse, who knows?" Indeed. Who does know. It is tempting, though, to think of it as the body's farewell yawn to a decade of stress, putting Atherton in a hospital and not on the field as his vast contribution reclaimed the 1998 summer of sport for English cricket amid a full house of mid-morning euphoria.

Sometimes, the cost of these things is such that what you have given means you cannot be there to witness its fruition. I think of Atherton then, batting with chronic back

Mike Atherton floored but survived – "Did I really do that? Am I really out there?"

pain and an auto-immune disease, then I think of Andrew's psoriasis and Lana's body failing her. I have a moment of thought for myself, too. Not for the person I am now, the one on the phone spouting half-read philosophical theories at the leading voice of cricket, but the boy in front of the television, as foreign to myself now as Atherton is to the batter I've just asked him to recollect. I think of the slow trauma that boy must have been quietly absorbing and wonder whether some part of that, too, was exorcised on the morning of that day in Leeds in 1998. I want to thank Mike for his part in inadvertently translating it all into some sense, but to do so suddenly seems hollow. It would not be my thanks, but a message on behalf of a 13-year-old boy, passed onto a stranger. Instead, I ask whether, despite it all, he remembers it being fun. "I do." The bright, hopeful tone, returns. "I loved it all actually."

14

Finding Home

Abla Assily was 15 and living in Haifa, Palestine, when Israel was created in 1948. In an overnight evacuation in which her family was forced to flee, they moved to the nearest city they knew: Tripoli in Lebanon. They kept their key, a huge bolt, half the size of a cricket bat, because, they told themselves, they were going to be back soon. For now, though, she was a sudden immigrant and, initially, treated like one. There was no schooling or work in Lebanon for Palestinians who had moved in and when finally there was, as a secretary, she would open her boss's letters to read complaints that he had hired a Palestinian. Her close friends, we know from surviving letters, were scattered, following different gambles of their own in forging new homes across the world, in Egypt and Canada to name but two. Home, to her, to put it mildly, had suddenly become a slippery concept. A year into their life in Lebanon, it became clear she would never be returning home. It was neither safe nor, for that, possible to get back in. The key became symbolic, rather than kept out of practicality. Even if they were to never get back to those abandoned houses, now with other people in them, they were still their homes and they always would be. They had the keys, after all.

Harry Odell was born in Teddington, to a separated, single mother, Elsie Neal. Word had been passed down in hushed rumours over time that his biological father was a philanderer and "not a good person", but that was as much as he was ever to know. At the time, between the wars, to be a child brought up without knowing who his dad was, was to live as a shame-tinged social anomaly. A different man brought him up alongside his mother, whom I met in her late years, a terrifyingly old figure in the corner of their dimly lit rooms at Christmas. When she died, she had a small black-and-white photo of a man no-one knew, presumably taken at the turn of the century, clenched in her hand.

In his young adult life, Harry began as an apprentice for a man called Harry Christmas, travelling in a sidecar to fix telephone lines in Clapham Junction decades before I would meet the mannequin cricketer there. He joined the army and fought through the entirety of the Second World War, moving through landings in France into Berlin before eventually being assigned captain of Royal Signals and posted to India. He left in 1948, moving into telecommunications and petroleum jobs across the world. As he would tell it, on one such posting he saw Abla Assily boarding a bus in Tripoli and told his nearest colleague that he was "going to marry that woman". His colleague softly consoled him that he didn't have the smallest chance of marrying that woman, now out of their sight as the bus passed them. A couple of years later, he had made true on his promise and they had two children in Lana and Paul.

They moved where his work took him: Syria, for three years until the English were thrown out in a people's revolution. Iran, until the same happened. Iraq for a short time. Their happiest times were in Abu Dhabi, now part of the UAE, which then was almost completely desert and barely populated with any people at all. Lana and Paul would play all day in the open expanse with their dog Skippy. There was no education in Abu Dhabi so, despite the years of oasis-like bliss, the children, it was decided eventually, were to be sent to boarding schools in England.

Harry and Abla in Tripoli, Lebanon.

Lana and Paul in Lebanon.

Atherton's small revelation about his physical condition during the '98 series, combined with my aborted read of Gabor Maté's *When the Body Says No*, is cause for a momentary dismantling of my own series of events. I am plagued with a sudden reframing of what happened to my mum and why. Do our bodies, when pushed, voice some trauma or stress we haven't been able to process for ourselves? I spend a week or two with a stark sense of creative stasis, having small flashbacks and reinterpreting tiny recollections. I remember Andrew, in a warning to me when I seemed overrun, taut and uncommunicative, telling me that Lana would spend hours on the phone, listening to her mother or a friend vent. When she came off the phone, having hardly contributed a word, she would respond to him, when asked, by saying, "It's fine." These alien stresses, he suggested, latched themselves into her mind, and in there, I elaborate to myself now, they would stay, looping and deepening themselves into her tissue.

Then I imagine the actual mechanics of being sent from a desert in Abu Dhabi with your family, to a boarding school in England as an eight-year-old. I haven't spoken to Paul for a number of years, the two sections of the family having slowly parted with the passing of time, and I decide this is a good excuse to do so. He tells me that the only problem is remembering it all himself. In the same breath, as if the act of allowing himself to remember opens a door where all the information is instantly available, he is recounting himself as a six-year-old in Abu Dhabi. "It was literally desert. There were six English families in the whole place." He is flooded with immediate recollective affection. "We spent the entire time right by the sea, lying in the sun and playing." The interruption, to be sent to boarding school, is something that he doesn't have to search for either, because he happens to have been reliving it to his wife, Tricia, only the week before. "It was extraordinary, actually, when you think about it. We would make our own way from Abu Dhabi to a boarding

Lana en route to boarding school, aged eight.

school we'd never been to in England, completely unsuper-vised. I'd get off the plane and go to Paddington and find another train from there."

Lana, eight when she first went away, was very popular at her girls' boarding school (Paul was sent to a different, all-boys school), and she would send him a letter every Sunday to make sure he was OK. "She really managed to look after me, even from so far away," he says, sighing that he didn't always write back. Though being left with hundreds of chil-dren his own age had its adventures and joys, some of them cricketing, he has spent years since unpacking being one of a vast collection of children, all hiding their own sudden aban-donment trauma, engaging in ways to fit in. "Because we were living with so many people, we were encouraged to hide our feelings. You didn't cry because you were missing your parents. You're almost a little..." – he searches for the phrase – "untruthful to yourself."

I feel a stirring new awareness of a handed-down, transgenerational displacement, my grandmother moved from her home, her fatherless husband constantly changing his and in turn sending their children away during their most formative years and half-nurturing them through an exciting yet rootless understanding of the world. "I can't speak for Lana," Paul says, "but for me, I never knew where my home was. I remember always thinking that I just wanted to be from *somewhere*."

Many years later, Paul would move his family out of London, to Reading. Paul wanted to have a home, a place that was constant, and that's what he found in Reading, where they, in my conscious mind, have always lived. Paul, inexplicably, was a Wolverhampton Wanderers football fan throughout his childhood. He'd never been to Wolverhampton. "That was so irrational, I eventually felt such a fraud," he says, not in a Brummie accent. Lana decided, in turn, the football team she belonged to was West Brom. This wasn't to create a Midlands rivalry with her brother, although it does sound like the kind of gesture she might affect, but because her parents had moved to the home in Purley that would become my playground 30 years later, and she assumed West Brom was an abbreviation of Bromley West, just down the road. This confusion about where home was, though a comical misunderstanding of geography, is nonetheless telling of their blindfolded reaching for home. With my grandfather leaving home and working, and only Abla in the house that decades later would have green stumps and the twirly whirly in the garden, my grandmother had begun to feel her own sense of abandonment, as well as possible guilt, and recalled Lana from her boarding school, to go to the local girls' school in Purley, so she could be closer to her. Lana, by now having absorbed enough displacement to cover several lifetimes, was no doubt further disorientated by not finding her beloved West Brom playing next door every Saturday in Bromley. Paul now supports Reading, where he and his family live.

The key to the house in Haifa sits in the living room that he has called home for so long.

My dad, from his packed working-class home within an island mentality, left school at the earliest age, just six weeks before his 15th birthday (the last year it was possible to do so). After a move to the "mainland" two years later, getting a place at university by 21, he too had his own ideas of what finding a home would mean. Through equal parts their own felt displacements and coincidence, Andrew and Lana found each other in London and, with that, something that was natural, simple and, more importantly, as close to a certainty as anything they had ever known. It was home.

And it was in this home that they had created – one in which they had encouraged each other to break the cycles they didn't want to hand back down to their children – that the carers for Lana, slowly losing her speech completely now, became more and more frequent. In part, it turned the home into a kind of adventure playground, the house constantly moving with upwards of 11 or 12 people in there at different times in any one day, vibrating with an enlivening semi-chaos. The spirit of fun from the earlier years of drawing on the walls and the *Top of the Pops* performances and International Rescue still lay inherent somewhere in the ever-evolving everyday. Andrew, somehow marshalling the entire situation, simultaneously became mindful of making sure that the house was a real home and not, as he felt it was in danger of becoming, a care home. Where it could be, he decided, it had to be as tidy as possible. Pencils were lined up exactly parallel, facing one another. The blinds were left exactly symmetrical and perpendicular to the floor. Surfaces were left empty and open. Cheese, one of the few items in a fridge resembling a minimalist art piece when you opened it up, sat exactly adjacent to the drawers and slightly off-centre. Salad, he said, would occasionally be there in case the "fridge police" came round. I'd open and close the door, walk back to the television, check the county cricket scores and team selection on Ceefax (page 340), briefly turn to look at myself in the mirror and pretend to be Noel Gallagher (I'd begun to imagine myself more as Noel than Liam of late) and then walk back to the fridge, opening it up again to see what was in there. There was still just cheese. He did continue to cook on odd occasions, but small things, like the smell of our own rogue frying of bacon sandwiches, became further off limits. Cooking meant mess, and mess meant less control. Retaining what control there was to be grasped was becoming of primary importance, as he tried to facilitate a functional life for his children around the dysfunction the illness had caused.

*

I've begun to return home – part semi-riotous thoroughfare, part as if it needs to be tiptoed round – from school and, knowing Lana will be in her now permanent residence in the room immediately to the right, walk straight upstairs. Each time I do it, I feel in conversation with myself, telling my own mind that I will regret it one day. I know, almost physically, as a part of me glazes over into a starched nothingness, that time is running out and she'd want nothing more than to see me. But still I decide not to go in. Spending too much time in the room provokes a sort of restlessness in me, in which I feel I need to do *something*, and something big, but have no idea what. Sport and music, both largely male worlds, are now a complete fixation for me. I can pour large amounts of feeling into them, exhibiting a feminine sensitivity towards them, and I feast on them, as if forcing myself to eat cake, in search of loss and love and pain. I don't just want to enjoy them. I want to get deep inside them. I still want to climb inside the television or the record player, stretch myself out across the landscape and hug the people inside. I want to tell them that they need not ever be worried about anything again. What they have given is enough. I need to let them know they are safe, and in turn, I hope that they will make me safe too. When I have done that, having earned their respect, I half expect to take them by the hand, climb back out of the television with them and bring them back to her. In that gesture, she will see them and realise that, despite the pain, it has all been worth it.

If I do achieve anything at all, I suddenly spring next door to tell her. That is when it is worth her seeing me. During the same time, our cats begin to turn up at our beds in the morning with writhing, half-alive pigeons, and stand behind them, doe-eyed, waiting for us to wake up, awaiting some praise for what they have brought in. I scream and run out of the room, while my poor dad, who has banned cooking bacon, let alone half-dead pigeons, has to shovel the manic, dying birds into the garden for impromptu funerals to honour their premature ends.

*

Christmas had, over the years that had dented the walls and seen a stairlift taken in and then out, turned into a slightly odd anti-tradition rebellion under Andrew's guidance, too. There were no longer any trees. Trees were mess. Trees were what the happy families in the adverts did. The annual tree, now, was a sliced cardboard cut-out, undeniably artistic and swiftly produced with a scalpel by him the night before. Christmas lunch was baked potatoes or takeaway shish kebabs from Tooting, the only area of South West London that decided to ignore the festivities. I took pride in this complete juxtaposition of a day, our alternative Christmas, as we sat in the back of the car on the return journey, Lana often in a hospice, driving back with chicken wraps through the eerily deserted roads of South London.

The next year, struck with a responsibility to bring a bit of Christmas back, on the last day of his own primary-school venture at Honeywell, Will had asked the school if they needed their Christmas tree anymore. They didn't, they said, so he dragged it back across the road I had been hit by on a Ted-less day when I was his age, and to the house. Andrew answered the door, to find his 11-year-old son arriving with a tree four times the size of him and, impressed with his tenacity, conceded it could live in the garden where, during a holiday in which South London was pelted with near-constant freezing winds, Will spent his days on differently fashioned stools, trying to keep it upright and decorate it with the box of decorations that had been for years untouched in the attic.

As the Christmases changed, so did the rest of the year. Harry and Abla, beginning to panic with their daughter's health tangibly worse with every visit, were suddenly convinced, with the illness now completely entrenched, that a treatment could be found. There must be a cure, it's probably just been missed somewhere, they suggested. They were told about the doctors' meetings long ago and the lack of a cure anywhere, and the decision that Andrew and Lana had made to be with each other and not waste the years searching in vain. This time, *they* could not hear this, though, and began to visit unannounced, armed with speculative leaflets and information.

*

They have turned up on one such mission, when Andrew is at work, when another buzz comes at the door. I open it. At the door is Hugo, smiling. He is flanked by two policemen, not smiling. "Is one of your parents in?" they ask. Technically they are, I say, and let them in. I walk them to the room immediately to the right, where they are met with Lana, in bed, her speech failing her, and Abla and Harry, standing beside her, armed with brochures and magazines and leaflets on MS. The policemen are visibly slightly taken aback by the sight and, suddenly minimising the reason they are bringing Hugo home, nonetheless proceed. There was a stationary helicopter in Battersea which Hugo had been throwing biscuits at. "Now, if one of those biscuits was to get lodged in the propeller," one of the policemen continues, "there could have been quite a serious issue." We all nod gravely, even Lana, somehow forcing her head up and down to match his tone. I have never in all my life been so impressed with Hugo, who gets away without a sentence.

*

Andrew continued, working, parenting three children, caring for his wife every day. It was a resolve that stretched further and wider than any brave opening bat, but which I could nonetheless continue to draw a comparison with. He was, essentially, keeping the whole thing together despite the ongoing shit-show of circumstances. I'd continued to see him as a borderline-unapproachable hero, like Damon Hill in the helmet, whom I needed to give space to do what he needed to do. With that, a slow numbing of each of us inside the house and a thawing expression outside, we found little escape routes, homes away from home, excuses to be out of the house and to feel as alive as we could while we were at it, unhooked momentarily from our tentative responsibilities. I saw it briefly in Andrew who, at any opportunity, would want to be outside or by the sea. We would be urged onto the upper deck of ferries back to the Isle of Wight, praying for central heating and air conditioning as we were force-fed salty sea air from the blustery wind. Hugo developed an obsession with bikes and affiliated himself with a bunch of local kids who christened themselves the Wannie Massive and took to weekends bunking trains to Caterham to do "the jump" and, plainly, throw biscuits at helicopters. Will found skateboards and created, at 11, his own skating company. I stared in the mirror pretending to be in Oasis and, when not occupied with that, left the house and went to watch sport.

As always, it was a team effort. I'd badgered Andrew about going to watch football and, being of architectural mind, he'd considered lower-league Fulham, with its ground on the lip of the Thames, to be a suitable club for his son. Some years earlier, I'd been taken, by Paul, to Stamford Bridge to see Chelsea, in a cup quarter-final draw with Sunderland, and considered myself a Chelsea fan, especially enamoured by their 4-0 FA Cup final defeat to Manchester United a couple of years later and the performative pain that went with it. While Chelsea enjoyed a swarm of popularity, though, I sensed myself disassociating from them and, reading it as a sin to switch clubs and feeling as if I were right on the cusp of an unreturnable point, I severed my ties with them before I reached the age where it would have been considered stone-cold betrayal. Andrew took me to Craven Cottage. We took the train, from Clapham Junction, just beyond the horizon where I had seen the mannequin batter and then walked to Our Price with Secunder Kermani, to Putney and then walked down towards the river, over the bridge and through Bishop's Park. Craven Cottage was beautiful: arcane and sullen. It looked as if it had never aged or been modernised, with its terracing and wooden seats completely frozen in time. It was, at best, half full, mainly of older men who grunted and rolled their eyes and filled the place with a kind of never-ending sigh. Although, on the day, Micky Adams's Fulham beat Barnet 2-0, it somehow articulated to me in a single trip that this was a club built on an acceptance of losing, which it had learned to embrace with a yawning stoicism. It couldn't have been more what I was looking for.

It cost five pounds to get in, at the door, to stand in the Hammersmith End, behind the goal. From that point on, with the journey etched in a map in my mind, that is what I'd do. With Oasis on my Walkman, its shockproof function broken so now wrapped in a towel, I'd make my own way to Fulham and stand right at the front, ensuring I was there an hour early to collect the same autographs from the same players during the same warm-up. The walks to and from became a kind of religious ritual and over the years I slowly moved further and further towards the back of the Hammersmith End, as if it were some form of initiation. I would listen to the anti-Chelsea chants, which were the only songs I wouldn't sing too, and hide my face slowly in my Fulham scarf, praying for them to sing something else, plagued by a low-level guilt at the decision I'd made at the age of ten: to do what I was told no man should ever do, and switch clubs.

Regardless, alongside cricket and music, Fulham lived as another complete constant, always there to complain about and pour in hour upon hour throughout my changing life. I began to feel a very deep sense of belonging and responsibility to the club and, somehow, it was easier to tell everyone I loved a place and a thing than that I loved a person. Fulham was simple and uncomplicated to pledge allegiance forever to; after all, I was safe in the knowledge it was likely to be there forever, like cricket. As soon as I saw Craven Cottage, I imagined myself as an old man, doing the same walk, maybe with children of my own. My search for a footballing home, though not without flaw, had at least been slightly better informed than my mother's.

So it was Craven Cottage, and it was The Oval. They were like siblings. I enlisted a gang from school, cricket lovers or general misfits of different descriptions, and we would head to The Oval, with one pack of cigarettes between us. We'd share the solitary pack around the back of the stands and then lean out across the empty seats to watch the cricket. This didn't necessarily only land on summer holidays or weekends. County cricket tended to sprawl itself out through working weeks and schooldays. We worked out that, if we left home in uniform and with a bag, changed out of the uniform and stuffed it into the bag and headed to The Oval, we could spend safe truancy, in a haven where we knew no-one would look to find us, learning how to smoke during completely empty games. For the others, this was an act of small-scale rebellion that had very little to do with cricket and more with trying to stick chewing gum on your mate's back or, as the day progressed and attention dwindled, hair. I half played along with the gags, while letting the less telling part of me focus on the Surrey team who, led by Adam Hollioake, would build dot-ball pressure on the visiting sides, swarming the bat and breaking partnerships through intensified periods of bowling absolutely spectacular areas.

The only thing we hadn't accounted for that year, beginning to study for our GCSEs, was that they had Sky Sports in the school staffroom. What with it being seldom that any crowd, let alone young people, went to county cricket during the week, the television cameras considered us prime cutaway territory one week. We were regularly being cut to, pushing and kicking each other and throwing things into the deserted empty chairs. The next day at school we were all asked, separately, why we hadn't been in. We were ill, sir, must have caught it off each other, sir. They told us we must have caught it off each other at the cricket, then, and we ended up in Saturday detention doing lines about the importance of honesty. I didn't write in my lines that I had shouted at Ben Hollioake, who had turned and waved, and that that moment of recognition between him and me was worth a thousand detentions.

The same summer, despite my cricketing outings and watchful eye on every smallest detail of body language of the Surrey champions, my on-field performances were cascading further into the futile. I was now shot of any real confidence or purpose of any description and, while Phil Tufnell was about to resurge into my television set bowling venomous spin, my own lovely, loopy stuff was completely limp. Tuffers's bowling which, of course unbeknown to me, he had formed with a vicious kick of unprocessed grief, was sorrow and ecstasy. Mine was solely of sorrow. Like the staged beatings, my bowling needed evolution in order to survive, but I was unable to engage with anything resembling anger which might translate productively; so it was just numbness and distraction, traits that weren't particularly helpful in bowling to ever-towering boys three times the size of me. What's more, the ever-towering boys were beginning to bowl fast. Fast enough for my Tufnell batting leg, the one intent on running away to square leg, to have complete control over my conscious mind and result in me being the first name to be sure of his batting position, at number 11. I was getting better and better at batting in the mirror, which competed for space with my Gallagher impression, but in real life, I could barely bring myself to stand in the way of the ball. Given these unquestionable chasms in my ability against my undimmed and continued willing, it at least gave the school coach less ethical selection headaches when Daniel Rodea-Ryan accidentally broke my arm in a lunchtime football match, leaving me to score the school final at the out-ground at Lord's with my plastered left arm, watching him play in my place. They were a better team for it and I knew it too. I so wanted to be better. I prayed to be better. I just wasn't.

Talking of which, England were still under the captaincy of Alec Stewart, who had, despite his sudden burden of both opening the batting and keeping wicket, perfectly kept the "what if?" burning by losing in Australia that winter, but not *that* badly. England were staging a home series World Cup that same summer. The build-up to the 1999 tournament was a strangely transparent public brainstorming of trying to find ways that cricket might be, gulp, cool and, oh no, fashionable. Nineties model Caprice was photographed in the one-day kit sandwiched between Alec Stewart and Adam Hollioake, all three of them with startled contractual commitment glistening in their eyes. Anneka Rice, whose television show *Challenge Anneka* had been nationwide essential viewing a few years earlier, was hired as an ambassador for the tournament and conceded at the ceremony itself that she found cricket "as boring as fishing". The fireworks, set off against low-hanging grey clouds, hardly went off and the balloons, as if deflated by Rice's admission, floated off in various half-arsed directions at a half-full Lord's. It didn't bode well. England, after a rained-off half day against India at Edgbaston, duly turned up the next day and collapsed, being knocked out at the first stage. "All Over the World", the official England World Cup song, by the Eurythmics' Dave Stewart, came out the following day, the team already unthinkably eliminated. The next day London's two biggest music stores reported zero sales of the song, which contained no reference to cricket.

15

The Worst in the World

I t was booked. I had the ticket. The Oval Test. Saturday, 21 August 1999. England vs New Zealand. I was finally going to be *inside* Test cricket. It returned; the dizzying, nameless feeling, not much different from the one I'd felt with the Spanish girl in the pool or dancing with Rhianwen Davies to The Prodigy: a horrid anticipation of exposed potential belonging.

All I had to do was sit and watch the series bumble around the rest of England before it came to South London. The World Cup elimination just gone had come at a cost. Alec Stewart was replaced by Nasser Hussain as England captain. Hussain had been born in Madras (now Chennai) in India and, after he had moved to England as a child, cricket had been his entire voice of expression. You didn't need to know that about him to understand it. Everything Hussain did was with an intensity bordering on self-flagellation. I had been taken by him in the previous South Africa series, playing his not insignificant role in the Atherton–Donald duel, where he would face a delivery and then take himself for a walk, muttering to himself, jutting his head forwards aggressively as if a little voice was just repeatedly shouting, "Come on, you idiot" as it echoed without relent around his cranium. It was like batting was tantamount to his existence. I would feel for him at times, worrying that he would only ever find himself one side of disappointment or, at best, relief. Still, he recalled Phil Tufnell to the side, so he was obviously sound of mind. Plus, he added to his first selections one of the beloved Surrey players I had gazed at while trying to pull chewing gum out of my hair in the summer of truancy just passed, Alex Tudor.

As I wait for the circus to come to town, at the first Test, Tudor magically transforms the game as the nightwatchman, disregarding the position's usual motive to just survive and instead taking it upon himself to win the game for England. Unbeaten on 99 at the conclusion, he stands there, slightly stunned, not anticipating the crowd running on to mob him, and is last seen under a deluge of drunk, sunburned men. From there though, it's the usual fare. Symbolic of the general cascading to which we'd all grown accustomed, the new wicketkeeper, Chris Read, although a gloveman of considerable talent, operates the first two games with a nearly visible quivering bottom lip. While batting, he misreads a slower ball from Chris Cairns which must have appeared, out of the hand, to be a beamer heading directly for his head. He turns to shield himself and crouches, side on. The ball arcs slowly, goes through his disengaged foetal shape and bowls him. He stands up, as if to ask what had happened while he'd been down there, partly in shock, and then, his stumps dismantled, walks off. It is an image, like Warne and Oasis, that immediately seemed as if it had in some form been around forever and, in its small way, came to summarise the tragi-comedy of English cricket in the '90s. The next day, every newspaper in the country led their front pages with the picture. He batted very well in the second innings, which is remembered less well.

So, with the score 1-1 and Chris Read back in the Battersea Dogs Home for discarded international cricketers of my mind with the Marks and the Martins looking for homes, to The Oval, where I am finally meeting them. The England cricket team. Me, Mark Knight-Williams and Kunal Patel turn up in the morning in completely giddy excitement. The Oval, our empty space of truant relief, is suddenly awash with conversation, pints being spilled and burger-van fried onions thick in the air. Somewhere in the background, over there, is the cricket. It is an undeniable thrill, to be so close to each and every shape of cricketer that I have been inhaling all summer, but it comes at a considerable cost. The hullabaloo is incredibly distracting. What is this, a fucking social? Does nobody care about the grave cricket unfolding in front of us? The two men behind us discuss their separate divorces and who has custody of whom, interspersing it with commentary on the game. An England player in the distance manically chases the ball to the boundary in vain. "Who was that, Graham Thorpe?" one asks. "No, it won't have been. No-one chases a ball like that who's been playing for England that long." And back to the divorce settlements. Man 2 is right. It is debutant Darren Maddy. Then the other part, the least comfortable part, where men in wide-collared shirts nudge each other at the bar while we smoke as professionally as we can a safe distance away from them, and they point at passing women saying, "Cracking tits, Jonesy" within their earshot as they go by. It is deeply disturbing to me that this is what Test cricket might actually be like inside, and I'm suddenly very concerned about what it says about me to be sharing the space with these men. I feel myself slowly retreat inwards, gauging how and what this thing is that I have already pledged all value to.

It is all like an incessant tick, the element of distraction the ground provides. Unlike at home with my television set, where carers and fuss phase into the background, I find myself less able to zone out and back into the game, and enter a more self-conscious, nervous reverie. It is only when the England wickets start to fall that the day settles into a blissful state of loss. The rolling-eye brigade begin. The old men discuss how they would have played the ball differently.

People start complaining. I am there, too, quietly willing on the loss, sucking in the pain, finding myself wanting to see this England team, to which I feel achingly attached, be cruelly beaten and force some feeling out of my blocked throat with it. We will all be there if that happens, focused on the same thing, hurting together.

The batting collapse is glorious, and just how I had imagined it. Darren Maddy is out to no shot to Daniel Vettori. Maddy will be occupying the Battersea Dogs Home for Cricketers in my mind soon. Mike Atherton trudges off as if he'd left part of himself at Trent Bridge in 1998. Graham Thorpe edges the ball and then stares back at it, nuzzled in a Kiwi slip-fielder's hands with a final cursed, Hollywood-worthy "Oh", as if all the alpha has finally been sucked out of him. Nasser Hussain, most cinematically of all, hooks a short ball from Chris Cairns to square leg, thrillingly holding in the air as the crowd rise, only for it to die and be caught by Matthew Bell at square leg. Nasser stands there, arms forlorn, staring into the gasworks in the distance, in total disdain with himself. I watch him, looking as if he has had every paranoid, contorted nightmare about himself confirmed, and feel a sharp, actual pain for him. It is right in my chest, just where the ribcage meets itself, and it surges back into my already blocked throat. I do not show this, as Mark and Kunal are busy tearing up their 4 and 6 scorecards in order to throw them up in the air when the Mexican wave comes back around. I've kept mine unharmed, for sentiment. England eventually lose the match, with Phil Tufnell being run out at the non-striker's end, hunched over on his hands and knees and, for the first time in their history, they are confirmed as the *worst Test team in the world*. Nasser is booed on the pitch at the conference, which I watch back at home with a pang of guilt that I have wished it all upon him.

16

Nasser Hussain and the
Winning That Counted

"It's odd, because I remember most of my dismissals, but I don't remember that. Felix, you have a better memory than me." It definitely happened, I assure Nasser, and he takes my word for it. "I do remember the wheels coming off, though – you were probably there booing me, weren't you?" I promise him I wasn't, while still harbouring slight guilt at having morbidly enjoyed the way his first Test series as captain unfolded.

Now sharing duties with Michael Atherton as a leading voice on the game with Sky Sports, Nasser Hussain has come a long way since that day at The Oval. In the time that has elapsed, I've let myself while away hours stacked into days turned into weeks, no longer watching him bat, but listening to him dissect cricket matches from his commentary position, lovingly smirking at his commitment to phrase-making, describing game pressure as "under the pump", bad deliveries as "absolute filth" and exciting matches as "crackathons". His omnipresence at the highest form, moving seamlessly from being a player to the media, has allowed for a public and slow unpacking of the man I first saw in person hundreds of yards away, staring into the gasworks. He seems to have learned, publicly at least, to reflect on his own career with a now bottomlessly self-effacing nature. So, unlike with Mike

Atherton, in whom you sense a creative instinct to reinvent, Nasser's responses are those of a man who at some stage learned to laugh at himself and, finding some release in that, has never looked back since.

Hussain has never missed playing. When he arrived in England as a boy, cricket was placed front and centre as life's only vessel of expression. "I'm a victim," he starts, before correcting himself, "I mean a product, of my environment. There was never any of this 'It's not life or death.' It was never about the fun or participating, it was winning and losing that counted. Cricket was everything." His playing career thereafter never allowed for much perspective. On tours, while Tuffers and Co. were going to see the alligators and the hammerhead sharks, he preferred to stay in his hotel room and prepare for the match. "I used to read all the press, I'd trawl through it and go and try to prove people wrong."

Prove people wrong, to his eternal credit, Hussain did. Being joined by coach Duncan Fletcher at the end of the New Zealand series, he took a side full of new selections focused on reinvigorating England and, despite losing the series in South Africa immediately after – a consolation last Test win being one Hansie Cronje turned out to have thrown for a leather jacket and, on being caught, banned from cricket for life – things had begun to improve. The following summer at home, England won against the West Indies for the first time in 31 years. I watched at The Oval, taking a picture in my mind of Courtney Walsh and Curtly Ambrose leaving an English cricket field for the last time, while a West Indian fan, in defeat, stood next to me scream-ing, "Thirty-one years! Thiiiiirty-oooonnnee years", as if he were a captain on a sinking ship who would rather drown with it. From the same range I had felt Hussain stare into the gasworks, I watched with a distanced awe for him then, walking back triumphant to his dressing room. Out of sheer force of character and, of course, ensuring cricket was absolutely *everything*, he was beginning to change the narrative of the past decade.

"A dressing room, I'm afraid, is like life," Hussain reflects on the slow shift in fortunes under his hard-edged rule. "It's a variety of people with different egos and different fears of failure." He then reels them off as if they were movie stars. "Gough, five feet nothing, he shouldn't be a great fast bowler, but he is because he loves the centre stage, he shows up knowing he's born for it." Gough's partner Andy Caddick: "Six foot five, perfect physique for fast bowling, massive fear of failure, worried about everything." Then his fellow stalwarts with whom he'd weathered all turbulence. "Stewart, meticulous in his preparation; Atherton, scruffy, hadn't washed his stuff for months, gear everywhere." I can almost see the dressing room as he recalls it, as if the ghost of Christmas past is pointing to each character from the corner of a '90s folk tale. The resurgence continued and peaked in a double series win that winter over Sri Lanka and Pakistan, where Nasser and Graham Thorpe famously ended up hugging in pitch black to secure a rare subcontinental sweep in the Karachi dusk. "That was my favourite series," Hussain says. "To be there with Thorpey at the end meant a lot to me. It still does."

English cricket, under Hussain, if still uptight and paranoid and twitching, had begun to feel good about itself again. It didn't look like fun, per se, but it did look less like losing; a cardioversion driven by all the devilish gnawing that pressure brings. "The fear of failure was always there for me. I once asked Graham Gooch, 'How do you overcome nerves?'" Gooch looked at Hussain like he had two heads. "He said, 'I don't have nerves, Nass, it's just a game of cricket.'" Hussain could never consider it just that. I think back, then, to the Hussain staring into the gasworks, unaware that the limp nothingness he is obviously feeling is about to provide the catalyst for something undeniably positive, then to myself, watching my friends tear up the scorecards. For Hussain, cricket was everything, and about winning. For me it was everything, too, but it was about losing. For neither of us was it just a game of cricket.

Hussain does, for a second, allow himself back to occupy the mind of the man he was then, as if none of it is painful anymore with the years between. "If you ask me what the best job I ever had was, it was being England cricket captain; it was the greatest job, even with the lows. It was hard waking up the next day and no longer being that."

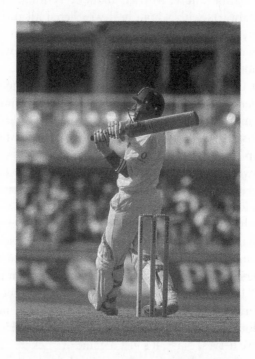

Nasser Hussain pulls the ball towards the gasworks –
"You were probably there booing me, weren't you?"

17

The Storm

I n late 2001, Nasser Hussain had added to his Test series
victories a comfortingly formulaic Ashes loss, in which
Mark Butcher this time had kept the "what if?" embers
burning with 173 not out at Headingley to win their single
Test. Meanwhile, my life at The Oval, Craven Cottage and
various gigs across London continued to expand. I'd seen
Oasis at Wembley Stadium, where everyone else seemed to be
pretending to be from Manchester too. The background chatter,
like at The Oval, proved oddly distracting, only dissipating
when the band walked on stage and filled the stadium with a
brief swell of united purpose. Lana, now unable to speak at all
but for huge agonising moments in which she would try and
force short sentences or one-word answers out of her mouth,
had developed a new, terrible tremor in her arm and neck.

By now, it is obviously agony for her to simply do nothing
at all. Just lying still involves a frantic wrestling with her body.
Her neck shakes quickly, and each time the side of her face
touches the pillow, she tries to hold it there before it is released
and swings back again. It has become violent enough that the
cats, ever-present either side of her head, have become less
inclined to rest there; yet nonetheless they stay, usually at the
foot of the bed. They have stopped bringing in the dead birds,
too. I watch it, watch her, and feel almost nothing where I
should feel everything, only a growing notion that the outside
world is moving quicker and quicker, and that I need to get

back into it and make something happen. I am not sure *what* I want to make happen exactly, but I know it is something.

Over time, through the influx of not just carers but doctors too coming into the house, pressure has been growing to take her away. She should be in a hospice at least throughout the week, they begin to insist with more regularity. My parents had made their decision, though, repeatedly over many years. Lana has found her home, and she isn't being taken away. Andrew knew that and she did, too. The fear, on his part, is that once she is in a hospital, getting her out again will be impossible. In their younger years, they had often passed a neurological hospital in Putney, the entrance of which was adorned with ominous, Victorian writing: "For the incur-ables". Each time they passed, they had shared a nightmare of somehow finding themselves inside. She was not going to end up there or any place like it. He knows, even if she can't express it, that she wants and *needs* to be with her family. One Monday morning the doctor, beginning to see him as quite difficult, informs him that there would be a meeting in the house and that he will not be involved. They suspect that he is in some way influencing her to say one thing when she needs another. Closing the door and locking Andrew out, six specialists gathered around the bed and asked her whether she really wanted to stay at home. Somehow, maybe with her eyes or in some forced gesture under insurmountable pres-sure, she managed to show that she did. They came back through the door comfortable that it was indeed her own decision. As they left, they told Andrew that this was the only case in Wandsworth, with this severity of illness, in which they had allowed it. Somehow, they had both managed to convince the board of doctors that this was the best place for her to be. It was her home, and she was staying there.

One concession was that she would visit Trinity Hospice with more regularity, as she had done for the last few Christmases. She went for five days and stayed eighteen, including Christmas

Day, which now rolled out almost wordlessly between us three boys, as we sat by the side of her bed, pre-kebabs, smiling gently. There came moments, after she returned home, when, as I turned my head around the door to say hello, she communicated a different kind of urgency in her eyes. I would detect it and walk over to her, leaning in and wincing to make out what it was she was trying to say to me. Usually, after slow, painful periods, she would shake and try and try some more, before eventually, deflated, dropping her head and giving up. I would tell her to not worry and leave. One time, however, in a flurry of sudden inspiration in which her body allows her a sentence, something comes. "I was just wondering," she says, "who's going to make my money." I don't know who is going to make her money, I say, and I run next door to tell Andrew. He responds as if it is an emergency and, charging in, he sits next to her and tells her that she never needs to worry about money and that it is all sorted. It was not the only time she asked that that year. He felt as if she was asking it not literally, but in an Egyptian burial sense: did she have enough money to take with her in death? It could have been that, or, more typically, she could have been concerned, as so often she was, not to be a burden to anyone.

It had come close a few times. Leaving the hospice one evening, Andrew was stopped by a nurse, who suggested that it'd be a good idea to stay. He didn't realise that she meant because Lana might die. He did and she didn't. There had been enough moments that it generated its own routine, each near-death situation playing out in its own cyclical course of familiarity until it was impossible to imagine that it might genuinely happen. He booked an appointment with a neurologist at Westminster Hospital that had taken six months to materialise, in an old hospital building. He wanted to know whether, in a last fix of trying everything, in some way he had missed something *still*. When they arrived, there were several people there, in a worn waiting room. A notice was up that the consultant couldn't make it, but a registrar was going to see people in his place, turning the appointments into a first-come first-served situation. On seeing Andrew and Lana, the whole room suggested that they go first. It occurred to him, as if for the first time, that she must *really* look terminally ill if this room of anxious, seriously ill people had noticed she should be the priority. The registrar saw Lana then and, moving outside to talk privately, Andrew asked her what more could be done. She simply said, "Well, in these situations, it's only a matter of time." He translated this to six months, or a year. He always pushed it forward.

Five days later, a group of us went to see Oasis at Watford Colosseum. My absolute commitment to the Gallagher brothers had continued to increase and stretch further across my everyday. I had worked it all out at school a week before. I'd bunk in the morning, phoning the ticket line as soon as they went on sale. Andrew, by then, was operating with a scale of perspective that understood getting Oasis tickets was more important than anything school was going to offer me. I'd got the tickets and walked back into class with a genuine sense of euphoria halfway through a lesson, punching the air. The teachers said nothing. On the day, we bunked again, making sure that we queued up from early that afternoon to be at the front.

*

When the doors open, we sprint to the fence in front of the stage, in a slightly more purposeful, aggressive version of my running to greet Chris Lewis some years earlier. We get there, front and centre, and we wait. Watford Colosseum is a comparatively tiny place for Oasis to be playing, and the sense of being closer to the Gallaghers than would usually be possible is causing a fuss. I feel the crowd growing, squeezing and packing people closer and closer around me, pressing on my ribcage, clamping my arms tightly next to my sides, making me part of one moving and sweaty mass. When

Oasis take to the stage, hardly a yard from me, I gaze and think that I never want it to end, trying to remember each frame so I can always re-access it. I search for their eyes and sing every single word and every guitar line, screaming myself into a hoarse, dehydrated frenzy. Eventually, increasing on every song, a force of momentum pushing hundreds of people forwards and into the barrier fence has begun to make me feel sick. I tap a sweaty stranger on the shoulder and, without further communication, they instantly know what I mean. I look bad. I should go first. I am lifted, on top of shoulders, limp and lifeless over the throng, momentarily rendering me closer to eye level with Liam. I point my finger at him, in a sort of messianic worship gesture, and he locks eyes with me back, underneath his tinted, if probably unnecessary sunglasses, very slowly tilting his head up and down in acknowledgement. On the other side of the barrier, two men take me by either arm and escort me out of the premises and onto the streets of Watford. It is the best night of my life.

The same evening, catching the train back, I am in a continued state of complete hysteria. Friend in tow, we bundle through the door, Oasis t-shirts on. I put my head quickly around the door. My dad is sitting beside her with a blanket on too, as if he is staying the night in the room. I don't stop to contemplate that it is unusual, I just have Oasis fizzing around my head. "It was amazing. Amazing," I say, hardly waiting for a reply before I bolt upstairs. I leave the next morning without saying goodbye. The whole day at school, I am full of exaggerated tales of the gig and how Liam had waved at me, each time elaborating the way we had acknowledged one another, and on a rare sunny winter afternoon full of adrenaline, decide to stay and bowl some blissed-out left-arm spin in the nets after school.

I haven't expected to see Harry on the street outside when I get home. It is a good surprise. "Grandpa!" I shout. He freezes for a second and, guiding me into the house with a very gentle nod, says, "Some bad news." Inside the door are Andrew and Abla. There are two words. Mum died. Then, as if I suddenly can't sense my legs, I float into the room, maybe partly guided there, where she is lying, exactly as she has been for the last few years, only now completely still. Her face is slightly set back, strangely static, frozen but not relaxed, and her eyes are closed, her mouth slightly apart. It looks exactly like her. "You can touch her, she's still warm," says Abla.

Still warm? What did she mean, "still warm"? I am left with her and I turn, away from her, both arms bent against the wall, and cry. For a second I see myself, leaning at the opposite side of the room, and see her too, as if I were above both of us. An hour earlier, she had begun breathing irregularly. The grandparents had happened to be round and, sensing something was wrong, Hugo phoned Andrew, who came back immediately. They were all there, by the bed, watching her die, telling her it was OK, as her last few breaths left her body. I was playing cricket.

I go upstairs to find Hugo, who is collapsed against the stairs, sobbing. I reach out for his arms, and he reaches back. Will is in his room, underneath his bed covers, immersed and completely still. I try to speak to him, to move the sheets, but he doesn't move and doesn't speak, and I give up to go to my room. I have planned what I might do when this happened. After all, there'd already been a few false alarms. I listen to Oasis, a premeditated selection of sad live demos in which Noel turns usually frenetic songs into melancholy little strum-alongs. Thirty seconds into the first, I am sickened by my own staged sadness and turn it off.

We have that evening together. If it had been a hospital, it would have been 15 minutes and the body would have gone. But we have as long as we need. We are home. I trip slowly downstairs again and, as if some kind of switch has gone in Harry's head, he walks back through the door where she has been and says, "Something's wrong with Lana. She's not moving." I am confused that this is the same man who had alerted me to bad news only a few minutes previously. Eventually they leave, driving home. With my brothers now upstairs, I watch my dad take the rings off her hands. The evening lasts a very long time, as if it is in some way equivalent to the 13 years she has been ill, and the five of us, not yet four, just sit together, staring at nothing, saying hardly anything at all.

At some stage into the timeless night, I am watching my dad flick through the Yellow Pages and then phone a funeral home. "Where are you going to take her?" he wants to know. I listen. "Where specifically are you going to take her?" Another pause. "Where the hell is a place of rest?" Another silence. He hangs up. He wants to know where the body is going, and they have already blown their chance to take it there. The second funeral home, after a bit of probing, tell him it is a morgue in Kingston, and they are round soon after: an older man and a man not much more than my age, in grey undertaker hats. They walk into the room and when they emerge again they are wheeling the body, zipped up in a black bag. "Don't worry, we'll take good care of her," the older man says to me. What does he mean, take good care of her? She isn't moving. Andrew, he doesn't tell me then, thinks to himself as she is wheeled off, "Wait, what if she's not dead?" He doesn't want her to wake up in a morgue, terrified. If she does, at least he knows where he can find her, in Kingston.

That evening, Hugo sleeps in my room. We both lie there very still, him in the middle of the room under temporary sheets and me in my bed. I stare at the ceiling, listening to him crying very gently, occasionally asking if he is OK, to which he always says yes. At some point, there is silence. I don't know if he has fallen asleep, but a storm comes that evening, which taps and taps on my window, just as gently as Hugo has been crying. I lie there tingling, experiencing the whole house being hugged by the storm, and, beyond thinking or asking or feeling, I *know* it is her saying goodbye, and that it is just between us. The house feels as if it has been lifted by its roots, the wind circling and wrapping itself around us, suspended in the air, before, just as gently as it came, dropping the house and leaving.

Photo of the four of us taken by Lana, many years earlier.

18

Adam Hollioake and the
Relative Grief

I took one day off school, the next day, when some friends of mine had arranged that they could do the same and meet me at Jessie Ware's house. That's where I tended to go. There were ten or more of them waiting there. We played games and laughed and I lay on a sofa and we watched *Almost Famous*. It was a strange buzz, the net of attention that was suddenly triggered, encasing me in a peculiar mixture of pity and projected wisdom. I felt myself full of an alien energy that pulled me through the days floating, at times almost blissfully and always completely present, enjoying the kick of constant communication. The occasional teacher held my eyeline and mouthed, "Are you OK?", to which I nodded. I knew people were talking about me and, in a way that I did not let on, as if by doing so the attention itself would also leave, it felt very good. I was seen everywhere, completely alive, moving through the world, brave and unique. I had been projecting forms of loss in a million amateurish ways for years. At Craven Cottage. Through the staged fights. In those tapes in the car. On English cricketers. There was finally some sense of soft completion in it, in which I silently revelled. My mum's death had somehow kept me alive in the minds of others; the badge of loss that I had so clumsily tried to pin to myself was now fastened there forever, where everyone could see it. I was complete, the real deal, the loss completely pure.

The side of the house so full of carers, chaos and movement suddenly gave way and was totally still. There were four men there, each in their own silence across an open and empty stretch of time. When the funeral came, the next week, her body was wheeled into the house, the casket open. As we were called for, and walked into the room that she had died in, to say goodbye, she looked the same as she had when I saw her last, but paler: an unusual chalk white. In some indescribable way, it was the youngest she had ever appeared to me. We stood over her for a second and, sensing as the oldest I should somehow take the lead, I kissed my fingers and placed them on her forehead. I can still occasionally recollect the coldness at the end of my fingertips, the lifeless chill, setting my teeth to chatter as if I am flushed with ice. Hugo did the same, and then Will. I felt guilt, as if they were following some custom which I had completely made up.

*

The funeral is carried out in a packed local church, full of school friends and people from her life. I sit there, sort of looking forward to the event, watching my brothers and dad cry, and turning around to see Paul and his children, my cousins, all crying too. For a moment I pause to wonder what they are crying about and ask if they are OK. After the ceremony, the coffin, which Andrew had asked me to help carry but then obviously thought better of it, is borne across the road and into the cemetery. I notice my uncle slightly tensing under the weight of it and trying not to let on. I reach the plot of land, the dug-out grave, first, immediately behind the coffin, and as people behind gather around and the coffin is lowered in, which must have been done by the undertakers on some kind of pulley system, but in my memory floats down, I look over into the deep, darkened hole and, knowing that I am being watched, feel the propulsion to spit into it. I

152

witness the thought, imagine myself doing it, playing it out in my head as if I actually had done so, but resist the temptation in the real universe and, peering for a second into the hole, turn and walk away.

I float through the next six weeks on this same secret buzz, not feeling life pinch or pull at me, asphyxiated in a pocket of time that doesn't have to change. Until the news comes. In the middle of the night, in Australia, driving home from a dinner with his brother and his parents before flying back to England, Ben Hollioake has lost control of his car and crashed it into the Mill Point Road exit of the Kwinana freeway. He has died instantly and on impact. He was 24. Their sister, Eboni, had been in the car behind, and watched the car slip on an oil slick and into the low wall. Adam had taken the other route. England, led by Hussain, are in the middle of a Test match in New Zealand, for which the Hollioakes have not been selected. It is suspended when the news comes in, before resuming the next day.

My imperceptible bubble popped, I step into the chasm of feeling and grieve for Ben, who had waved at me all those years earlier. This, I say to myself, is an actual tragedy, stirred by a strange sense of guilt for Ben being even younger than my mum. I don't deserve any attention at all. What Adam must be going through, that is *real* pain. A week later, the Queen Mother dies and England is cloaked in a national service of mourning in which flags are half-mast and black armbands worn everywhere. I consider it an umbrella of grief which is not so much for the Queen Mother herself but, firstly, for Ben, and latterly, my mum.

*

"I enjoy talking about him," Adam Hollioake says, from the Australian Gold Coast where he now lives. "The more I talk about him, the more I bring him back to life. It's funny you've got in touch now," he continues, "because I'm coaching the Queensland Bulls out here and the head coach's son committed suicide recently. I've been reliving it all."

On the evening of Ben's death, Adam told his family that he was going to retire from cricket immediately. His father, who had been so proud of his two sons and what they were achieving in the game, turned to him and said, "I've already lost one son, don't let me lose another." "That sounds disturbing now," Adam says, "but he was the biggest person in my life and he said, 'You go home and you do what you've got to do.' I went back with those words ringing in my ears."

Adam returned to England, to the team he had left earlier that year, minus Ben, and captained Surrey again. He had his most successful year with the bat. "I just played the ball," he says. "For me, it was an escape from the pain of being inside my own thoughts." Ben would turn up in Adam's mind for a split second, but the thought would be interrupted by having to prepare for the next ball, and so Ben would leave again, and Adam would sink into the relief of concentrating on the leather rock heading towards him, away from the loop of the pain. "People said to me, 'You must be so mentally tough', but I think it was the opposite. I was fighting on instinct. There was no *thinking* involved, it was all physical." He scored an otherworldly 117 in 59 balls against Sussex in the quarter-final of the one-day cup, which to this day he doesn't recognise or remember. "That wasn't me," he said in *Wisden*. "I can't bat that well." It was tempting, for everyone witnessing it too, to see Ben in that innings, lending himself to Adam for an afternoon, making him pull and push and punch down the ground in the image of his younger brother at Lord's against the Australians six years earlier. *Wisden* named Adam one of the five Cricketers of the Year.

The "mental toughness" to which Adam refers sits in my mind as we speak. Only a year before our conversation, Alzarri Joseph, the West Indian fast bowler, turned up to play in a Test match against England when his mother had died the previous evening. In a stir of well-meaning if potentially clumsy plaudits, he was praised on air throughout the day for his "mental toughness". It was as if, had he decided not to play, he wouldn't have been mentally tough. It is a topic that takes a profound hum in cricket, mental toughness, in which the amount of time the game takes and the amount of thinking that you cannot deny yourself while playing it, can deceive you into perceiving it as a survivalist battle of the strongest wills. Adam Hollioake, who had forged a formidable unit at Surrey in which he glued a side of big characters together, found this received wisdom landing him in a state of prolonged exhaustion. "If anyone hit me with the ball, I wouldn't rub it. It's just the way it was. But that summer, I'd begun to not be able to feel anything but exhaustion. Looking back now, I just didn't understand what was going on." As Adam describes it, I can locate this feeling of complete exhaustion and a recurring desire to do nothing but sleep.

Hollioake continued to score runs, carrying the weight of his family and his team. In doing so, he found himself in the surreal and disturbing situation of beginning to console his teammates about his own brother's death. "I think people were so caught up in their own grief, that they didn't stop to think. We were all very young, and we were all *men*." It wasn't the only young death at Surrey in recent years. Five years earlier Graham Kersey had also died in a car crash, one year older than Ben had been. He considered his grief for Graham, and realised that his teammates were going through something similar with Ben. He encouraged them to come to him if they wanted to talk. He was the captain, after all. The barrage that year was only silenced for brief moments when he turned to face another ball.

Adam retired the next year at the age of 33. T20, a lucrative short form of the game in which he would have undoubtedly been a forerunner, was taking off, he was captain of Surrey and at his peak. "Everything, from the outside, was good, you know? But I just thought, I need to move on. If he'd still been there, I think I would have carried on." Adam's portrait now sits in the Long Room at The Oval among the other legends of the club, yet it is the only one that is drawn from a photograph because he "couldn't sit still for long enough for them to do it". There has evidently been a propulsion in his life since, to illustrate just that, a restlessness. It has been full of so much: ultimate fighting in a cage, hypnotherapy, launching a business, creating a TV show, coaching in Afghanistan. I can identify with the hoarding of activity as a response to young grief; the bringing back of achievements as some kind of bargaining device, coupled with the understanding that we *really* are not here for that long, and there is no time to waste. I want to discuss this, but for fear of making general assumptions, I stop it in my mouth, and instead find myself enquiring as to his balance as a grieving man, of holding quiet resentments against those teammates who seemed to be moaning far more about far less. "I had a period where I was thinking to myself, I can't believe he is coming up to *me* with this problem." Adam stopped and had an awakening, to think of himself while Ben was alive. "When I first had my heart broken, I was inconsolable. I recovered. I didn't lose a game of any sport for two years. When it happened, it was like a depression. I was so low, I could hardly move." I feel for him, being from the England side in the '90s. "If I'd known then how many games I'd lose!" he laughs. "But my attitude after Ben died changed, for example Graham Thorpe wanted to discuss issues he was having with his wife once." Hollioake listened to Thorpe as they were running laps of the Rose Bowl cricket ground. "After 20 laps I was going, Jesus, man, can we take this to the bar, it's just your wife." He continues to reflect. "But I was completely disrespecting his grief. It's all relative to what you know and what you've been through."

It's an understanding that it has taken me a long time to

reach myself, often choosing in my adult life to align myself with brilliant but melodramatic people with whom day-to-day things are turned into huge issues, and then silently resenting them. I have spent my own time working it out, too. I'm not prepared, though, for where Hollioake takes the theme. "This is being completely 100 per cent honest with you here, Felix, but I would be lying if I said that when you say, 'I lost my mum', that my default position isn't 'They're just your parents, mate; parents are *supposed* to die before us.' But I have to fight that when you say it and realise that's your journey." It sticks in my throat for a second, while he continues talking. I consider how what he has just said is so bizarrely close to the punishment I silently rotated in my own head when Ben died, almost as if it had been placed there by someone as some kind of test.

I observe the feeling gathering to block my throat and I momentarily want to bite back and say that watching your mother die from a degenerative disease as a child is not comparable to anything either, but I let that subside and feel his words settle in me, almost as a gesture of respect, which then allows me to feel some sympathy for the people in my life that I have judged for not having someone close to them die and still having the audacity to find life hard. I thank him for his honesty. I mean it. I asked him for this, the truth about his grief, and I feel touched he is giving it to me. I let him continue. "I remember, when my brother died, believing that when I stopped thinking about him, that would be the day I'd be happy. But it was only when I appreciated that there's 150 things I can be happy about during the day, that I did. It might be a good song on the radio. It might be a great coffee. My child smiles at me. I have a good conversation with a stranger. It isn't something looming on the horizon, it's right there, I've already found it. That's happiness. The sun always has to come up."

At last, I ask how the grief has changed over the years. "I found that five years after Ben died, I went through a relapse. Then five years later, when I was going through a divorce with my ex-wife, it happened again. I feel like I found my peace then. Instead of thinking of all of the things he didn't experience, I had a moment where I went, 'I might never have met him! How lucky was I?' Someone was saying the other day, 'What a moment that was for you and your brother to make debuts in the same Test match.' They asked what it felt like. I said, 'It didn't feel like anything.' It was just a game of cricket. It's only when I look back now that I think, wow, that really was a big deal. Some people go through periods of their life where they don't work for one day with their brother. I'm grateful for knowing him. That's been the catalyst to being at peace."

I thank Adam, think of my brothers and silently acknowledge the life we have shared together, and tell him maybe he should reconsider writing his book. He's happy just peacefully going along, he says. With that, I wish him well and, completely exhausted by all the recollected feelings that have surged through me and remembering how tiring grief can feel, I fall asleep.

Adam with Ben Hollioake on England debut - "I'm grateful for knowing him. That's been the catalyst for being at peace."

PART 2

19

This Machine Kills Time

I didn't know who Woody Guthrie was when I was 17, nor did I know that he had etched "This machine kills fascists" onto his guitar, while laying down the folk protest-song fabric that Bob Dylan would follow in the 1960s. So, unarmed with this information, in the hours after we had watched the coffin float into the ground – and I had resisted the temptation to recreate my vision of spitting into the hole into which it was lowered – when Steve Blake unboxed his acoustic guitar and revealed "This machine kills time" written across it, I didn't find it a funny or ironic reference to Guthrie's modus operandi; I saw it as a calling. Steve played some songs, hashed out on the spot as I watched, momentarily filling the same room I had been restless in, reluctant to enter, then had seen myself and my "still warm" mother from outside of ourselves with new promise.

A guitar is not an elusive instrument. It requires a combination of left and right hand, joining them together in an act of kinship, completing a body in its own loop, as if to make sense of having one at all. It takes a relatively short time to sound good, not least because one of its unique selling points is that, if it is played with enough conviction, even the bad noises it makes – to a specific ear – sound good. This knack for connecting the senses, both inside the person playing and then with whoever is listening, has allowed for untold variants in its use since the 15th century.

As with Guthrie's anti-fascist agenda, I did not knowingly see any of that in it either. I just looked at Noel Gallagher on the cover of *There and Then*, the live Oasis video in which Liam had beckoned me towards him years earlier, and studied Noel's arms, guitarless, stretched out in messianic crucifixion, both palms turned upwards, while Maine Road stadium bathed, euphoric and connected, in his presence. I studied every single face in the crowd on that picture, each of them fixed exclusively on him, all joined together in one motion of communal worship. He had achieved all that with a guitar. I looked at the sleeve and knew the only way I was to make sense of my life from here, to feel something other than a kind of guilty grief-stricken bliss or a numbed-out vagueness, was to, somehow, get myself there too. *That* was where the absolution and cumulative feeling were. If the tool that was the conduit to getting there would kill time too, I was in.

So, from there, with any sort of academic demands on me forming a constant yet discarded panic in the background of my conscious mind, it became my solitary mission to learn to play guitar, or more specifically to play Oasis songs. It was like a map, I imagined, and if I couldn't follow the path to what it took to play cricket for England, or even my school team, here was another. Learning an Oasis song was like retracing Noel's thoughts, where I could feel myself, as he must have done, putting the progressions together and forming the backdrop against which so many lives congregated. Noel himself had escaped to playing his guitar at a similar age in a home in which physical abuse from his father was a part of life, creating his own mental fortitude of escape in which he required only his imagination and his guitar to survive. He later, in the film *Supersonic*, thanked his dad for "beating the music into him". I, of course, didn't know this either. But still I followed.

The only thing was, I was not a natural. I was anything but. In a few early lessons, for starters, I'd picked the guitar up "the wrong way round", holding it left-handed. The acoustic needed to be restrung and turned around. Once it was, I found that holding chord shapes was agony. I'd fashion my hands as I'd remembered on a shape and wince as I felt the strings scrape and mute as I tried to pluck each one individually with my left hand on the way across the chord. Once I'd formed, for example, an open G, which requires your hand to be playing both the bottom and the highest string, I wouldn't let it go, as if releasing it would mean it would be gone forever. I'd sit in my room, swamped by posters of musicians endowed with a kind of grace I could only dream of, and I would stare at it, my right hand tensed and pulsing as my left plucked each string as I had been told, to allow the chord to ring.

It was months before I had formed a G, and after it the slightly less taxing shapes of E minor and A minor and so on. I would count the chords I knew, closing my eyes and projecting how many I would be able to play by this time next year. Who knows, it could even be five or six? My stilted progress was in stark contrast to the abilities of my friend Jack Peñate. Jack had played guitar for years and would bring his instrument into school for seemingly no reason but to play it to us in the hall. His hands would surf across the neck, never going anywhere near the rookie open-chord end of the guitar in which I was forever bound to paddle. He improvised Hendrix guitar solos and all kinds of jazz chord shapes incomprehensible to me. Plus, most importantly, he wrote his own songs. He wrote songs about struggling to do his homework and having a broken heart and concepts he'd picked up from his classical civilisation GCSE. I somehow convinced him, after months in which I'd bizarrely begun arranging gigs for which I didn't have a band to play in, that *we* should be in that band together. Joel Porter, the third in our central circle, was enlisted on drums. Joel couldn't play the drums, but he loved Oasis. That was the most important thing.

*

It is our first rehearsal. Jack announces that we should write a song on the spot. I watch him doe-eyed, as he riffs on a chord structure that *looks* like a C shape, but then moves up and down the fret too quickly for me to be sure. I force my guileless hands to copy him, always a couple of frets behind, as he begins to sing, searching for the premise of his new piece of improvisation. "I've got it," he says, with the urgent confidence of a man suddenly inspired and needing to concrete the vision before it leaves him, and he grabs a piece of paper. Shyam Prajaparti has swallowed a fly at school that week, and it has been the sole topic of conversation for the days that follow. Jack is going to write a song about the incident, but from the fly's perspective. I gaze at him, with a small pinch of jealousy, but a far larger dose of loving awe, as he writes the words, "Now I see why I, 'Mr Fly', I want to fly south, into Shyam's mouth." It is fantastic. The chorus, as if to make it easy for me to catch up, stays on an F major barre chord. An F major barre chord hurts, but as long as I don't need to move it in a hurry, I can do it. I play it over and over, downstroke after downstroke, as Jack tilts the pencil back and forth to his lips, searching for the missing piece to our first song, before finally singing, "Now I see what I see, cos I see what I see, and I see what I see cos I see it right now." It makes absolutely no sense whatsoever. That doesn't matter. Oasis have taught us that. With "Shyam's Song" written within the space of an hour, we are on a natural high, a sudden burst of the possibility of where our chemistry will propel us. We need a name. I look around at our surroundings, in Jack's basement. Wait. That's what we are called. Jack's Basement.

*

I felt, personally, that given our obvious brilliance, which we'd had immediately validated by Jack's mum Clare saying it sounded good through the floorboards, we should leave school and concentrate solely on the music. Maybe we could move into Jack's basement permanently. It was the only way to accelerate what was already inevitable: our eventual arrival on the front cover of *There and Then*. Jack, though, cautiously eyeing his bandmates, me like a frantic dog demanding communal discipline yet not being able to play myself, and the drummer entirely incapable of playing any part of the kit apart from the snare drum and, occasionally if given enough time without pressurising him, the kick drum too, perhaps did not see the future in Jack's Basement that I did. Or maybe he did and projected the extent to which the workload would inevitably fall on him. In fact, I had already known this and, on some level of deep-subconscious manoeuvring, had suggested the band had his name in it in order to appease this undoubted truth. We did not, under a vote of two to one, leave school to pursue the band.

Nonetheless, new songs came, every fortnight on a Sunday in Jack's basement. "Hego", a classical civilisation-inspired meditation on a man with an ego, complete with a sort of spoken-word rap. I listened through once and played a kind of three-note riff that sounded a bit like a Balearic record jumping and just repeated and repeated and repeated as Jack moved through his continuous chord phrases. When we finished the run-through, Jack turned to me. "I love how Jessie will probably say that your riff is in the wrong key, but, come on" – he rolled his eyes at this imaginary conversation with Jessie – "we know that already, that's the point." I nodded. Totally. So true. (I didn't know it was in the wrong key.) There were more: "Only Me", a love song about a girl who was "everything", in which I repeated my trusted technique of playing a three-note pattern again and again throughout the entire thing. Nobody said to change it. So I didn't, assuming that the lack of discussion meant it was brilliant. That was a band-dynamic truth I would stick with from that point on: if no-one said, "It's rubbish" or to change it, they meant that it was brilliant. Men, after all, found it hard to articulate that they thought each other were brilliant.

Slowly, in between every rehearsal, soaking up whatever new chords Jack would show me and going home and looping them on repeat to virtual sickness in my room, I had begun to be able to move between chords, and not just the basic ones at the beginner's end of the neck either. I knew that maybe, to keep Jack's Basement afloat, I needed to contribute some songs too. I was nervous about this and, so that my brothers or Dad wouldn't hear, I locked myself in my room and muttered the beginnings of my songs to myself in the evening. I hadn't planned them to be, but – a bit like my bowling – they were extraordinarily melancholic and earnest acoustic songs. Every line I would sing to myself, over a chord I softly strummed, I would repeat in my head and then, like Nasser Hussain playing and missing and giving himself a personal whipping, I would spit back into my own brain: "That's *shit*. Do you think Noel Gallagher or Bob Dylan would ever write anything as shit as that?" I found myself completely handicapped, never moving past Nasser's voice in my head, telling me to give up. I did eventually complete two, recording them onto a cassette recorder with a blank tape, one called "Plastic Eyes", about a person who "saw the world through plastic eyes", and another that had a bit about "whisper you'll miss her". They were embarrassingly underdeveloped and adolescent strum-alongs and I knew it. Slumped, I would listen back, hoping the song might have miraculously improved, before admitting to myself that actually, if I was to have any chance of recreating my own *There and Then*, it would have to be with Jack. If I could stick with him, I thought, everything would be OK.

My humiliation and embarrassment of myself in my room – the constant trying and the constant failing to produce anything that sounded anything close to musically passable – oddly subverted itself every time I got back to Jack's basement on a Sunday. Buoyed by Jack's natural showmanship and propelled by an uncontrollable wave of inner excitement, I'd find myself suddenly very confident when flanked by Jack and Joel. The music that we were making, that we were intent on being straight-ahead universal stadium rock music yet accidentally sounded like it *might* be good in an incredibly conceptual and dissonant art-rock-funk band, made me feel completely alive. We were taking our unintentionally oddball three piece for our first gig soon, which I had of course arranged, and, in an Alan Wells-ish been-waiting-all-my-life-for-this-but-not-quite-actually-ready-yet frenzy, I scrambled to the last rehearsal before the show finally with one song. I wrote a chord progression of A, G, D and then A again, with little twiddly bits in between each one, that I felt looked impressive while buying me time to reach the next. I called the song "Spirits Die", its chorus landing on an E major while I shouted, "I'd give you my soul but my Spirits Die." It was the biggest load of nonsense potentially ever recorded to a blank tape. When I presented it, though, to Jack and Joel, I half-pouted while playing it, to lend it an air of confidence, and made sure to scream the chorus, making it 1) far enough from Jack's singing to give it a unique selling point and 2) not like the melancholic strum-alongs I was writing that, however many times I listened back to them hoping for them to show their inner beauty, I knew were shit. Jack and Joel didn't say it was brilliant per se, but by them not saying that it *wasn't* brilliant, I did the rest of the maths internally. They just weren't saying that because men found it hard to articulate brilliance.

We added a new section to the song, a final minute where it sped up and sped up and sped up until Joel was just sort of smashing the snare as quickly as he could. Being able to speed up really fast was a skill unique to us, surely? Jack had one last touch, too. It needed something, he said, and that something, it didn't occur to me until he did it, was for him to begin the song with a two-minute guitar-funk solo, which he carried out completely unaccompanied and then nodded to me to start the song when he had finished. Perfect.

Our first gig, at Clapham Contact Centre, a converted small church hall, was a support slot for Intentionally Blank. I worked myself into the mindset that the gig had world-ending stakes to it and, with my microphone sellotaped to a table, performed with Black Rebel Motorcycle Club and Oasis stickers on my starter-kit electric guitar. Will recorded the entire thing, standing in front of me stage right, on a handheld hired video camera. I relived the gig via his footage, making notes, bathing in the realness of it all, and Jack's Basement evolved, beginning a Spinal Tap-esque conveyor belt of changing personnel on drums, Joel becoming a bass player with far more organic dexterity, and eventually finding Tommy Stubbington. Tommy was into bands far beyond our comprehension: post-hardcore groups like Fugazi and Minor Threat and, well organised and a borderline actual musician, he gave me a kind of logistical teammate. We sorted two London gigs, back to back, in real pubs. On Friday, the Brixton Windmill and on Saturday, the Bedford Arms in Balham.

In the run-up to these shows, a mini-tour of South London in our eyes, we were filled with the fear of being inside the actual adult world of gigging. More than the gig or the songs or the playing, I fixated on what the experience of a sound-check was supposed to be like. Soundchecks, for any musician who has played enough, are usually a mind-numbing regulation in which the sound engineer checks all the instruments in isolation, asking each musician to make some noise on their own, and then the band plays briefly to ensure it sounds good in the room. This is usually followed, as if it were an industry law, by a complaint by one of the members in the band about how it sounds and the sound engineer saying, "It'll change when there are people in here." I had, however, misinterpreted the concept of a soundcheck into the anxiety-inducing fear that it was a sort of vetting process to weed out non-musicians. In my mind, when it was my turn, the sound engineer might say something like, "OK, 12-bar blues in the key of B flat, please," and I would be found out, stranded, with the eyes of the bands waiting on the floor setting up their equipment all suddenly upon me, incriminated in the white glow of the stage.

*

Luckily, we soundcheck second at the Brixton Windmill. We watch the first band's drummer studiously (a drummer always soundchecks first), each of us being careful to learn the ritual on sight. It is their first real gig, too. The sound engineer instructs him. "Kick, please." Drummer plays kick repeatedly. "OK, thanks. Snare." Drummer plays snare repeatedly. "Hi-hat." Drummer plays hi-hat repeatedly. And so on. On completion of the last piece of the drumkit, the sound engineer, happy everything is working, barks coldly, "OK, everything at once." The drummer pauses for a second. He looked confused, his face contorted in an expression of bewilderment at what is required of him and then, protruding his elbows and forcing his knees towards the cymbals, he stretches out and, in a single strike, including his forehead for the hi-hat, he attempts to hit every part of the drumkit at exactly the same time.

Ba-dom-chish.

There is a pause but for the sound engineer, incredulous enough not to find it funny, simply sighing inwards, "No, play a beat with the whole kit." I turn to Tommy who, relieved, is also digesting what he's seen. "Don't do that," I whisper.

He nods. When it comes round to my turn, I am safe enough in the knowledge that I am not going to be asked to reproduce grade eight classical guitar, and so when asked to play, I proudly and loudly play my Balearic loop from "Hego", again and again and again.

*

The gigs, as far as we were concerned, went very well, but not well enough to convince Jack and Joel that we should quit school, where the female teachers had taken me aside after lessons and explained things about when they had encountered death, or apologised that part of an English lesson had accidentally covered a novel that dealt with grief. These tiny graces, if genuinely helpful, did also in essence give me the impression that I now had a free ticket to daydream through my A levels without any expectation whatsoever. I revelled in this freedom. I had learned a new technique for practising my chord progressions when at school: I'd imagine my teeth were the frets of a guitar, the back of the right-hand side of my gums the first fret, and the back of the left-hand side the high end. The root of the tooth was the highest string and the crown the lowest, and I would place my tongue on a certain part to denote which note I was playing. I then switch off, safe in the knowledge I would not be called upon, phase my attention out into the middle distance or through a window, and go through the chords to "Like a Rolling Stone", or whatever Oasis song it might be. When I realised that I might look a bit odd, my mouth half ajar and tongue waggling around inside, I'd pause for a second and silently plan my outfit for the next Jack's Basement gig.

This attitude permeated my cricket, too. My undimmed enthusiasm for the game and for practices meant I was still guaranteed a place in the school team despite my recent form – a five-year wicket famine. I wasn't in the first XI, of course:

that consisted of what looked to me like elite-level, international-standard cricket. A rag-tag selection of our year, alongside the misfits from the other two, formed a second XI which was left largely to its own devices. This allowed for a kind of anarchic haggling system of batting orders despite what we had been told by the coach, who would be on the field umpiring while we argued. It also, somehow, provided quite fertile conditions for our growing obsession with weed. First Mark Knight-Williams, always ahead of the game, then Matt Weeks, had begun to find the numbers of various random people dotted around South London with pseudonyms, who would wait a left and a left again from the school gates and drop off little transparent "baggies" with sugary, pungent skunk in exchange for money we had collected for our lunches.

Standing at slip, playing "Like a Rolling Stone" on your teeth while intoxicatingly stoned, is quite a hazardous occupation. Given our sort of left-field hijacking of the team, despite none of us being considered captaincy material, the four of us would lurk needlessly in the slip cordon/gully region, with bloodshot eyes, squinting as the bowler ran in and flinching when we realised our reactions would be significantly delayed by our paranoid state. We'd giggle in between balls, before repeating. It was quite a subversive thrill. I didn't realise then that I had maybe made it into the slip cordons that defined bands. My slow left-arm spin, needless to say, still had not infused the grief-inspired anger and purpose that Tuffers had. If anything, it had become more lovely, more eager to please and far more hittable. I was throwing up lollipops that almost literally pleaded to be loved and never were. My customary two overs a game (I batted 11, so I had to bowl) would play out with my team, even my stoned slip cordon, rolling their eyes and ringing the boundary, while, with a fogginess of artificial super-skunk clouding my senses, I'd trot in, be duly dispatched and then get back to practising guitar on my teeth.

Our group stretched out beyond the handful moving up batting orders in exchange for packs of Twiglets and cans of Coke, and we spent weekends slowly learning which pubs in South London would let us in if we wore dark enough clothes, then walking home, all together to Matt's house, in a gaggle of 12 or 13 or more, bagsying who was going to get "roller's rights" and "twos" or "threes" on the spliffs we hadn't yet even made. Matt's house became a home from home over that period of a few years and, as I had done with Jack's and Jessie's and Mark's, I'd developed a sort of weighty connection with his mum, Annie, ensuring I always held her eyeline, unlike my muttering, stoned counterparts, and finding constant comfort in our every interaction. Like Clare, she had lost her father at a young age too and, alongside her natural maternal tendencies, I found myself pulled along by some kind of comforting understanding she managed to project without ever having to say. Matt's room became our universe HQ, where visitors piled in and out and temporary yellow foam beds without covers and sheetless duvets were thrown around the room for whoever was asleep during the day or going to sleep there that night. One evening, in a giddy fix of loyalty to the nights we had spent stealthily smoking weed together, Matt walked into a tattoo parlour and asked them to emblazon "Giggles" in gangster-rap style font, propping up an illustration of a marijuana leaf over the entirety of his left shoulder blade. "I will definitely never regret this,"* he said, without irony, when he showed it to me and my brain spiralled into the million sounds I wanted to make but couldn't.

Hugo, his refuge coming in the arms of the Wannie Massive, had been having his own non-cricket-related adventures. Where I was always keen to make sure my psychedelic experiments were as close as possible to a metaphorical handrail,

* Matt, 20 years on, has just begun the process of getting the tattoo painfully removed.

172

he had dived in in a more determined way. His school work had been completely dispensed with and his weekends spent away from home. Each school night he would quietly let himself into my room at the top of the house and would roll a spliff, levering himself up beyond my growing CD collection and, legs half onto the roof, through the window, leaving half for me to smoke. As our lives threatened to drag us in different directions, it was our unspoken yet never broken meeting point every evening. The cats would join us, purring into the side of the alphabetically ordered CDs, and we would sometimes speak and sometimes not, taking it in turns to silently clamber up and down from the window ledge. In the distance, through the roofs and telephone lines, you could make out the cemetery populated by ancient trees. The tallest one, which arched over the rest, stood immediately next to Lana's grave, a horizontal slab of minimalist stone curated by Andrew which punctuated a disturbance in the upright gravestones that shared its row. We never mentioned, as we smoked and sometimes spoke, that we were both staring directly at it. There was no choice. When Hugo eventually left, creeping downstairs, I would put on *Pink Moon* by Nick Drake, a present from Jack that year, so quietly that I could barely hear it and, lying completely still, eventually attune my sense to the near silence and feel it wash over, then through me, thoughtlessly into chemically enhanced sleep.

While the generally unspoken loss had sent my dad, my brothers and me into different directions, music had become a more vital connection than ever before. Bob Dylan and Loudon Wainwright III especially, the three of us suddenly homed in on with a different kind of affinity. We approached Bob, the bootlegged tapes labelled in Lana's handwriting that filled the house, as if he was suddenly a long-lost friend of our mother's. It was as if we felt somehow that he and Loudon had been friends of our parents when we were younger, and that their music might connect some sort of perilous void in time between then and now and us and them. With that, and my continued exploits in the accidentally-quite-good-but-not-in-the-way-we-thought-we-were Jack's Basement, Hugo and Will had also taken up guitar. They were good, maybe a chord or two behind me always, and rather than accepting my fate as I had with my cricketing inability, I saw it as a motif to stay ahead of at all times, being stirred into constant guitaring activity so as not to be surpassed by them as I usually was. I spent this time proudly assembling pieces of instrumental music for which I could not find a compatible vocal melody I deemed passable, so I'd present them to Jack's Basement during rehearsals and Jack, much as he had done with "Shyam's Song", would improvise lyrics and vocals over the top. I would watch these little songs, things that I had just made up and that had their being only inside my own room, turn into real solid entities, existing between four people, handed over in a kind of shared ownership, and I felt myself almost physically lifted up by it, as if I had grown taller through their creation. The music, of course, was shit, but to focus too keenly on that would be missing the point.

Matt and his older brother Orlando, introduced to me as Land, occupied the two rooms at the top of their house and, like most teenage brothers, communicated with each other as little as possible. During one Friday night post-pub-in-dark-clothes sleepover, I was sent next door to Land's for a Rizla. I snuck in and, while I was there, became distracted from my task by the guitar I had interrupted Land from playing. His room was full of DIY ashtrays and illustrations and, tripping into conversation, noticing that he was only really playing low E again and again, I ended up writing a sheet of all the chords I knew for him in amateur tab. I knew six chords by now. He asked me if I had any songs. Overcome by a wave of optimism, I played him one that for some reason I hadn't yet played to Jack's Basement – a heavy waltz using the chords E minor and C7 again and again. They were

174

useful chords because you didn't have to move your fingers much to get from one to the other, enabling me to deliver this impromptu performance with conviction. I had lyrics which, of course, were nonsense. I was still under the impression from Oasis that songs that had lyrical meaning were in some way wimpish or laughably try-hard. Land had a four-track recorder in his room and, taken enough with my gibberish wordplay, suggested we record the song immediately. He sang the backing vocals into a rolled-up piece of paper, fashioned into a kind of megaphone, and with the guitar completed in one take, we were listening back to our song in 20 minutes. I returned to the next room, not just with the Rizla but with an entirely new sense of self. Land had made me feel, *and* sound, less shit. It gave me an odd sense of worth, a current of connection which, of course, I would never mention, but which I had never felt before.

Land phoned me up the next day. He was looking for a guitar player to join his band. "My brother's nearly as good as me," I said, as if that was of some kind of credit to him. Hugo turned up at Land's the next day, guitar in hand, also meeting Robert Dylan Thomas on drums. Rob was *actually* named after Bob. Hugo came back saying they had three songs (none of them from the perspective of a fly being swallowed), Orlando was brilliant and he had a chord chart stuck on his wall that looked as if it was in my handwriting.

20

That Sounds Like the
Name of a Good Band

G uitar culture had dived in popularity since Oasis and Britpop's mass rule of the early '90s. Unlike the rest of the country, I had not queued outside a record shop to buy Oasis's third album *Be Here Now*, the most highly anticipated album of the decade, but I *had* done for their two subsequent records, for which, with the cultural focus having shifted elsewhere, there were no queues anywhere. I liked that it was only me queuing for these records, standing there with my flag in the sand like Atherton or my dad when all other hope was evaporating. By 2002, though, when I was armed with visions of being a guitarist myself, it was slowly forcing its way back into vogue. My news, as it had done years ago on *Top of the Pops*, now came every week through *NME* magazine, which was especially keen on putting America's new myth-made-flesh guitar groups on the cover. I had seen and read about The Strokes, Black Rebel Motorcycle Club, Kings of Leon, Interpol, The Yeah Yeah Yeahs and The White Stripes before I'd heard them, and already decided that I loved them all. When I did eventually hear them, my CD collection gathered pace, each album I'd been recommended sounding even better than I'd hoped, every one clearly delineated on the map of guitar history my parents had laid out and, with the

CD rack becoming bigger and bigger and harder and harder to vault over silently while we smoked in the evening, me and Hugo listened to these records, that really needed to be played loud, very quietly and stared off into that arched tree, imagining the life beyond it.

As I collated this new intake of bands from America, irresistibly close to me in age, I continued to chase back all of Oasis's influences. If learning the songs on guitar was like a muscle-memory tracing of how making good music must *feel*, they were littered with lifts and references to music from the past, too. My life had become a process of joining the dots between those three records in the car from the trips to and from Purley, past the waving woman, to Oasis and the new-wave American groups. In each record or new band that had clearly influenced the one before, there was another clue. I did this dot-joining, in part, in the huge HMV record store on Oxford Street.

*

Here, there are old Oasis singles, each with three new B-sides, that I have saved for and am deliberately collecting one at a time, and albums from across the decades slewn in bargain bins, that I root through looking for a group I have read Noel citing as an influence. Today I have made particularly good progress in the bargain bin. I've ticked off three big records by three big bands, names that are thrown around all the time that I haven't yet formed an opinion on beyond constant written praise: The Smiths' *Hatful of Hollow*, The Small Faces' *Ogdens' Nut Gone Flake* and Love's *Forever Changes*. I am queuing to buy the records when Jack, always leading these shopping trips, reeling off facts about every record that I am looking upon for the first time – the names of the band members and which instrument they play – runs up to me. His face is completely drained of colour, a shocked, sudden white. He holds my eyes for a second, with an expression that tells me what he is about to say is not fabricated, before, after a quick intake of breath, announcing, "It's," then another breath, "Noel Gallagher." I process the information for a second, as if unable to hear the words, staring back at him, with the records in my hands. Jack continues, "Quick, he's leaving." Without having consciously made a decision, I have left the queue and I am running. I am running through aisles and barging past shoppers, to the huge exit, in a bid to grasp my only opportunity to see Noel. When we reach the exit, wide enough to house three shopfronts, he is there, leaving the store. "Noel," I shout. He turns and nods, and then continues walking out. But without thought, I am following still, out of the record store and into the throng of London pedestrian traffic, the unpaid-for CDs in my hand.* As I continue to follow, needing to speak to Noel, I set off a chain reaction of alarms that suddenly encircles me and, awash in flashing red, with two security guards flanking me, it is now Noel that turns and looks at me. The security, one on either side, move towards me. I plead, "That's Noel Gallagher, and I just need to tell him that..." Noticing that it actually is Noel Gallagher, they briefly abate. I say something like thank you, then something else, then something else, too fast for me to even know what, and then it is over as, each arm hooked by a security guard, I am dragged back towards the store. Noel has disappeared in the distance and, tears settling just behind my eyes, my only moment gone, I explain to the staff that I will go and pay for these records in my hands, and that I am only buying them because that man walking off into the distance told me to.

*

---

* Oxford Street HMV has, give or take, the highest security of any store in London.

That winter, of 2002 and into 2003, dots between fantasy and reality being delicately formed, my focus returned to the Ashes. It was Nasser Hussain's turn to take his rougher, tougher England side to Australia. Winning the toss on the first day of the series at Brisbane on a cloudless day on a grassless pitch, he opted to bowl. It was a terrible decision. Simon Jones, England's promising young fast bowler, slid chasing the ball on the first morning and, his knee bouncing off the hard ground as he did, bent backwards to a series of repeated gasps over the in-ground television replays. He sat up, in tears, as fellow new young hope Steve Harmison helped carry him off on a stretcher. It was alarming, the stretcher. A desperate part of me imagined him being taken to a morgue in Kingston and, with him sitting suddenly bolt upright, I fizzed inside myself. Maybe she *had* sat up too, when we were gone?

Alex Tudor, in and out since last being seen deluged under the beer-bellied crowd invasion in 1999, was hit so hard in the head later that winter by Australia's new fast bowler Brett Lee that, having ducked towards the ball, he went staggering left and right, hands on his head before ending up flattened on the floor, just as Simon Jones had been a couple of weeks earlier. It was Mark Butcher who carried the stretcher this time. Tudor didn't sit up. The silence as he left had its own sense of funeral-pyre starkness to it and I flashed again, as he shot out of view, to where he was going and prayed it would be safe there. As Tudor, shaken but all right, was being carried off, he said to Butcher, "Tell my mum I'm OK." It was the most visceral and physical manifestation of defeat, even by their standards, that England had ever been subject to.

This slumber back into another calamitous English cricketing winter, exactly the same as each I'd known, was momentarily reassuring and, voicing once again the healthy reminder that everything is always fucked and there is never really any hope but a relentless "what if?" that age cannot dim, it saw the beginnings of my new temporary home, the sad cricket cave. The sad cricket cave could be built anywhere there was cricket. In the cave and with the cricket, I began to feel – not understand, but feel – a deep sadness within me that I almost impressed myself with. Cricket and I had a little pact with each other where, whether it be radio or TV, I had a solitary space to sigh into. I knew that nothing would be asked of me other than to watch, which I'd begun to do with my guitar ever present, my head concentrating on the cricket and my hands just playing without instruction. I'd look into the vacuum and feel the screen eerily continue to articulate a deep sense of hopelessness that I could dive into but not yet name while I killed time with the machine that killed fascists, my hands producing a soothing, mindless repetition, creating a little pocket of looped sound to forever live inside.

Hugo had now installed his best mate Rupert Jarvis into the group: he'd got in by coming round and playing Lenny Kravitz's "Fly Away" on the guitar to us, as we watched jealously awestruck. Ru owned a bass, albeit one that required batteries and sparkled with glitter, but a bass nonetheless and, without further discussion, he was in the band. Another friend had been one of the rolling guests at the Weeks' of late, and had put their finger down on a line in the Bible, saying, "That would be a good name for a band." They were going to be called The Maccabees.

With The Maccabees and Jack's Basement now making two functioning groups worth half an hour of material each, we started to book shows together. We stumbled from pub to pub promising each one that we would bring a crowd of not so much fans, as friends, to fill their spaces. That was enough for the Pleasure Unit in East London and South London promoter Zaid. With these semi-regular London shows, we began to practise all our combined rock-star would-be-isms to our net of mainly drum'n'bass interested friends. They made it clear that they didn't think we were particularly good – it was sort of the trade-off for their time – yet they created a big enough swarm of bodies in front of the stage that while I was playing, I could suspend reality for a second and feel a pulse of belonging that elasticated time. Even when I was jolted into reality by the sheer haphazardness of it all, it offered enough glimpses of what I imagined being in a real band would feel like for me to daydream it into a bigger show than it was when I was back in my sad cricket cave.

The Maccabees, it had to be said, were becoming worryingly taut as a unit and the songs, centring around Land's tongue-in-cheek recapturing of adolescent relationships and love of smoking, would consist of the band playing as fast as they could for the duration. Rob, comfortably the most complete and gifted musician in the two-band scene, could play as quickly as the band asked him to, with 16 rhythms on the snare that he would hit from the side on rather than straight down among hi-hats and complex kick-patterns, all with a cigarette perfectly balanced off his bottom lip. In part, it appeased our drum'n'bass friends. The sheer pace, though, would leave Land, a brilliant singer but still an unconfident guitar player, giving up moving through the chords and simply finding the last one, resting his hand there, waiting for the last note and clanging it with the rest of the band.

Silently, I was sad to leave school, where I had felt safe and protected and, for the most part, understood. With it only two weeks into the past, I got a call from Jack. He didn't want to be in a band the same way I did, he said. He didn't want to rehearse every day. If I wanted to join The Maccabees, he went on, he'd totally understand. It was as if he had always known that I was meant to be in the other band. I put down the phone and, like I was suddenly floating adrift in the middle of the ocean, desperate and alone and gasping for air, I cried to myself, completely taken aback by the strength of feeling my gut had just kicked back up through my throat. I walked downstairs and told Hugo about Jack's suggestion, about me playing in The Maccabees. He was reluctant for a second, using this inversion of power to dwell on his own thoughts on this matter, tears not completely swept from my eyes, as I waited for a response. He eventually put me out of my misery, bargaining enough in this unexpected agency by saying, "OK, you're in. As long as you know, I'm the lead guitar player. You're rhythm." Anything, I told him. Anything he wanted. Privately, I knew that I had got out of the deal very well, as neither of us could play anything remotely resembling guitar solos in any case. Next, I phoned Land, who spoke with relief and joy down the phone before confessing that he wasn't really playing the guitar at the shows anyway, apart from the first and last chord of each song.

The Maccabees had a work ethic that I could immediately tuck inside. They were all very serious about the band, it was universally understood that it was the most important thing in their lives. We looked a complete mess, each person trying to be in a different band, all in various forms of post-pubescent self-discovery, but when I looked across the room in my first rehearsal, as Land sank to his knees in a kind of jubilance, saying, "It sounds so good! It sounds so big!" – I felt like I really belonged there. The Maccabees were my new family.

Cricket, as it always tended to, met my new rush of purpose and excitement that summer with the South Africans back in England for a manic and thrilling series. After a rainy first-Test draw, Nasser Hussain resigned his captaincy with immediate effect. That first morning of not being England captain fell in the 48 hours between Test matches in which Michael Vaughan had to get his head around being the leader himself. It was a fitting induction to the challenges in store, with England being beaten by an innings and 92 runs. Across a series that I rehearsed outside of and then zoned back into, Vaughan introduced the new components which his England would be built on: a lessening of pressure and a prioritising of expression. I was there at The Oval as Alec Stewart

– in his final Test – was lifted on Vaughan and Flintoff's shoulders to celebrate an end-of-summer victory at the same ground where he had taken the cameras and my teenage self, unrecognisable to myself now, into that dressing room, five years ago. He was 35 then, 40 now, and he had stretched his entire life across the tragedy of English cricket up until that point, leaving with a sense that maybe all the effort was for something eventually, and that something was to lie ahead, without him.

21

Alec Stewart and the Suncream

lec Stewart is a man of absolutes. There are do's
and don'ts, yeses and no's, hows and whys. It's part
of what made him the cricketer he was, dragging
England through the barren spells and leaving them just
about to spring into life, having survived a decade in which
any sort of success at all was because of his input. You'd
imagine that to anyone with any other mindset, international
cricket in the '90s was a pretty inhospitable landscape.

While Alec, now director of cricket at Surrey, is out driving,
on his hands-free, I am desperate to dig into his brain for
some previously untold emotional residue from his England
days. Impressively, there really does seem to be none. He still
thinks the most important thing about his last game, being
carried aloft around The Oval, was that "we won the game
and we squared the series", telling me, "It sounds a bit soppy,
doesn't it, the emotional side of it, but yeah I guess there was
some romance to it." I'm thrown by Stewart telling me that
being triumphantly held aloft by his teammates, while a sold-
out Oval stood and cheered him into the distance is "a bit
soppy", suddenly imagining how soppy he will find my entire
ramblings and emotional projection, much of which he is the
centre of, on the game of cricket.

The sets of absolutes in Stewart's playing career were as
well defined physically as they were ideologically. "I don't
know how it started, but I always had to put my left foot onto

the field first. I would always check my stride to make sure. It's stupid, but that's what I did." I don't think it's stupid, I tell him, just like I don't think considering the emotional ballast of your last England game is soppy, and I ask what would happen if he went right foot first. "I just wouldn't have done," he replies. That's that, then. It calls to mind Stewart's ritualistic quirk when batting: systematically after every ball pulling both sides of his shirt collar up, touching both pads, before standing tall and twirling the bat a few times, with it pointed to the sky. "I'm a creature of habit. I can't not do it. Even if one of the Surrey players shows me their new bat and says, 'What do you think?', I'll just pick it up and do that immediately. Even when I play charity games and people say, 'I'll donate if he doesn't twiddle his bat in a whole over', I can't do it." I tell him how culturally resonant it was to young cricketers in their early teens across South London, assuming that in order to bat "properly" you had to carry out that exact process first before the ball arrived. He laughs, "People are sad, aren't they? I don't know what that was, but it was my set-to. That was my way of dealing with it. To be honest, it was probably OCD, but it's what I needed to do. It is stupid, but cricket is stupid."

I get the sense, like most who dedicate their lives to cricket, that Stewart finds the need to both feed his addiction to the game and acknowledge the meaninglessness of it at every stage, almost to send it up. It's part of his life; he has no choice now. It is, after all, forever recurrent in his dreams. "When I was playing, my wife would be telling me I was talking in my sleep and it'd be about cricket. But now, I'll still talk as if I'm talking to a player in my sleep, apparently. The saying is true, you live, sleep, dream cricket. It is a part of you. So that's what the game means to me." Does he miss the playing itself? "I do miss the feeling of facing fast bowling. There is no adrenaline rush like it. I've been lucky to have been occupied, because so many struggle afterwards with not being able to replace that feeling of..." – he pauses – "...genuine danger."

Alec Stewart – genuine danger.

There is one thread I am desperate to search down. Atherton couldn't celebrate against South Africa in 1998 having conjured series-winning innings, his body sending him to hospital at the last minute. Stewart, too, on the last Australian tour, missed a game, I know by the deep recesses of my cricket badgery-brain, because he had a rash on his face. It was reported then that it went undiagnosed. I am curious about the cost of the '90s losing and the pressure and whether he feels his body too chose to articulate the stress elsewhere. "The rash?" He thinks for a second before laughing. "Oh, you've jogged my memory there. That was Sydney or Melbourne, I think. They didn't know what it was

187

at the time." I wait, searching down my next psychoanalytical cricket clue. "It turns out it was a reaction to suncream." Stewart hears the slight anti-climax in my response before very sweetly suggesting, "I mean, we can make it bigger for your book, if you want?" No, I tell him. The truth is fine.

22

I Just Know That Something
Good Is Going to Happen

Every evening our ritual continued, clambering expertly over the CDs to numb our minds a fraction as quietly as we could. I still couldn't roll spliffs, which was an impressive feat given that I was beginning to spend chunks of each day stoned. My general life philosophy was that something someone else could do would be beyond me and not worth the torture of trying; I was yet to discover this to be the baseline thought process of most musicians on anything other than, and sometimes even including, playing music. This accounted for rolling spliffs.

Regardless, now that we were united in purpose, where Hugo would once tiptoe back down to his room, the evenings sprawled out into very quiet Maccabees guitar rehearsals. The Strokes and Interpol, both strangely perfect groups from New York, had begun to reach out from the CD racks and teach us game-changing guitar-playing philosophies. Consisting of two guitar players each, The Strokes like the light and Interpol the dark, both relied heavily upon dynamics within the band for their songs to flourish. It was not about strumming a song and the band forming a general backdrop, while everyone gazed at the singer, as was Oasis's defining aesthetic. It was about weaving an ever-moving sonic tapestry, where the guitarists would play down-stroked constant percussive patterns, relatively simple in isolation, but becoming vital components in the context of the song. They were organisms dependent on a variety of moving parts, inconceivable to any single member. This was wildly appealing to us all. Especially to me. I'd been drowning in self-hate at my inability to communicate anywhere near my desired standard with just my voice and an acoustic guitar. The pairs of guitarists in these unbelievably perfect groups managed to convey purpose and reason, the small things I was trying to find, in their playing alone. It spoke in a way that didn't necessarily need words to connect or, more precisely, didn't put the lyric front and centre. The bands, we decided, tripping head-first in love, were who they were for a couple of reasons: a cohesive idea of what they were trying to achieve (which we hadn't landed on yet) and a group ideology of playing as part of one piece, for the greater good (which we absolutely had).

This merged purposefully in our heads with the collation of The Clash footage we were collectively beginning to assemble: most specifically *Rude Boy*, in which they acted half-heartedly in between live footage from packed clubs across the early stretch of their career. The Clash played with a similar, if much more direct, down-stroked debt to the cause. As they did, the packed clubs moved with them, as if something vital was unfolding in front of them. Joe Strummer, Mick Jones and Paul Simonon lined up at the very front of the stage, each a front man of sorts, in a gesture of both confrontation and affinity with their audience. As they bounced across the stage in cartoonish anger, they clearly meant it. That was important. We did too. We weren't exactly sure *what* it was we meant, but we really did mean it.

The lightbulb development in song construction gave Hugo and me a focus to our evenings. We worked out that, rather than playing chords, if one of us played a note continuously, repeatedly pushing on a D for example, and the other one did the same thing but an octave up, it sounded really good. Much better than just strumming a chord. It was slick and purposeful and it needed the other part to make it whole. The Maccabees, back in our rehearsal space, bought into this idea wholesale and, poring through a big Clash book at Land's house, we began to string together what it was our band was trying to be. The Clash really enjoyed dressing up. Their hair was detailed and slicked back, a kiss curl left flicking the tops of their foreheads, their clothes generating a mission statement in themselves. It was "like trouser, like brain". Hugo took to this literally, rolling up one jean trouser leg and putting a banana skin inside it, with a sweatband on each wrist and a cap that read "little devil". I found myself caught between all my Manc Oasis inclinations and this new slicker, tighter look of The Clash, while trying to incorporate The Strokes's obvious taste for having clothes with holes in, blending the three into a sort of three-for-one history of guitar music. Needless to say, with little at my disposal wardrobe-wise, it didn't really work.

Of course, trying to be that band, our own version of the groups we had developed crushes on, and actually being that band were two entirely removed concepts. My first gig with The Maccabees, at Kingston Peel, in which I positioned myself in the middle of the stage in a bid to make myself immediately indispensable, had some teething issues. Our show, my left-handed guitar head stock regularly clashing with Ru's bass among some alarming pirouettes that, to even my surprise, were suddenly part of my stage schtick, was sabotaged halfway through when the drummer from the support act came on stage to take his drumkit back. The song collapsed mid-show as a long conferral between the drummer and our band took place, entirely separate to the sparse crowd. "I'm so sorry," he said, as we wrestled parts of the hardware back that he was beginning to pack up amid feedback and clanging, "but my mum's outside and she says I have to go now." We completed the show with Rob playing

191

a floor tom and crash cymbal alone. Like Jack's Basement before, it sounded quite good, but not in the way that we had intended it to.

That's how we continued, sounding quite good, but not exactly in the way we thought we did. Rehearsals every weekend would stretch over eight hours, playing our songs again and again to each other. All of them "needed another bit" and, despite never finding the "other bit", we'd play them on loop as if eventually we might form one brainless unity and the music would just mutate the next section for us. Land's lyrical material became frequent and more idiosyncratic, songs about things like pointy shoes. With his sketches on guitar, we'd go home and quietly practise them every evening, bending them into some kind of slightly evolved piece to bring back into the rehearsal room, knowing he would have done the same. The gigs slowly developed with it, always incorporating a new song, or an idea of one song going into the other, but would be frequently stopped by our one tuner having to be passed around the band as the rest of us waited. The tuner we owned cost a tenner and was prone to picking up any noise. So, if you were tuning in a pub among chatter, which of course was routine for all shows, it would pick up the pitch of the chat above the guitar strings and send you tuning your low E to a low G, just by your speculative following of the free-form arrow.

I had not learned to tune by ear. I assumed, like the spliffs, that it was something way beyond my technical ability. This quite serious issue for a musician was compounded when, at the Pleasure Unit in Bethnal Green, I decided mid-set that the chatter was too much and took my guitar to the toilets to tune it up, leaving the band on stage. Two minutes later, as I had packed myself sweating into a cubicle, trying to get the fucking strings in fucking tune, my dad came in. "What are you doing?! Get back on the stage!" The pub, sat in music-less silence for a minute, watched as Andrew led me out from the toilet, dressed like Oasis on my bottom half, The Clash on my top and beer in my hair à la Strokes, back onto the stage. I apologised and, plugging my guitar back in again, deeply humiliated, I strummed a chord. It was definitely still out of tune.

Regardless of the mishaps, infinite and achingly apparent, we definitely improved. We went to see Interpol at Brixton Academy, watching the four of them make a sound so familiar, but so much louder, in front of us, both completely attainable and completely mythical, as we grabbed each other's heads to listen by the floor to "really hear the bass", leaving telling each other that we thought we could do that, too. Every week, we stretched ourselves into different excuses for competency, more able to execute the complete dead stops and starts together as The Strokes could, gently infiltrating moments of our own brand of Interpol-inspired beauty into the framework of racing each other to the end of every song.

As we did, the England cricket team – blurred out into a non-priority and more of a contextualising backdrop – spookily continued to emulate life and make their own newfound flawed but tangible progress. Michael Vaughan was still juggling his side and next to the weathered names that had lurched cricket through the dark days of the '90s, Butcher, Hussain and Thorpe, it was becoming familiar to come across a new set. Marcus Trescothick, an opening batsman with an unfathomably lovable demeanour. Matthew Hoggard, the Yorkshireman tirelessly running in to bowl like a panting shepherd's dog. Steve Harmison, a menacing fast bowler from the North East who you sensed wore his fragility slightly more on the surface than he knew, producing steep and intimidating bounce. Freddie Flintoff, constantly involved in the game, bending matches to his will with both bat and ball, yielding destruction and soft charm at the same time. And Michael Vaughan, with every passing Test looking more like a *joie de vivre*-installed leader of men. All of them, like The Strokes or Interpol, were tantalisingly close in age to me, and rather than striking up a kinship of distant, remarkably fragile superheroes, they now took on the form of the inspired older brothers I didn't have, merging to make one unit inconceivably bigger than the sum of its parts.

Then there was left-arm spinner Ashley Giles. Unlike Tuffers, who had retired a year earlier, Giles wasn't really a romantic proponent of my lovely, loopy stuff. His lack of grace or devilish magic was such that Henry Blofeld on *Test Match Special* would soon call him, affectionately but uncannily accurately, a "big old wheelie bin". Despite this resemblance, he found a way to make his moving parts, each one a systematic hauling of a limb to carry out his main function, work. His success in finding his way into the England side was of no small note to me.

When England arrived in the Caribbean in March 2004, they had not won a series in the West Indies since 1967/68. A West Indies tour, much the same as an Ashes series, was loaded with a roll-call of the inevitable, a montage of carnage as English stumps tumbled and batsmen flew despairingly out of, and occasionally into, fast bowlers' trajectories. A flashpoint of alarmingly low scores, too, the one that still haunted them the most being all out for 46 to Curtly Ambrose's unplayable streak ten years earlier.

*

As Steve Harmison receives the ball in the second innings at Kingston, the game, much as has been anticipated, is tantalisingly in the balance. Harmison, a slightly awkward giant of 6 foot 4, tends to run in with each stride marking what might be three for any other man. When he arrives at the crease, he propels himself in to deliver the ball by pointing both hands towards the sky, like the arms on a faulty grandfather clock set to 12 o'clock, then, before causing them to spin in fast-forward, himself pausing for a second mid-flight, he unleashes the ball in a continuation of his last stride. His action, explosive and, as with so many of the great fast bowlers, entirely idiosyncratic to him, means that the ball jumps from an unexpected length at batsmen's throats when on target, and at others stays low and skids through on wearing surfaces. Matthew Hoggard, his counterpoint, scuttles the ball out of a propulsion not created by his body parts as Harmison's is, but by the harrier energy in his run-up, skidding on quicker than batsmen would give credit to and often swinging the ball late, to make him deceptively dangerous.

Harmison forces Chris Gayle to flash at the ball and Graham Thorpe, as rugged as ever, dives to catch it. Ramnaresh Sarwan, jumping onto his toes and misjudging the bounce, is struck leg before wicket. Shivnarine Chanderpaul blocks the ball only to watch it pass through his legs and roll back, as if propelled by cyclical fate, onto his stumps. Then Lara, receiving an alarming ball from Hoggard and visibly disturbed, can only palm the next straight to Freddie Flintoff at slip. England are away and jubilant, the old guard in the catching positions awed by their young teammates' lack of fear. It doesn't stop. In a series of moments in fast-forward, Steve Harmison cleans up the last two, running in with a child-like joy, wickets constantly falling, stunned by the harm he is causing. When it is done, Harmison has bowled the West Indies out in the second innings of the first Test in Kingston, taking 7-12 in their score of 47. He walks off the pitch hiding a giggle, as if he is moving back to the dressing room he left as a boy, now as a legend of the game.

*

The rest of the series played out pretty much like the first Test: an oddly accurate retelling of the same old story, just the other way around. England's cricketers stretched themselves across the series, at first unsure of their own worth, then slowly, giddy and puppyish, whooping and laughing, punching each other, drunk with newfound power. The West Indies, meanwhile, managed to collapse from just about anywhere after establishing brief, hard-fought moments of almost parity, just like the English side they had tormented for the last couple of decades. The change in power was so telling that, during the fourth Test at St John's in Antigua, when Brian Lara reclaimed the world-highest Test score with an almost chanceless and genius 400, the celebrations, unlike the first time he had done it, where there were scenes of genuine elated abandon, were in front of a largely English crowd, the ground awash with St George's crosses, and tinted, if softly, with a strange, hollow sadness, too. The new England side, all old guard now gone with the exception of Butcher and Thorpe, galloped from there around the world like a new family, completely in love with each other, forever enveloping one another in celebration, pressing their cheeks against one another, high-fiving and always laughing. Flintoff especially turned the summer into a moving parade around himself, bowling quickly and sharply in constant game-changing spells and, lurching over his bat with his shirt undone, regularly smashing the ball around the ground with a charmed arrogance, his helmet thrown at jaunty angles on either side of his head as he emerged from whatever stroke landed the ball into the crowd next.

As all this played out in the background while I rehearsed or sat learning chords, it said something about where my life was heading. The past was gone. The past meant nothing. The future was to be taken. Freddie made it feel as if you could make something you wanted to happen, happen, just by imagining it. It was as if the difference lay in his audacity to imagine it at all. I channelled these life lessons into my day-to-day and, as The Maccabees rehearsed daily in some form, in constant communication with each other, changing songs or sharing records or smoking weed, I imagined us to be a cricket team, rehearsing slip catches if slip catches needed to be practised, or ground fielding if it had been sloppy last time, slowly honing every aspect of what we were, a new family of men given the free pass of being able to tell each other we loved each other amid substance-fuelled weekdays in a world that otherwise did not allow it.

Land, a year older than me and two from the rest, had already gone to Brighton University that year but – hell-bent on keeping us going and much to the confusion of everyone around apart from the members of the group – he travelled back to London and we travelled to Brighton every weekend. We decided we'd all follow him to the coast the next year, to keep the group together, and we gathered excuses for degrees, mine at Sussex University.

*

I arrive at the coast with a disorientatingly sad feeling under-neath my stomach, forcing itself back into my throat, blocking my voice. A part of me feels disloyal in some way, leaving home. I still want to be bringing experiences or people or achievements back into the room in the house that, for the first time, I no longer call home. I hug my dad to say goodbye as he leaves me in my new room in Kent House Halls, on the university campus, both of us doing odd impersonations of people not about to cry. Kent House is a huge block, where groups of 12 share a kitchen, two toilet cubicles and a shower. The rooms, small box rooms with an all-in-one wardrobe and sink at the end of each, flank the floors.

Within a week, I am inducted into my new group of friends, the people who live immediately around me in Kent House. With no ability to cook anything whatsoever and no intention of turning up for any lectures either, I turn slowly grey on microwavable Rustlers' burgers (nought to tasty in seconds) from the campus shop opposite. With the members of The Maccabees occupying different parts of Brighton while flunking our different excuses for degrees, we begin to find some serious acceleration in popularity. There are hundreds of late teens, all bred on the indie music which we are in thrall to and exponents of, ready to find a band of their own. Land and I make flyers, different photocopied illustrations stuck to times and dates, and stick them extensively across the town. We begin to rehearse almost every day, finding ourselves rehearsal spaces in which to keep our gear and simply show up and play, through the night. The songs, too, begin to get *actually* good. Ru has recorded a bass line over a drum'n'bass tape, which he brings in and plays to us. We play different kinds of similar single-note riffs either side of it and Land etches out a song about a girl he's read about in Russia who claimed to be able to see holes in people's hearts. It is called "X-Ray" and, in a rare flood of sudden vague inspiration, each member hashes out their own part on the spot and the song, dependent on each bit, is just there. With it, song upon song follows in what will become the music that initially defines us, music packed full of hundreds of restless ideas, played with enough gusto to just about see them over the line. "Latchmere", a paean to the small things in life, in this case the swimming pool where we grew up that had a wave machine. "Precious Time", a song I assume is about friendship – but never ask – that we fill with hours of development of tiny riffs and patterns and volume shifts and as much drama as we can with our instruments, as I occupy Land's "Let's make time work for us" section with a riff that I think sounds like my newfound loves, The La's.

As it happens, suddenly and very quickly in our new unloaded homes, Brighton becomes a sort of information centre, ingesting musical DNA into the pores of our skin. We are at club nights three times a week, jumping on each other's backs to The Strokes, asking DJs what music that we haven't heard yet is and noting the t-shirts of all the alternative bands that we have not yet absorbed: Sonic Youth, Joy Division, Pixies, all of whom will become part of our sonic compass. Every club-night venue becomes a place to be conquered, where we turn up, stay all night and end each evening working out how we are going to be the best band in the world. On one of these nights, I walk past a girl I vaguely know from home, who has moved to Sussex too; as we cross, without any preconceived notion of romance, we reach for each other's hands and, just as we motion to walk past each other in the opposite direction, hold onto one another until it is just our outstretched arms and then our fingertips, simultaneously pulling each other back towards one another and kissing. It is there again – I am swimming front crawl and head-banging and doing Oasis/Blur polls, yet this time neither out of my depth nor deliriously separate, just safe. Jess* and I become relatively inseparable and from that moment on develop a kind of half-sibling, half-paternalistic romantic relationship. With her in the South Lanes one week, I walk into a shop and see the most beautiful woolly hat. I need to have it. I wear it every day, at shows, in town, at the few lectures I attend. I need a look and, at last, I have found it. It is only the next year, on further inspection, that I realise it is very close to the colours of the Jamaican flag.

Jess and I develop little homely rituals in which we save one spliff for every evening, after her lectures and my rehearsals, sit cross-legged facing each other on one of our beds and smoke it together before falling asleep cradling each other. I'm not sure when it happens, but during this time I slowly develop a dependency on weed that means I can't sleep without it. Finally being able to roll, not out of conscious will but by a form of osmosis, any evening when I can't smoke and am forced to negotiate a night sober becomes a time of

* Not Jessie Ware, a different Jess.

serious and genuine panic. I carouse the halls of Kent House, turning tables over and rooting through cupboards, looking for remnants of weed. This moulds into adventures of mushroom taking through the forests that run around the back of Sussex University. I stop with friends in front of fluorescent lights and cry for hours at how beautiful they are, before realising it is a sports hall; tripping around the muddy outgrowth pointing to where we swear there is a hole in the sky.

Abla has become beaten by the world since her daughter's death and, with her and Harry ordering more and more alcohol to their house ever since, she had fallen ill about the time I leave South London. She has been in hospital for a week when, during one of these night-time trips across the back of the university, my dad phones me three times. Back from the latest adventure, in a green woolly hat and tripping out, I watch the phone scuttle around the table and I *know* what it means. I don't pick it up. She dies that evening. I make it my responsibility from there to ensure that I am never without weed, even if it just means an indecipherable pinch is left in the bag, safe in the knowledge that I can always retreat to an unthinking haze where I need nothing but sleep.

The Maccabees on Brighton Level.

23

The Ashes, the Studio and
the Stairs In Between

I am sitting in the Sussex University bar, East Slope, on Sunday 19 June 2005. I should be working towards something, or studying, but I'm not. I'm drinking snakebite (half lager, half cider and blackcurrant), dressed like a confused student member of The Strokes, complete with the green woollen hat I haven't yet realised is possibly the colour of the Jamaican flag. Courtesy of myself, flyers for The Maccabees gig next week at the Freebutt are now distributed all over the empty bar. They look quite sad, I think to myself, scattered across a table, competing with littered cut-outs for '90s nights (all shots 90 pence), and the R'n'B events that Brighton is staging that week too. I think about hiding the other flyers, then feel a pang of low-level depression that I have even considered doing that – that hiding flyers is what my time is amounting to – and I sink, alone, back onto the wooden bench.

Sky Sports's sole broadcasting custody of the one-day series that preludes the most anticipated Ashes series in memory means it's even harder to watch cricket in my usual private cricket sadness cave. It's not even on in the communal, largely unoccupied Kent House television room, which has big wooden doors that must be unflapped, then all the blinds shut so that the screen doesn't project a distracting reflective glare. Instead, not yet stoned, I must try and muster some kind of comparative cricket sadness cave locality in the bar – not especially difficult while staring back at my own flyers – to watch the game.

It's an ODI at Bristol and it's the first time Australia, still undisputed giants, and England, in a perplexing white heat of form, have met this summer. Despite our recent successes, this is Australia. England, set a chaseable target, are in trouble, of course, at 160-6. Kevin Pietersen is at the crease. I have only read about and listened to his innings last winter in South Africa: I've not watched him in action before. He is indeed colossal and athletic, already a figure of curiosity in his general swagger, bookmarking himself as untied to anything before him in an England shirt. He begins to flex his batting impulses. Aussie fast bowler Michael Kasprowicz is mowed over mid-wicket. Then he is heaved over cow corner. The camera cuts to captain Ricky Ponting, looking slightly confused. He's not used to this sort of thing. Brad Hogg* is then hit so high into the air, the camera jolts to find it. As the camera veers left and right, it eventually decides to give up entirely and settle on the crowd, celebrating, in the assumption the ball must have landed somewhere in there. Pietersen has 50. He punches gloves. He removes his helmet to reveal a skunk-like white streak across his hair. Ridiculous, I think, pulling the peak of my woollen hat across my head for a second. But he's not done. The Australians seem slightly frozen. Gillespie attempts a yorker and Pietersen nudges it, as if sending a ball back for a cat to mess around with. It sails for four. Nasser Hussain, these days on commentary, is becoming more and more nasal. "There's not a lot you can say," he says. "This is…completely different." It really is. Pietersen is hitting the ball everywhere and the target is becoming smaller and smaller. Feeling a swell of foreign excitement, I zone out into the real world for a second, and notice the bar is becoming full. I am now accompanied by other students, all staring at the TV, punching the air

* Left-arm spinner.

with increasing commitment at every boundary. They mould into the crowd at Bristol, who now look like a re-enactment of beer-fuelled street parties to celebrate war being over.

East Slope is celebrating on a Sunday afternoon. Pietersen, hitting the winning runs with 16 balls left, has turned a deserted flying stop-by to a moment of genuine joy. I am overcome, suddenly emotional, and in the middle of hugs and high fives and cheers with strangers, I run out of the bar, much more drunk than I had realised, pull my hat out of my eyes and, both arms horizontal, greeted by nothing but the odd student carrying books from one place to another, I scream, "We're going to win the Ashes! We're going to win the Ashes!"

*

I'm not sure if it was provoked by Pietersen's giant-bashing in Bristol as the 2005 Ashes build-up began in earnest, but I had decided, from this point, that the way forwards in my own life was to make clear, to myself and anyone around me, that I didn't care that my mum had died. If I found myself alone, which was very rare and usually just for the purposes of rolling spliffs (I was now an expert), I'd repeat the phrase to myself silently as if it were a mantra. I don't care. I don't care. I felt it acting like a plug at the top of my throat, creating a dam for a surging, unexplainable feeling that would threaten to immerse me in these stolen solitary moments, blocking it, before whichever distraction came next dissipated it. Whatever that was, racing occasionally inside my body, I chose not to name it and let it get in the way of a bounding, montage-perfect summer in which The Maccabees were slowly becoming bigger and bigger. Each local show was getting a little more like The Clash gigs we had memorised: the crowd big enough to move as one beautiful mass, tussling to get a view of the stage, one trip causing a mass domino effect of falling bodies over my feet as I dripped head to toe in sweat like a dog that had jumped into a lake, down-stroking my guitar, catching falling bodies as if everything in the world had paused and centred around our show that evening.

The gigs had suddenly become full of people our age and younger and, most encouragingly, that we didn't know, who had ingested the songs from our uploads on our MySpace page and would sing them back at us, and I would sing too, off the microphone, half in the band and half in the crowd. As I stood on the stage, armed with all the not caring about my mum being dead and the buzz of these moments rushing through me, I realised that I could really scream. I could scream incredibly loudly and alarmingly naturally. Sometimes I was so loud that it competed with my guitar amp for volume, completely unaided. It was not a scream of conscious anger, more a rejoice, and every time I did it, as we incorporated it into part of our sets, me offsetting Land's softly delivered lead lines behind him, I felt a pinch of that same swell that came to haunt me in my moments alone, except this time

Half in the band and half in the crowd.

bathed in and absolved by a crowd, I let it go, putting it to whatever words Land had written, finding a belonging in the guitar strapped around my neck. It was magical.

Though gaining a reputation as odd local upstarts of sorts ("hedonistic punksters", the Brighton *Argus* genuinely wrote), The Maccabees were not yet big enough to have to pretend that we didn't have heroes of our own. My room at university, to which I returned stoned and drunk and joyful, became a pit of my life, with layers upon layers of clothes and books scattered across the floor until there was no more floor at all, and walls full of the bands that we had brought to Brighton as influences, plus a new batch: The Futureheads most notably. Among the bands, dotted around, were cut-out pictures of the England team, too. In all of the images on my wall I saw a new abandon, a vehicle for mass escape of the mind. The Ashes were coming and we were fearless, we didn't care about past hurt. This time, it was going to be different.

*

When the first Ashes Test of 2005 comes, at Lord's, to begin with it is everything I've hoped it will be. Channel 4, under Mark Nicholas, has become a broadcasting bundle of unabashed selling of all things cricket and Nicholas, desperate to present a game that isn't the sole property of a privileged class, greets the television camera that morning, his eyes alive as if this is the moment he has always waited for, knowing that this set of players are the ones to deliver to a country with their attention fixed. Australia win the toss and bat. Hoggard, his hair longer to give him even more of an air of a sheepdog running in, both more lovable and more dangerous, bowls Matthew Hayden, who, as if slain and fallen on his sword, pauses for a second hunched over his bat. Justin Langer is hit on the arm. It looks as if it hurts. No-one comes up to ask if he's OK. Then Ricky

Ponting is hit in the head by Steve Harmison. The camera cuts to Ponting, himself momentarily bowed. When he lifts his head, a distinct slice of dark red has appeared on his cheek, and it is seeping blood. Again, no England players are running up to see if he's OK. Harmison gets him out, fending to Andrew Strauss, soon after. The wickets begin to scatter, just as they have for the years in build-up. Flintoff, like Hoggard and indeed the rest of the England side, appears simultaneously cuddlier and scarier than he has ever been before and forces Langer into a pull shot in which the ball arrives more quickly than Langer judges, leading him to spoon it into the air. Simon Jones is in form, too, forcing Damien Martyn into an outside edge to Geraint Jones behind the stumps and trapping Michael Clarke LBW while screaming him off. England bowl out Australia for 190 inside the first day. I am watching in the pub in Brighton, softly nudging Jess on the arm. I told you, I'm telling her, as she gazes half into middle distance, making a fist of being happy about a game she has no real reference for. I told everyone. We're going to win the Ashes.

The rest of the match does not fall quite into place. On the same day in the final session, Glenn McGrath takes advantage of the conditions on offer and, metronomically landing the exact same unplayable ball on repeat as he infuriatingly always does, has England 21-5 before too long. From there, it plays out exactly as it used to do. The pre-written script. Shane Warne, all those years since Mike Gatting, flummoxes this new generation of my adopted bigger brothers in exactly the same way. He ends up with six wickets in the game, McGrath with nine, and Australia win by 239 runs. I find myself irrationally upset at Geraint Jones on the final morning, chipping the ball to Jason Gillespie in an already doomed run chase. I certainly am not angry at the world for the death of my mum. I definitely don't care about that. It is Geraint Jones I am angry with. It was a stupid shot.

While my finger had pointed at Geraint Jones for extin-
guishing the brief hope, the media, in the week between
Tests, pointed at Ashley Giles. Playing with him, one paper
observed, was akin to playing with ten men. It was hard not
to take this personally on behalf of not just Giles, but all
left-arm spinners. This was, after all, in truth, how we all
felt about ourselves anyway. Ashley knew when he turned
up at Edgbaston for the second Test that all his resourcefulness in the art of left-arm spin was going to be under the
microscope. For myself, too, under pressure from everyone
I had shouted at for the month building up to the Ashes, I
had to double down on my predictions. I couldn't go back
now. We were still going to win the Ashes. When I shut
my eyes, I couldn't actually imagine this happening and I
was at a loss to explain how or why we would – I just saw
jarring visions of McGrath bowling the same ball again and
again to different English batsmen, all of them nicking it
or being bowled or trapped LBW and him wheeling away
celebrating, finger occasionally to his lips. As I reached
further into this daydream, I used Giles-esque resource to
plunge into the reverie, persuading my imagination to twist
the truth and bend an England win, and it delivered to me
a McGrath-less Australia. *That* would be different. That's
how we'd win the Ashes.

*

By the start of the Edgbaston Test, The Maccabees have been
packed off to 811 Studios on the outskirts of Brighton. We now
have a manager in John Reid, connected by local promoter
and our new accomplice Laura "Curly" Davidson. The first
thing we need to do, they say, is make some proper recordings, and that's what we are doing at 811: a residential studio,
its upstairs room with camp beds opened up to fit five tightly
into it in front of a TV, and a recording room downstairs.

It being the first morning of the Test, my priorities do not sync with the other band members on arrival. They run around our communal bedroom, manically darting from bed to bed, testing the springiness of the mattresses in an effort to gauge how their week of sleeping might be best spent, as I, my back turned to them, desperately try different remotes to turn on the television and, finally seeing a red light turn green, wait for the old television, faintly coming in and out of focus for reception, to come to. When it does, it isn't the image I'd expected of Mark Nicholas's hyper eye contact and satisfyingly hyperbolic build-up. It is Glenn McGrath, his practice shorts on and white jumper limping, his arms across two Australian teammates, being carried from the field of play. I'm a little bit disturbed at what I'm seeing. A McGrath-less Australia? The news is coming in as fresh as the injury itself. He's slipped on a cricket ball on the outfield while warming up, we're told. I feel my eyes widen and my heart rate leap. I can't leave the television set, inches from the front of it. Is that real? That can't be real! The next few minutes might determine the entire summer. Finally, the news comes. Glenn McGrath has been taken to hospital and will not be playing. It's there again, the rush, the strange sensation with Rhianwen or the Spanish girl in the pool, the weird foreign sense of anticipation. I feel myself bouncing on the balls of my feet, clicking my heels like Dorothy, except I'm repeating the mantra, "We're going to win the Ashes" and not "There's no place like home". This, after all, is my home – whichever room The Maccabees are in.

Ricky Ponting wins the toss and, in an act of brazen arrogance, a stitched scar now on his cheek, he decides that his McGrath-less Australia will still bowl first. When I turn round, the room, which the last time I checked in had been a hive of activity, is empty. The beds have been made, each Maccabee designating his clearly with his stuff laid out on top, leaving one camp bed that won't fold down much further than a half-reclined armchair. That'll be where I'm sleeping this week, then.

We have, by now, become accustomed to spending the near entirety of our waking hours in small spaces together. When we rehearse, it is in damp rooms with low ceilings where the microphones smell of a thousand chain-smoking, auditioning rock stars wrapping their mouths around them. We tussle musically, forever within touching distance, stopping for breaks and huddling in even closer proximity from the rain while smoking, discussing the songs. It means that for our early recordings, playing the songs that will carry us through the next few years, it makes sense intuitively to just play live in the live room. That's what we do. We are yet to come across the studio concepts of simple things such as click tracks, where bands play to a metronomic pattern that keeps everyone in time and allows for over-dubbing and retracking with ease. We do not know what reverb is. We just plug our instruments in and, effectless and stoned, we play as fast as we can. It is, actually, quite a specific art form. The routine of setting up, like the beds, has become a sort of sibling jostling for space. That's my corner. Can you move over? You're way too loud. There are only two sets of headphones, I'm having one. These are the conversations that pepper our existence. Every single tiny decision is made with us all in close physical proximity. It makes for the beginnings of a fraught permanence that will prove unresolvable, but also a wildly productive tension, where we hem ourselves into an always moving unit, buzzing with ceaseless activity. The loading in and out of gear, forming a chain from studio to van and back to studio. The plugging in of equipment. Sleeping always in the same room and forming a kind of constant awareness of each other. It is all the non-negotiable requirements for being able to play together fast and tight and very loud.

The constant manoeuvring that forms part of being a Maccabee, though, leaves very little space for anything else,

and that little space for anything else I have chosen to dedicate, rather than to Jess, to cricket. We set up to play that
morning and, eventually finding a little angle for my guitar
and an enclave in the live room, far from the best one because
of the time I have wasted on Glenn McGrath's injury, I run
back upstairs. England are 90 for no wicket. Wow, we are
going to win the Ashes. I catch a glimpse of Andrew Strauss,
in between takes, just allowing myself a minute to watch him,
wedding ring around his neck as always, hammering Shane
Warne down the pitch. I feel the back of my eyes slightly
water with giddiness. I run back down, we need to record
another take.

We have recorded a new song this morning, racing each
other as ever to the end of it, called "Lego". It has dropped-
down sections in which Hugo and I both play down-stroked
guitars, face to face, the parts moving in and out of each
other, just as they had in my room the couple of years before,
but now, with no fear of waking anyone, as loud as we like.
We are alive with the promise of the song, hearing in it all
the things we love about all those bands we saw then read
about before we heard. The lyrics, which Land continues to
write on the other side of the transparent glass as we play,
positioned right on the end of a sofa, are about childhood
nostalgia with a chorus that borrows from the Green Cross
Code: "Look left, look right, cross the road, hold my hand."
It happens very quickly, each instrument interacting hyperactively with the other and making a wiry, frenetic sound.
When we are ushered back into the control room to hear our
take, though trying to remain aloof – imagining that if I let
on how much it means to me, it might be taken away from
me – I find myself quietly overwhelmed by hearing our music
back loud. I am not sure what I think it sounds like – that
capacity is beyond me. I just know that it sounds at all and, in
listening back, I have certifiable proof that I am alive. A part
of me wants to take the recording with me, back to South

London and to the room where she died. Then I remember I don't care, and shove that surging feeling back down my throat where it belongs.

When I get back up to the television, covered in sweat and feeling myself pumped full of all kinds of promise, Kevin Pietersen and Freddie Flintoff are batting together. The noise from the crowd, and in the tones of the commentators' voices, is something close to disbelief. England are not going to go quietly into the night this time and Australia, disturbed by the sudden absence of McGrath, are being attacked. Pietersen whips the ball with dominance. Flintoff takes long, unabashed, full swipes at the ball that consistently sails over the ropes. Brett Lee, running in faster and faster and more disturbed, eventually sends one towards his head. Freddie turns and, half playing a pull shot and half trying to get out of the way, makes contact with the ball. He is the last person to see it fly, accidentally, for six. When he brings up 50, he hugs Pietersen, forcing his helmet to tilt over the top of his eyes for a second. It is a quirk of Freddie that when things go well, his hat or helmet sits just over the top of his forehead, slightly concealing his view as he half-smiles, like a mischievous child. It is as if the entire country is ruffling his hair. My own hat is now thankfully dispensed with. The country does not want to ruffle that. I run back downstairs again.

I hardly sleep that night, with all the adrenaline of the music being made in the studio and England's surge of eccentric cricket and the bed not actually being a bed. The next day rolls into it, the room upstairs with the cricket and the studio downstairs with the music becoming a metaphor for my own brain, the staircase providing the only moments to pause for any reflection or silence in between, shoving the feeling back down. Australia reply with the bat, Hoggard removing Matthew Hayden immediately, then Ricky Ponting, from what I can gather from the fragments of time I can steal between each take, looks to be making easy work of the England bowlers. A take is finished. Everyone else goes outside to smoke and I run back to the TV. Ponting is faced with Ashley Giles. I'm glad I've caught Giles's first ball, I think. He needs a friend. Nicholas introduces him as "England's beleaguered left-arm spinner". Flicking the ball between his fingers as he moves his fielders around, he indeed does look concerned. He runs in to bowl, and for a second I see in motion the wheelie bin that everyone describes. There is no magic or flick or deception. Instead, his long-limbed action churns the ball out, as if it's an invention patented by Wallace and Gromit and, being slightly quicker and flatter than Ponting has imagined, it arrives in a hurry. Ponting is not quite on one knee, looking to sweep the ball over said beleaguered spinner. He can only top-edge it. For a moment, reality is suspended as it harmlessly sits in the air and heads straight to Michael Vaughan. Vaughan, slightly shocked at his opposing captain's decision-making, catches it, then throws the ball in the air. Suddenly Giles is swamped, every single one of his teammates engulfing him. Giles is worth something and they are showing him how much. I run back downstairs. I'm very excited. Later, in a motion of synchronised fate, I manage to catch him bowling Shane Warne, who marches down the pitch and tries to heave him in a statement of spin-to-spin confrontation. The ball does not spin. Warne misses. Giles hits.

This is how the week continues, me darting up and down the stairs to try and combine the two parts of my life, keeping them from each other like an affair and yet letting the marks from each flood into my interaction with the other. We record the takes quickly, the songs thrashed out and continually, to my genuine shock, proving themselves to indeed be real-life actual songs when played back in the control-room speakers. I remain beyond criticism of our work and just in a flow of doing. The songs exist and that's enough. I miss England's collapse in the second innings. I can only get back to see Freddie at the crease. Freddie, in a week in which everything he does turns out to be timeless, settles on his bat in an essence of rugged simplicity, hitting the ball everywhere – at one point smashing a perfectly decent ball from Michael Kasprowicz into the crowd and following it with his eyes, himself in disbelief, mouth ajar, a wide grin on his face.

Over the course of the three days, the other Maccabees, recording engineer and studio owner, all of whom have been, as is the norm, treating the cricket like inconsequential yet jarring white noise in the background, have begun to slowly change their behaviour. With Australia requiring 281 runs to win, the general drama that seeps through the television means that on my darting missions to run upstairs and catch the score and a ten-minute passage of play, I find myself accompanied by another member of the band. Then another. Then another. Then someone else (I don't even know who they are or what they do). By the time we have reached the afternoon on day four, an hour into Australia's reply, I return to the television joined by every single band member, each deciding that a glimpse of the cricket might this time be worth more than ten minutes outside.

We sit on our respective beds. I am charged with a strange pride on behalf of the entire game of cricket that it is finally capturing the begrudging imagination of the public. Australia have sailed relatively unharmed to 47 without loss. Michael Vaughan throws the ball to Flintoff. Freddie's collar is upturned, his chain showing. He looks less cuddly now. For his second ball – running in like a train that has been forced off a track at high speed and, struck by his own momentum, just trying to slow down in order to deliver the ball at all – he is in at Langer. The ball is quick and Langer forces on the front foot, chipping it straight onto his stumps. For a second, I can't believe that Freddie has given me the gift of providing drama when I've got other people around to watch. The boys are suddenly half up, propelling themselves towards the cricket as they never have been before. Ricky Ponting, his own collar turned up, is next in and he is slammed on the back foot onto his pad first ball. Freddie goes up in appeal and with him, in the same action, so do the crowd, the England infield and, to my pride, The Maccabees with me. Billy Bowden gives it not out. We settle down. The next ball Flintoff roars towards the crease, still looking like a faulty train trying to brake to avoid a cliff edge. Ponting is squared up and edges the ball just short of Ashley Giles, who stops it and, on one knee as if bowing in grace to the magnitude of the moment, fields it. "Flintoff has changed the whole feeling of the occasion," Nicholas says. He's changed the feeling of the recording session even. His next ball, roared in louder, again strikes Ponting on the pads. It's outside the line and given not out. The next, the last in the over, is outside off stump and Ponting leaves it with a flourish, as if in relief that that's over. As we jump up to move downstairs again, there's a pause. Bowden has no-balled it. "What does that mean?" the others ask, suddenly keen on understanding the laws of the game. "It means Flintoff gets another ball," I say, para-phrasing. "He's stepped over the line." So, we settle again. Freddie is in, the braking train, the roaring in. He unleashes the ball, on a perfect in-between length and Ponting is neither forward nor back. He plays at the ball and edges it. Jones takes it. "Beauty! Yes!" Nicholas shouts, for a second forgetting his impartiality. The boys too have forgotten their antipathy and we are all within inches of the screen, creeping further towards it. Freddie is standing in the middle, arms out wide, bathed in joy and absolution, about to be mobbed, gazed upon adoringly by the entire country. He didn't even need a guitar to get there.

The next morning, it is less simple than England have hoped. After an hour of trying and failing – bar Shane Warne stepping on his own stumps to Flintoff – Brett Lee bats without alarm. Australia require an unimaginable 107 more in the morning and yet, an hour later, chipping away painfully under increasing silence, they only need 20 with just one wicket in hand. The match is a cause of distress for me now, running up and down the stairs to absorb all of this. Because it is distracting to the point of non-productivity, recording is cancelled until it's finished. We are all upstairs, the band, the studio engineer and Mikey, the guy who runs the studio, the people I don't know, all crowded around the television. The camera is cutting between every delivery to people in the crowd with their heads in their hands. The required 20 becomes 15 and Michael Kasprowicz, the Australian number 11, is on strike. Flintoff bowls to him, dropping one just outside of a length on the off stump. Kasprowicz ramps the ball, nervously, in the air, to third man. Simon Jones is waiting there. It's hard to judge. Jones is running towards it. He gets there, the ball in his hands and then, desperately, it bounces out as he lands on the grass for more Australian runs.

Now *I* have my head in my hands. I can feel the silence around me, all The Maccabees wishing the ball back in his hands too. My heart is beating out of my chest, my face drained of all colour. Maybe that is it? The runs required keep going down. Thirteen. Eleven. Ten. Nine. Eight and, eventually, four. Harmison, his radar skewed by all the commotion, bowls Lee a full toss. Lee hits it hard, along the ground, towards the off side. The camera panics to find it. It's momentarily lost in the mêlée. When we do settle on it, it's safely in Simon Jones's hands. A yard either side and the game and the summer would again have been Australia's. The boys are by now taking an obvious pleasure in my distress. Rob, such is his general spirit occasionally, has changed tack and decided he wants Australia to win. It's a perverse emotional experiment which I have no capacity to challenge. I just sit, completely still, waiting. Harmison is in again, this time to Kasprowicz. The ball is short and

Kasprowicz is fending it off. It looks like it has hit his glove. Richie Benaud shouts as the ball flies in the air towards the wicket-keeper, "Jones!" He catches it. Then to umpire Billy Bowden, the camera resting on him as he lifts his finger, "Bowden!" It is all that needs to be said. England have won by two runs. I'm overcome with joy, screaming and screaming, but there is nothing coming out, the week has run me hoarse. Suddenly, I'm in tears too. We are going to win the Ashes. I knew it. I knew it. Rob, picking up the remote, decides I've had enough time in the sun. "Well, if nothing else is on, let's get back to it, then, shall we?" He turns the television off. Two minutes later, I'm back in the room, sweating, eyes bloodshot, guitar around my shoulder, thinking of the last time I saw Ashley Giles, running around the outskirts of Edgbaston punching the air, while I play as fast and as hard as I can.

*

The rest of the summer of 2005 spilled out with a continued bubbling joy. The win at Edgbaston, quickly christened the "Greatest Test Ever" and broadcast on terrestrial television, of course, had made cricket as popular as I had ever known it, by some distance. The series began to envelop the world outside and suddenly during gigs in Brighton people would shout out in mock-Adam Gilchrist accents, "Well bowled, Shane" in between songs. The streets were littered with tennis-ball games, everyone pretending to be Freddie Flintoff or Kevin Pietersen. I spent my summer at Jess's house, being cooked for and slinking off during the day to Land's student home down the road, where his housemate's bed had literally fallen through the first floor but they'd chosen when given the option to not pay rent rather than fix the hole. There we would watch the cricket all day – its drama feeding itself into the possibility of the day and the music – working on

Maccabees songs before rushing out into the tiny garden in lunch breaks, playing games in which bowlers would nominate their field from the various implements that happened to be down the narrow alley. That summer I imagined myself not as Flintoff or Pietersen, but as Ashley Giles, wiling away to a conservative field of the drainpipe and bins, bowling to a plan and squeezing every ounce from my limited skills.

Trent Bridge, the fourth Test, unfolds with a similar fervour. It is Ashley Giles, at every mysterious corner of the series proving himself an inimitable functional aspect of the side, who sees them home, punching Warne through mid-wicket for two in front of 8.5 million viewers. Giles, a week later, has to bat for three hours in an Oval decider that still could go to Australia, watching and supporting Kevin Pietersen as he compiles his 158, guaranteeing that England can't be beaten. We *do* win the Ashes. I knew it. It is the first time since 1986 that England have done so.

When the team celebrated the next day, in an open-top bus parade across London, greeted by thousands upon thousands, I watched from home, smiling softly and stoned at Flintoff and Pietersen, obviously still up from the night before, alcohol almost visibly swilling around in their eyes, waving and shouting from the bus. Everybody wanted to talk about it. Cricket was no longer something to retreat to in a cave and melancholically play guitar in front of, but a genuine source of enthused conversation with the world in general. I felt it infuse into me a reckless joy that I could feel artificially filling me up, like eating only popcorn for months on end; being buzzed and full yet strangely malnourished. I knew this had reached some limit, for I had begun, by the end of the whole thing, to search for visions of Lana, disturbingly starting to lose the recollection of her voice and only see her face undefined in images that I had once held in my mind. I feared I had done this to myself with the not-caring-she's-dead schtick, and yet I squeezed that guilt too back down my throat with every rising tide of feeling. Every day was manic and busy. There was music to be made. There was cricket to be watched. The only two things I needed.

The Maccabees improved and evolved and surfed a wave of momentum that in some surreal yet genuine sense I felt had been aided by the cricketers that summer. The same way the game had articulated sadness and hurt, this year it had also explained optimism and the cyclical nature of all things. If you wait long enough, it comes back around. A lot of people had waited long enough to see England win the Ashes. I'd just had to wish it true hard enough.

*

The Maccabees had become the go-to local support band for big shows moving through Brighton; that year, as well as our own gigs, we played before Arctic Monkeys at Komedia, just months before they became the biggest-selling group in the UK since Oasis. We watched their set after ours, taking mental notes, and decided we needed a tuner each now, and that you could buy some that worked as foot pedals too. That looked much easier. A month after that, Curly phoned me in barely containable excitement. We had been asked to support The Strokes at the 6,000 capacity Brighton Centre. I ran around the streets of Brighton, the same way I had earlier in the summer when Kevin Pietersen had played his symbolic one-day innings, stopping only to phone my dad.

*

When we turn up to play, The Strokes are soundchecking in the huge empty arena. We walk in sheepishly, herding ourselves in a tight pack through the pitch-black standing area, and sit at the back, watching the figures we know so well, silhouetted perfectly. I find myself moved to nausea. It could have been the lights they are bathed under, while the rest of the venue is plunged into afternoon darkness, but they genuinely glow. As we play later that evening, I look to my left and, having to check for a second that it isn't a mirage, see that they are all there, standing side by side, watching us play. The most perfect slip cordon I have ever seen. I have half a mind to ask whether I can take them home, back to that room, just to show Lana it is all real.

We play the small and infamous London club The Water Rats two months later and as I am coming back onto the stage to clear my equipment (amp and personal foot-pedal tuner), drenched in sweat and unplugging leads, a big, bearded man called Jim Chancellor and A & R scout Alex Close introduce themselves at the lip of the stage. Jim is the head of Fiction Records. The Maccabees sign a record deal with them that summer. Jesus, I thought, as Ashley Giles must have done at Trent Bridge, this couldn't really have worked out any better.

24

Ashley Giles and the Letter

Ashley Giles, in his own words, "screwed up" his A levels. "I worked in a petrol station for eight months after leaving school and while I was trying to find a professional contract. I used to open and close it up, working behind the till." I'm trying to imagine Ashley Giles, these days the managing director of English cricket, in a service-station job, and find myself unable to do so without envisaging him wearing the reflective wrap-around sunglasses he was barely seen without during his playing days. It's as if he catches me doing so, noting the pause. "I'm sure you can see me with my Shell polo shirt on. There used to be the odd customer that would walk in and throw abuse, and I'd just think, right, I really need to get the cricket going."

Cricket was proving, at that time, quite elusive to get going. Giles had played so much even by then, as a teenage seam bowler, that running in fast was becoming hard, "My body couldn't cope. I was sometimes playing two games in a day. I probably had an undiagnosed stress fracture." As a result of this injury, Ashley was demoted to Guildford's third XI to get back to full fitness and work on his batting. However, during one particular game, in search of cheap wickets from anywhere, his captain asked, "Can you bowl some of that filth you do in the nets?" In cricketing vernacular, filth is another phrase for lovely, loopy stuff, depending which way you look at it. Giles, as properly as he could, took the ball and ran in to bowl left-arm spin. He took five wickets. Just as importantly to him, he found that he could do it without pain. Unlike the other left-arm spinners, who tended to gravitate to the quirk out of sheer natural survival instinct, Giles found he had something dormant, formed from years of fast-bowling, that worked. "I had a really solid, repeatable action. I just did it again and again. To be honest with you, Felix, I don't think I ever cracked the game." Darting to his defence against his own self-defeatism, I am quick to remind him about Ricky Ponting mistiming him, sparking the rhythm of the greatest Test match ever played. "Yeah, that was great. I still get shivers thinking about it. That ball really felt like it was in the air forever."

We recount the moments in the series like cricket fans sharing memories, Giles sometimes forgetting he was actually the one taking the wickets. Damien Martyn being bowled. Batting with Kevin Pietersen at The Oval: "I think I just had the best seat in the house to one of the greates Ashes innings of all time, to be honest." Getting Shane Warne out. Hitting the winning runs in the fourth Test in front of 8.5 million people. "No wonder cricket didn't get figures like that again, they were all watching me bat."

Giles, to this day, seems so aware of not being the star of that England side that his memory feels slightly leaden from the pressure. "There's a lot of time, if I'm really honest, where I didn't enjoy what I did. I wasn't the most natural or the most gifted, so the game was really tough to keep up with, and all the pressure that came with that." The experience of keeping up throughout the Ashes series, one of still obvious joy, instantly sparked the end of his career, where even bowling spin was painful. "My hip suddenly started to become a problem. It was all my life's work really, all my dreams, wrapped up in that one summer. It's hard to know where you go from there. I think it affected everyone very deeply."

In his case, only playing another four Test matches, he chose to chase that same feeling in his own way. "It's one of the reasons I've followed my career path. That tension, that stress, the winning and the losing, the deadlines. It keeps you alive. It can't replace what you do on the field with a team, but there are similar pressures and similar sleepless nights."

Years before my own sleepless Ashes nights during that second Test, for reasons beyond my recall, I'd found a website run by Ashley's brother and sent him an email asking, and I quote, "whether he could ask his brother whether Ashley would have ever liked to bowl with Phil Tufnell". A week later, on Warwickshire County Cricket Club headed paper, came a hand-written note, from none other than Ashley Giles himself. "I'd love to have bowled with Phil Tufnell," it said. "Lovely flight." I held this note, unsure how to comprehend that this very same paper had been in the hands of a real left-arm spinner.

Ashley Giles during "the greatest ever series" –
"I think it affected everyone very deeply."

Does he remember signing letters for fans, I ask, who may or may not have been asking whether he ever would have liked to bowl with Phil Tufnell? "I think you were probably one of the only people in the fan club, Felix," he laughs. "My brother used to run it. Warwickshire had sent off for some mugs with 'King of Spin' on them for the club shop and the printers, obviously not cricket fans, sent them back as 'King of Spain'. We decided that's what the fan club should be called." It stuck. Giles still gets people who notice him from 2005, turn around and shout, "Wahey, King of Spain", on a near-daily basis. It's better than being abused at a petrol station, he says, and just before we go, he asks, politely, about my career as a musician and adds, "I had decided to listen to no radio and read no press in 2005 after that first Test and all the criticism. I only had the James Blunt album in the car, *Back to Bedlam*, and I just listened on repeat all summer. No wonder I was depressed."

25

Dissonance

The 2005 Ashes winners: Strauss, Trescothick, Vaughan, Bell, Pietersen, Flintoff, G. Jones, Giles, S. Jones, Hoggard, Harmison. Those 11 names, mythologically carved in millions of imaginations, would never play together again. From hereon in, they had to deal with the messy business of their moment being gone, every day moving further and further away from it, hauling their living, breathing, fleshy selves somewhere else, separate from one another. This truth, that you can build towards a moment for the best part of your life and, in a flash of adrenaline that your body remembers better than your mind, it can be gone forever, was bequeathed to the entire cricketing community too. Cricket was taken from terrestrial television that summer and the game, finally at its best, the point finally made, was from that point on whipped from the view of anyone who didn't seek it out or pay for it on Sky Sports; it was so perfectly cricket in its self-sabotage. The game was there, better than it had ever been. The players were there, better than they had ever been. The attention was there, wider than it had ever been. Then it was gone. Hidden.

It meant that cricket, as quickly as it had become mainstream, was tucked away again like a regrettable national fling. From now, if I was to watch it, which of course I had to as a matter of physical need, I had to go during the day to pubs that had the television on in the corner. The conversations in these pubs on entering, stumbling across them somewhere between Jess's flat and the studio in Brighton, would run one general way; "Do you have Sky Sports, mate?" "Yes." "Can you turn it on?" "Why?" "The cricket is on." This would be followed by a bartender at first pretending they hadn't heard the request, then, on my asking again, a long sigh and finally a concession with a catch: "OK, but no volume and I will turn it over the minute anyone asks." That was me. Perched in the corner of these various pubs, sidelined with an obsessional compulsive cricketing problem, drinking whatever it was that would take the longest to drink, as slowly as possible, wincing towards a TV set, imagining what the commentary might actually be saying, wondering where '05 had gone, guitarless in my multiple, ever-changing, sad cricket caves.

Nevertheless, England had beaten Australia and The Maccabees had a record deal. I dropped out of university, handing in my resignation at the secretary's desk, proudly giving my reason as becoming a professional musician* and watched her look over my attendance record, a passing "this is no great loss for us in any case" moving across her face before she signed me out.

Just as we had promised each other in the years of the empty pub gigs with one dodgy tuner and five half-working leads, we now belonged to each other. I, without hesitation, pledged my life to the four other people in the band. We were only The Maccabees as the five of us, we said. Without any one, we were nothing. Rehearsals became daily, the only requirement in our lives. The music we were making, that for so long had only existed in the vaguely soundproofed rehearsal rooms and between our own memories – slightly changing every time we played, depending on how each of us had remembered our parts at the next rehearsal – was

---

* Despite still not knowing how to jam in B flat or tune a guitar by ear, I technically was a professional musician.

becoming its own force in the world outside of it. Now there were recordings from 811, on a CD, in demo form, to constantly reference, which John and Curly and our record label had opinions on. Then a live agent and a PR team and a radio plugger and a TV booker. As it grew, our shows continued to grow too, the venues slightly bigger, more people of our age and slightly younger, more *people we didn't even know* filling the spaces. We didn't spend our time before gigs completely inconspicuous in the crowd anymore, watching other bands, before clambering on stage and playing ourselves; instead we hid in small and dank dressing rooms, covered in defaced bands' stickers, then onto the stage to what felt like a condensed hysteria, then off again, back into the dressing room, back into the van, packed even tighter together. The next day, we'd be back in a rehearsal room together, nursing hangovers, wearing the same clothes, earnestly poring over the ways we could have been better when leads were pulled out in a stage invasion that I may or may not have encouraged in a fit of overexcitedness.

The vague mush in which I remember it is, at least in part, sustained by all the diaries and sporadic notes I had begun to collate. Books are littered with set lists, songs crossed out and etched back in basically in the same order. The set lists dovetail oddly into cricket scores, before moving to to-do lists, which usually end with things like 9) Pay rent. 10) Get better at guitar. 11) Keep on going, never give up. In between all of this, sometimes slightly disturbingly, are long, barely legible writings on how useless I am, punctuated by slightly incoherent statements. On one page, next to a list of things I need for a recording session, I have written, "The difference between me and anyone I know is that I'm not scared of anyone leaving me anymore." Then written into another among a few band admin notes, the usual pay rent, the cricket score, I suddenly write, "I don't like how Jess says she loves me more every day." The functionality of the everyday is constantly interrupted as the pages slowly unravel into further lows: "I'm guilty for encouraging praise upon myself. I'm guilty for lying about my mum. I'm guilty for what happened to my mum. I wished it upon her, for attention. That is disgusting. That is sickening. This band will be my sole achievement in my life and it is four other people's, not mine. The only thing I contribute is making sure everybody is OK."

When I read these words back, years later, I can remember the feeling, the guilt about prioritising cricket and Oasis on the day of her death, and find it again, in my throat and my stomach, for a second being able to step back inside the foggy head that wrote the words. The next page usually begins, as if written by another person, with "The gig was great", going into acute detail on the shows, before once again veering off and noting something about the cricket – the space between the highs and the lows and the band is filled with cricket and cricket alone.

Our first album, in 2006, was recorded in two halves, at Olympic Studios with Stephen Street and at Miloco Studios with Ben Hillier. Stephen had recorded all kinds of albums of which we were, in our wildest dreams, imagining ourselves to be one day considered descendants, records that had made up significant parts of the joining of dots of musical history. He'd made multiple Blur records, including *Parklife*, and before that, multiple Smiths records, like *The Queen Is Dead* – records that were deeply entrenched in the lineage of British guitar music. The fact that this man wanted to spend months with us, recording our music, set me into a deeply uncool spin to begin with. Olympic Studios in Barnes had a history so rich that photos of the Rolling Stones and Led Zeppelin lined the walls, playing in exactly the same space we had been given. The recording room was huge, so impressive it almost gave the feeling the record might somehow make itself in there, with boothed-off spots for each of our amps already marked on our arrival. I told the studio engineers not to worry as they gestured to carry my amp to its designated spot. I aimed to emit a kind of down-to-earthness despite, you know, making an album at fucking Olympic Studios with fucking Stephen Street. In an ill-advised gesture of "Don't worry, you're in safe hands", I flung my guitar around my neck, over my back, and then picked up my amp, in one highly overambitious trip to the far corner of the room. The guitar, as if to put me in my place, unhooked itself from the strap halfway across, and as I turned round to catch it (unsuccessfully), I dropped my amp, too, all three of us landing in a heap on the ground. I looked up and Stephen Street was pretending that he hadn't just seen the whole thing.

We recorded our songs live, as we had got down to our own specific skill, exactly as Stephen told us, standing to attention as if we were on some sort of psychedelic school trip. Ben Hillier, at Miloco, by comparison, had made recent records by the bands I had imagined as spiritual bigger brothers, like The Futureheads who I'd just taken down from my wall, and in his makeshift "swimming pool" room in Bermondsey, where there was no separation between the recording studio and the live room, we recorded live and into toy amps and did vocals in cupboards. I carried my stuff separately this time to set it up on arrival. Land had – very late on in this process – written a crooner love song on guitar that sounded like nothing else we had. I listened to him play it to me once, following what felt like a never-ending chord sequence, and, pretending to not be as impressed as I was, I plugged in one of Ben's toy amps and played a high guitar part. My part was there, in its entirety, in one pass, as if it had just fallen out of me. It ended up being the last song on the record, "Toothpaste Kisses". The result of both sessions, one a high-fidelity lesson in "proper" recording and the other a looser and jauntier affair, was our debut album, *Colour It In*.

The England cricket team, meanwhile, had found themselves emotionally depleted from the highs that had just passed. Marcus Trescothick, whose ever-presence and fear-less counter-attacking from the top of the order had been such a marker for all the success while blending it with a sort of innate goodness via body language, found himself shivering and sobbing on the floor at Dixons in Heathrow Airport. He would soon be diagnosed with severe anxiety issues and eventually have to concede his international career was over. Simon Jones, injured, was left out of the first game and, unbeknown to him, had also played his last Test. Ashley Giles too was unable to play, now bowling even spin in pain, and captain Michael Vaughan, with a recurrent physical injury that would render him never the same presence for England again, did not play a game on the tour.

In their place were a batch of young cricketers who, just as the men they were replacing had once done, approached their cause with a bounding simplicity. Monty Panesar, the first Sikh to represent England, a left-arm spinner slightly more from the school of Tufnell than Giles. His action was a beautiful motion of momentum, without the smoke and mirrors of Tuffers before him, but with more pure hopeful-ness. The ball he produced, if in form, was basically the same every time, and contained Giles's speed and economy, with somehow also the gift of Tufnell's loop and spin. It was left-arm bowling with commitment and quirk, somehow still slightly melancholic. What was even better, Monty really couldn't field or bat. He was borderline worse than Tufnell, a fantastic breath of fresh air in a game being modernised so quickly that all the reassuring flaws were being slowly chipped out of it.

In Trescothick's place was Alastair Cook, a young man whose helmet sat on his head as if it were a jockey's, always slightly uncomfortably, and who seemed to possess very little actual scoring shots yet still, immediately and forever since, looked as if he belonged. There were others too, Ian Blackwell and Owais Shah, a cricketer with almost too much natural hitting ability for his own good, neither of whom stayed in the team long, joining the Marks and the Martins, Chris Read, Chris Lewis, Alan Wells and the rest back in the Battersea Dogs Home of heartbroken cricketers that my mind stored somewhere, now completely full of young men frozen in time and stuck in cages, packed like sardines.

In the winter of 2006/07, an Ashes series in Australia returned. Jess, as people were tending to, had stopped smoking weed. We no longer shared our cross-legged last smoke of the evening and she now fell asleep at night alone as I turned the radio on, as quiet as I could so as not to wake her, and opened the window, just enough to smoke out of without letting in a chill. I dreamed of Maccabees songs for rehearsal the next day, occasionally remembering that we actually had a record deal and fans and played music for a living, and felt myself flush with the promise of how much life there was to come, staring off out of the skylight into the Brighton sky, waiting for the seagulls that would swoop down and steal your sausages when you weren't looking to come back with the dawn.

*

Jess is fast asleep as I tune in for the first Test. England are bowling first. Harmison has the ball. He runs in and, unveiling that clockwork action, exactly as he did so destructively a year and a half ago, he lets it go. It isn't the short ball with vicious purpose that hit Ponting or Hayden or Langer in the Ashes just past. It flies so far out of his hand, the wrong way, that it sails directly to Freddie Flintoff at second slip. Freddie throws it away immediately, as if doing so will give the impression that it hasn't happened at all. It is too late, it definitely has. The bubble has burst. You can feel it from Brighton. It casts a deflated tone for the series that remains unaltered. Australia win 5-0, reclaiming the Ashes and, in perfect images of The Nasty Boys, their greats – Warne,

McGrath and support-cast members Justin Langer and Damien Martyn – all retire, having done what they have done their entire careers, bar the one blemish that they've just corrected, humiliating England. I sink back into the warmth of my sad cricket cave, safe in the knowledge that I am always probably going to have that little pain to dial into every four years. However good England might get, they will never win in Australia. I feel by now that it is a deal we have, the game and I. In being beaten, the cricket knows that it can offer me some inconsequential pain, familiar and, in its own way, comforting.

*

Colour It In charted at number 24 in the UK when it was released the next summer, just before the cricket season returned again. To me, this was a wild and unimaginable success. I kept everything that we appeared in. The adverts, the cut-outs, the posters, the reviews. Even the bad reviews, I cherished. I found it completely unreal, the same way I had been awed that we sounded at all at 811 studio, and held each one as if proof of our own, and my own, existence. Outwardly, it was not deemed as much of a success as I had assumed. Britain was awash with guitar bands that, exactly like us, had grown up with Oasis and then been encouraged into action by the success of The Strokes and The Libertines. It was odd to burst out of our little scenes, all of them local to each of us, in a world where the internet was only just beginning, and notice the number of guitar bands that had sprouted up across the country, with exactly the same ideas and influences. All of them seemed, like us, that they meant something too, they just weren't sure what. We had quite a disadvantage as we did not really look like a proper rock'n'roll band, more like unassuming students, and we found ourselves vaguely critically approved of, with a passionate, cultish fan base that sat somewhere between the mainstream and the alternative, without being either incredibly successful or particularly groundbreaking at all. I found myself, in interviews with the *NME* or Radio 1, all the places I had memorised Oasis and Clash interviews, assuming a kind of half Manc, half slightly dropped t's Saaf London accent. It was what I thought bands were meant to do. I occasionally tried the odd "We're the best band in the country" line, too, as Oasis had taught me, but it felt awful coming out of my mouth, and it landed horrendously lumpen on journalists who, no doubt having heard it six times that week from other guitarists who looked roughly like me, looked directly through me, expressionless and unimpressed, as I said it.

Everything The Maccabees stood for as a band, then, happened in an inexplicable, implied way on stage. It was hard to explain how it happened exactly, as there was very little talking or showmanship and off stage we looked a bit vague when gathered together – on the stage it just, somehow, held its own undeniable small power. So touring, and playing live, is where we thrived and where we stayed. My life became a rhythm of routine, every day climaxing in anticipation of the evening's show. I came to recognise the same bubble of noise that I had been on the outskirts of and so disturbed by at my first Test in 1999, the sound of mass conversations, all in one space, an amount of lives clattering together for one singular purpose, and to appreciate it in a wholly different way. I'd prepare myself every night, checking that what we were going to do was definitely real, by repeatedly standing at the side of the stage and listening to it grow as people came in. That general hum, the buzz and conversation were congregating to see *us*. I could be sure that we were thought of, popped into conversations that we weren't part of.

It started to become clear to me that, even though The Maccabees were beginning to reel in teenagers who would wait outside the front of venues all day, to whom, of course, we would bring out cups of tea in slightly unnecessary gestures of friendliness, *I* was the biggest Maccabees fan in the world. I loved the music so completely, so without question, and the people in the group, that when we walked on stage, time would slow and my senses would become dimension-warped and heightened. I could feel all the eyes on us, and any disturbances in the rhythm of the event, any shirks in the way it was meant to go, became hyper-focused in my mind, in vision and in slow motion. A man, clearly having been dragged there by his girlfriend, yawning. A microphone about to fall over, watching the lead tangle itself, then be propelled from its position. A shoe flying through the air, just swaying inside it. Atherton. A pint doing the same, and not being able to. Tufnell. It was an addictive experience, a feeling of nothing in the world mattering but the exact moment, happening there and then. When I looked across the stage, blurred and, dripping in sweat, in a perpetual sense of euphoric fever, I'd see my brother and my best friends. They were all there, growing in their different ways, but for now, completely as one, all the tiny fusses of the day airbrushed into a mesh of unity. Then I would check back in and face the crowd and look out at the venues of my childhood, the venues that I had been in – London Astoria, the Roundhouse – and hallucinate versions of myself, back in the crowd, at Oasis gigs. I was happy here. After each show, I would collapse, feeling infinitely more worn by the experience than the other Maccabees seemed, into a heap. Sometimes I'd weep, sometimes just stare into a corner of a dank wall until it was time to leave again. Despite all the tiny things that I saw happen so slowly and in such detail, somehow it was always over so quickly.

Entranced in this fuzzy familiarity, our days were completely structured. I'd leave for tour, walking onto our splitter van, knowing that when I set foot back off it again, we'd be in one of three places: a service station or a hotel or a venue, where we would be told exactly when we needed to be back on the bus again. Ten minutes. Three hours. Nine the next morning. All I had to do was get back on that bus at roughly that time and, during this initial rush of purpose and half-success, I began not to know what to do with my hands if a guitar wasn't with them. In the moments in transit, I anxiously played guitar on my teeth while watching the real one being thrown onto flights in a soft case by airport staff. I'd pick it up on the other side, counting the chunks that had been taken off it, tutting and ferrying it back to my hotel room to practise. This machine, the guitar, it turned out, really did kill time. While it did, too, I felt it beginning to voice things through the other side of my hands that I couldn't express otherwise: a restlessness, a tension, a hopefulness and an unresolved low that where I had once painfully slowly forced chords from it, now it began to sound like its own extension of me, a necessary, unspoken part of my affiliation with the world around me, that via the sheer amount of time I'd spent with it had finally developed into something close to second nature. As we kept playing, honing our sets and debriefing our every move with a determined – if admittedly stoned – resolve, the splitter van was upgraded to a sleeper bus, with a living room in the back, and the venues we arrived at became slightly bigger, the hotels slightly nicer.

Being in the bus was like being in a shuttle or a submarine, where you could see the world outside, through the windows, as we lived our days in tiny variations of exactly the same theme. It made for a confusing concoction. The further we went, the more we were forced to evolve as musicians and push the band further and further into different spaces, and yet, other than that hour in the evening when we were playing, we were cemented in semi-forced adolescence. I enjoyed this to begin with. In backstage areas for a day, by the end of it, anything in the office that could be harmlessly practically joked on got harmlessly practically joked on. The venue's laminating instructions, left next to the laminator, would be laminated. A lighting engineer would be taped to a chair for an afternoon. Jelly beans would be scattered across the entirety of the backstage area like a yellow brick road. Another band's dressing room would be filled with bubble-bath bubbles for when they came back off stage. My shoes would be locked in a fridge, which was padlocked. It wasn't possible ever to cook anywhere, obviously, which was of no frustration for me because I couldn't, so we lived on constant visits to Pizza Express or Nando's or Wetherspoons or McDonald's. I felt myself evolving supernaturally at one rate, gazed at lovingly every evening as if we had some kind of secret answer to the universe, and at all others felt like a non-functioning participant in the human race. Regardless, I spent the days wandering through towns all over the world, completely buzzed out by where playing guitar had taken me and with visions of becoming REM or Blur or The Smiths in time, if we just held on and kept going.

*

Touring the United States entails days of long, never-ending drives. In part, the sheer scope of the continent is what makes it so hard for English bands to "break". On our first support tour there, Bloc Party are already playing to thousands of people. Our life involves travelling by minivan throughout the days, stopping at hotels for a few hours, half sleeping, then starting again. Being completely unknown in the States, we play to half-interested and half-full-at-best arenas, before doing it all again. I stare out of the window for hours on end, watching the desert landscape turn to neon across cityscape and back to desert, every single view as if it has been airlifted into the windows from different films. Driving through the night, much the same as all the others, in the middle of Bible-Belt America, between one show and another, I am sitting in the front passenger seat while our sound engineer, Joel Gregg, drives. We are doing 80 miles an hour through a desert landscape, the road sitting on a few feet drop either side, with the immediate view only revealing itself a few feet at a time, the rest sunk into an evening pitch black. I am half watching the road while dreaming of the shows we are doing and how big we are going to be one day.

Out of a sheet of darkness, a deer is standing in the middle of the road, in front of us. Like on stage, time suddenly slows, myself stretched out and yet powerless in it. As we plough through the wilderness towards the deer, it is looking straight at us. My eyes catch its eyes. Then there is a thud. It's a thud that forces Joel, already swerving left to avoid hitting the animal, to renegotiate as the van turns again on itself. For a second, the cliff edge is immediately below as we teeter on it before pulling to a standstill. There is complete silence. I sit there, rerunning the event, the deer a vision of every tailender in the '90s, helmetless and quivering. In my recall, it looks like me, startled in the wake of a fast bowler running in towards it. Its legs are not motioning to run away, though – it is dead still. When we spill out of the van, the boys sliding the passenger door open as if on the other side might be an inhospitable foreign planet's atmosphere, the entire right-hand side is painted red. There are parts of deer in the wheels. Maybe it's an eyeball. The van does not move. We are stranded in the middle of the night, in the middle of nowhere. The seven of us push the van down that highway, creeping it further forwards through American nothingness, caught inside a horror film.

We eventually arrive at a service station – our accents, dropped t's or otherwise, so foreign to the two men there, a man and his son, that they wince at us to decipher the words. They hear "deer" and simply ask, "Did you keep it?" No, we say, we haven't kept it. When we perform for local television a few days later, an unearthed microphone that I place my lips to at the start of the song sends me across the stage, landing astride Rob's bass drum. I am helped to my feet by the band and, eyes wider than they usually are, a sort of odd performative quirk Hugo and I have developed where we open our eyes as if they are clamped open and stare down any half-interested parties on support tours to try and inspire even the slightest bit of curiosity on their part, we perform the song again. It is the time of my life.

*

I took this wide-eyed, anything-is-fine-as-long-as-it-makes-me-feel-alive-and-some-people-are-watching attitude to the festivals that summer, where we opened up new bands' tents across all the European mainstays. The backstage compounds of festivals then, much to my shock, tended to house all the bands in one area. It meant that we would occasionally bump into Interpol, or Regina Spektor, or various other artists who had until only recently been unfathomable as humans to us, as we ran around like children, asking for photos and telling everyone that we were on at two o'clock at the far end of the festival, if they wanted to come and see us. This strange sensation of being inside my stereo, with all the bands that had formed so much of who we imagined ourselves to be, marked some endings. At T in the Park in Scotland, we found ourselves watching the football World Cup final with all the bands squeezed into the marquee tent. Jess had come with all the other friends and girlfriends from Brighton, our spot on the bill being quite an event, and when I turned to her, she was looking at Fabrizio Moretti from The Strokes – crying at the sight of him. Worse still, I understood where she was coming from. His cheekbones did look impossibly more pronounced than they were even on the posters on my wall. I knew that it was over. We split not long after, with me declaring in my head that "I didn't need a mother" and, on leaving her front door, feeling my legs buckle underneath me in a wave of heartache, lying outside Domino's Pizza, sobbing about the end of a relationship that was entirely my own doing. It was a feeling similar to the end of Jack's Basement, momentarily being completely lost and yet without any understanding of

238

why I would feel that way. I did not name it and forced it back down again.

So back to the sad cricket cave I retreated (with guitar). Even so, I was incapable of being alone for very long. Our first sound engineer, Steve Ansell, who had told me that he hated bands like us but liked us and wasn't sure why, invited me to see his band. They rehearsed in the room next door to us and they were so loud, I imagined them to be a six-piece of slightly techy, sweaty men. When I saw them, I was stunned to find they were a two-piece, Steve on drums and a small, unassuming Irish girl on guitar. Laura-Mary Carter played guitar in a way I had never seen it being played, as if it could only be her playing, in part because it was so unbelievably loud, but also because she had an untaught idiosyncrasy completely her own. She was incredibly shy, too, which made her a mystifying prospect. Blood Red Shoes' scene in Brighton was like a subsection of Brighton itself and on our first date, Laura-Mary, drinking sambuca straight from the bottle, took me to a local show. It was in a downstairs bunker, an airless room with no stage, an unadvertised gig with 30 people there. The aim of the music, completely devoid of melody or any of the strictures that I had followed so devoutly, was, it seemed, to alienate as many people as possible. The more people whose ears were accommodated to "pleasant" or middle-of-the-road music you put off, the better. Having used music as a vehicle to, if silently, try and get as many people as possible to approve my existence, I found this new enclave half compelling and half discombobulating. Laura-Mary and I spent an increasing amount of time with each other, eventually, despite my clear phobia of any commitment that wasn't to my band, becoming a couple and spending evenings at her and Steve's flat with them making fun of the beigeness of my music taste. Oasis, The Clash, The Beatles. To her, they were all evidence of a lack of imagination and discernment.

Laura-Mary introduced me to a musical world of dissonance and subversion and atmosphere: My Bloody Valentine,

Hot Snakes, PJ Harvey, L7 and all the riot-grrrl music. I had never even considered that the music industry had been embedded with sexism, or that 99.9 per cent of all the groups that I had developed attachments to were men. I even, defensively, at first argued the case with her. "The music industry isn't sexist," I replied the first time she brought it up, in some way inferring that her suggestion was that The Maccabees were part of the problem. It felt horrible in my throat immediately, as if just by saying it I had realised how wrong it was. The more we talked about it, the more I lived through her eyes until I came round to her opinion completely. People always assumed that Steve had written the songs or was the person with things to say, despite their clear intra-band democracy and her being the singer and guitarist.

Cricket, unsurprisingly, was a hard sell to Laura-Mary. The sheer maleness of the world, the sound of the commentary and the bubble of men talking in the background, in crowds or on commentary, all so sure of their opinion and that everyone needed to hear whatever had just popped into their head, provoked a sort of repulsion in her. Reticently, I kind of knew what she meant, and thought back to how disturbed I'd felt at my first Test match by the City-boy chatter. Where I chose to airbrush it out, it was all she could see and hear. It meant that, unlike with Jess, there was no tolerance or interest for cricket in the peripheries of this relationship.

I was spat out, to the Lion and Lobster next to their place, a dark pub that had a cosy, actual cave-like quality to it, and always had the cricket on Sky Sports in the back room. There, without exchanging one piece of information with each other, I shared my sad (literal) cricket cave with four regulars, each a few decades older than me. We never knew each other's names, but occasionally would roll our eyes or say ridiculously specific things very sincerely like "I'd have second slip a little wider", and discuss the point, before pointing to the other's pint and picking up the next round. I'd return drunk, sad and fulfilled, ready to take in whatever the next ear-bending thing Laura-Mary had on was. Coming out the next day, on the way to rehearsal, with my clear guidelines of what good music was indefinably altered, I began to consider that maybe The Maccabees needed to change. The most important bond of all between Laura and me was the unequivocal understanding in our relationship that our bands were the most important thing. We were very clear from the outset that we were the second, maybe third most important thing in each other's lives. And it worked for a while.

The first Test series of that summer of 2007, played out in the darkened shared space of the back room of the Lion and Lobster, saw the West Indies visit. It was a limp and sad series that England won 3-0, and it sparked a curious feeling, watching the one-sided non-event play out every day. I felt almost the same pinch of hurt, but on behalf of the West Indies. Maybe it wasn't about *England* winning or losing at all, the old feeling of hurt? Test-match cricket goes on for a long time and, when the sides are mismatched, even for me and the nameless men at the Lion and Lobster, it can be painful to watch. As the West Indies struggled, once so vibrant and dominant, I played back recollections of all the moments in films that haunted me at night. The ally in *Saving Private Ryan*, who has his own knife turned on him by a German soldier, begging him to stop as it is slowly forced into his own chest. A TV drama in which a woman police officer is thrown out of a window, the man holding her over the fourth floor of a building long enough for her to ask him to stop before he lets her go. Then, among it all, my mum desperately projecting with her eyes to tell the doctors that she wanted to stay at home, her husband locked outside.

My sore need for cricketing balance was fortunately corrected when India followed the West Indies for a three-Test series. They were awash with regal names of greatness – Sachin Tendulkar, Rahul Dravid, Sourav Ganguly, Anil

Kumble – and competed with an England team that had found Alastair Cook a reliable partner to Andrew Strauss and had Jimmy Anderson, returning to the potential he'd shown in the previous two World Cups. Sachin was the greatest batsman, possibly of all time, and he could play anyone in the world, apart from Jimmy, who had learned to bowl in Burnley.

*

Zaheer Khan, a seam bowler with a guile and wisdom that Anderson will acquire in time, is batting at Trent Bridge when he stops play. A jelly bean has been thrown onto the crease where he is batting. He removes it. The next ball, he stops play again. He calls the umpire over, pointing his bat at the offending object. He is clearly very annoyed. There is, indeed, another jelly bean there, nearly exactly where he removed the last. A chink, through the pub at the Lion and Lobster, strikes me cold. Throwing jelly beans at each other is the kind of adolescent thing The Maccabees do, the days disintegrating into long arguments about who put that jelly bean there. It hadn't occurred to me that cricketers might be the same, forever herded around, developing at a supernatural rate in one direction, and yet oddly frozen at the age when they had stopped being required to do anything else in order for the world to accept them, throwing jelly beans at each other. No England players owned up to the incident.

We had spent the time after our London Roundhouse show, which I'd had to play with a seriously infected finger after trying to superglue shut a cut on tour, writing our second album. Rob, now infamous across Brighton for antics as The Maccabees became a "proper" band, had begun to not turn up. He would be found days later, in a stranger's apartment or delivered to gigs with no money or memory of where he had been. It was a constant agony, what to do with Rob, whom we all loved and who had started the band in Land's bedroom, but clearly had very serious addiction issues that were beginning to derail the group. Eventually, and inevitably, he failed to show for an actual gig, at the Exeter Lemon Grove, having carried out the soundcheck and then decided to go back to the pub in Brighton. The venue was full, and when the announcement was made we were booed from our dressing room back onto our bus, which was parked outside, by 800 angry students. I sat on the bus, thinking maybe this is what it felt like to be Nasser Hussain, booed by your own fans.

Just after that we finally made the awful, wrenching decision to let Rob go from the group. I had told him, on many occasions, that there was no band without him and we weren't going to get rid of him. We all had. But with the promise that we would pay for all rehab and that we loved him, we decided the next record would not have him on it. Heartbreakingly, at a party weeks later, he got "The Maccabees" inked permanently on his arm by an amateur tattoo artist. It wasn't enough. The moment was gone.

This sort of changing of personnel with people I had envisaged would always be with me was mirrored that winter tour, when Matthew Hoggard and Steve Harmison, the listed buildings of English cricket, were also moved on. In their place, a resurgent Jimmy Anderson and Stuart Broad were picked. Broad had long blond hair that he would continually swipe effeminately out of his eyes and a boyish enthusiasm that instilled the whole side with a naïve new focus. Anderson took five wickets in the second Test, spurred by his newfound responsibility as leader of the attack, and Broad, opening the bowling with him, chipped in with wickets too. As for the band, Sam Doyle joined. It was difficult at first, to square the concept that the group was moving on because it needed to and not because of the friendship which had initially defined it. But Sam *loved* playing drums, and that was enough for us. He played them harder, with a more muscular and technical approach than Rob. It helped form an impression of what we might turn into as we searched to outgrow ourselves. We wheeled our gear from the lock-up to the room every morning, setting up and playing the songs that we just had workings of, repeating and repeating, trying tiny changes and throwing them away. There were batches of songs, at first ones that we thought were the album, then clearly were not, then another, then another, until something clicked. Land harnessed the conversations about Rob and they became woven lyrically into the songs "Can You Give It", "No Kind Words" and so on. They sounded bigger, the songs, if tenser, and slightly wider, like they were meant for bigger places.

Hugo, too, had learned home recording and wrote the beginnings of "One Hand Holding". They were songs desperate to leave the rehearsal room. I considered my role, as before, to keep everyone happy somehow, to keep the entire thing afloat and moving, and I'd go home between the Lion and Lobster and the rehearsal room and Laura-Mary's and play and play the guitar. I was a cautious writer still, but one desperate to develop, and I chipped in constant guitar riffs, and different parts, and arrangement ideas, and moved the songs along, knowing that when they were released into the world, I would be able to look people in the eyes again, punching the air, standing at the lip of the stage and screaming into a sea of faces.

*

Thinking it romantic, we eventually go to Paris to record the songs on our second album. Every morning, I walk through Père Lachaise, the cemetery which divides our apartment from the studio, passing Edith Piaf's and Oscar Wilde's and Jim Morrison's graves, listening to Wu-Tang Clan's *Enter the Wu-Tang (36 Chambers)* and Public Enemy's *It Takes a Nation of Millions to Hold Us Back*. It is a contradictory input to the senses, but I have recently been determinedly propelled into the history of hip hop by a Roots Manuva CD Will has passed on, and I like the idea that I am probably the only person in the world walking through a Parisian cemetery listening to hip hop, about to make a second record. We have chosen to work with Markus Dravs, who has just recorded Arcade Fire's second album, *Neon Bible*, with his engineer François Chevallier. We fall in love with them both and every day Markus makes us go and do his washing or sends us out on chores before taking us out to French restaurants and deboning my fish for me. Franky delivers us hash at night, on his moped that has Barack Obama and "hope" on it, and me and him listen to the beat from "No Kind Words", which Rob has written and Sam now plays, making it sound monstrous, sharing our dream with each other of what it might sound like if Roots Manuva rapped on it.

We are under the impression that working with Markus will give us some of the Arcade Fire (our new favourite band) maximalism, next to which our less wiry but still wiry sound has begun to feel feeble. In some ways he does, eventually hiring in the same brass players, who come to Paris and play back anything we hum at them, pitch perfectly, like real musicians. We spend every night switching off stoned, buoyant about where our new sound might take us.

We finish the album at Hook End Manor, a famously haunted old mansion near Reading, where there are tales of phones catching fire and old women appearing behind shower curtains. It is so big and the bedrooms so far apart that I am genuinely worried that my scream might not even be heard. I sleep with every single light on for a month. I have, at the last minute, written a small piece of music and we record it in Hugo's bedroom, about half a mile down the corridor and also permanently as bright as a doctor's surgery, sleepless through each night for fear of paranormal activity. It has no chord changes, which I deem myself probably incapable of, but, taking Franky into the room in downtime and having him hammer bottles against the guitars and deaden the strings, we patchwork and

245

layer it into something really soft and atmospheric, intentionally apart from the rest of the record. Land eventually takes it into his room and, inviting us in a week later, sheepishly sings the lyrics for "Bag of Bones". He has made it really beautiful, I think to myself, and leave his room at Hook End, remembering years earlier when I had first met him, on a Rizla mission, and had left his room feeling incomprehensibly taller.

*

Of course, the haunted evenings were not helped by England's tour of India, which I watched, exhausted, through the night, constantly checking the hallways and the bathroom for pale old women on fire. England lost the series and Pietersen, wielding the power he had been given as the new captain and determined he couldn't work with Peter Moores, a conscientious if unglamorous coach from the county game, told the ECB it was either him or Moores. To his surprise, in a storm of chaos and infighting, they decided it was both. Andrew Strauss, by default, was suddenly the new England captain. The Zimbabwean Andy Flower was the coach. He and Strauss were put together by chance, a complete quirk of circumstance, and they got on.

26

Them Crooked Vultures and
the Evening Ferry

It's 7 February 2009. I know it's the 7th because 5 February 2002 is the day I saw Oasis at Watford Colosseum and the 6th is the day I came home late to be told my mum had just died in the room she had hardly left for years. I have begun to feel the dates arrive every year, as if my body is warning me, my mind reliving each sequence of events as it does: being carried over the front of a barrier, mustering the strength to point at Liam Gallagher, who very, very gently nods back. Not saying goodbye to her that morning. Deciding to play cricket the next day after school. I have not discussed any of these details with anyone, and there is a shame ever-enveloping, folding itself again and again somewhere inside for missing that last moment in her life. Some years, despite the rhetoric that I don't care, I feel overwhelmed with this physical infliction that I nonetheless keep completely silent, my limbs extremely heavy, my conscience diving into a sadness that feels as if it only goes inwards, my reserves somehow suddenly very deep and accommodating for it, desperate for nothing but to be curled up, rocking backwards and forwards, alone and, preferably, stoned. Other years, for reasons I am not clear on, it doesn't even pinch. This year is one of them.

England are on tour in the West Indies again. I am almost reluctant to watch the West Indies these days: they have begun to be so obviously the wrong side of a power struggle that I am worried that going through it all will again leave me with those flashbacks – the roll-call of film scenes I can't delete from my memory, then finally my mum, jutting her head back and forth, trying to smile. Nevertheless, the time difference alone of a West Indies tour makes it too accessible to avoid. The Maccabees, getting ready to tour our recently recorded second album, have decided that we will only rehearse during working hours, as all the band have partners now. I am beginning to suspect that their girlfriends are their priorities, and that they have not made the same bond on which mine is agreed, which I, again silently, cite as some kind of misgiving on their part. I don't want The Maccabees, my new family, to leave me. Sometimes I don't even want them to leave me for an evening. If I had my way, we would be in that room, running those songs again and again until my hands bleed. The songs wouldn't benefit. Nevertheless, regardless of these ugly and exposing feelings circulating in me, I bow to their new (entirely reasonable) suggestion that we should only play during working hours. On the plus side it means, after all, that I can go to the Lion and Lobster/sad cricket cave straight after and watch the Test match, which will be beginning as we finish, with the men whose names I don't know. I have time: Laura and Blood Red Shoes *do* rehearse through the night, and I don't have the keys to their flat.

The first Test in Kingston, Jamaica, is well balanced. I have got into the pub slightly late, having offered to pack down all the band's gear, as if it might trigger a guilt in them so that they decide to stay and play all night after all. As I arrive, England are 11-2 and about to take the field after lunch.

When I settle down, nodding as unenthusiastically as I can with my new "friends", with whom a sort of emotional distance and personal vagueness appears key to our relationship, the projection of the game, which fills half of the back wall, shows Kevin Pietersen on strike. Jerome Taylor is into his stride and, in a beautiful rhythmical action, surrounded by an encouraging hum in the ground, he delivers the ball. It's full, perhaps fuller than Pietersen expects, and it's fast. Pietersen, a man of over-arching alpha, is already assuming his presence on the ball while it is mid-flight. He motions to whip it through mid-wicket. The ball straightens a touch. Pietersen misses it. His stumps are flying out of the ground. He doesn't even look around on the way off, knowing he will see at least one of them no longer in place. Nasser Hussain is on commentary, and he can barely contain himself with the nostalgia: "His off stump went flying, just like the old days!" There is an ominous silence in the Lobster, and a party in Kingston.

And so it unfolds. Strauss is caught behind off Taylor, trying to withdraw his bat at the last second. Paul Collingwood juts his bat down on another full one from Taylor and is bowled too, deflecting the ball onto his stumps. He's the only person not to realise it, only noticing his dismantled stumps when he turns to attempt a second run. England are 23-6. Sulieman Benn, the West Indies' own brand of left-arm spinner, the bat surrounded, forces Stuart Broad to hit the ball straight to bat-pad. It's caught. Benn is off celebrating, just out of sight to the camera's right, his giddy fielders all following. The camera keeps cutting to Englishmen in the stands, their tops off, their faces red, comically sullen, chins sunk against their chests looking down on their ruby bellies. They look a debauched, jaded version of themselves four years earlier – as does Andrew Flintoff, trying to shepherd the tailenders, his feet unmoving as if he is now simply a coconut shy, eventually bowled by Fidel Edwards. As he leaves, his helmet tilts over his eyes, as it used to in his childlike celebrations. He looks as if he's outgrown it. England are all out for 51. The ground is full, reassuringly full, in Jamaican celebration.

Amid the chaos of this collapse, I noticed a familiar sensation within me. Alongside the anger and the tutting and the criticism now filling the air, I was not only finding some private comfort in this nostalgic collapse, I was *enjoying* it. Suddenly, where the nods at each table had represented the limit of our communication only an hour earlier, now each man, a self-pronounced island at his own table, formed a hub of union and communication. "What are we going to do with this England team, then?" one asked. I rolled my eyes over-theatrically and looked into my pint as if genuinely searching for the answer. I needn't have done. Everyone, it turned out, had the answer. Wrong captain. Totally agree, mate. Wrong coach. Absolutely, 100 per cent spot on. Wrong team. It's the undeniable truth. Another pint, please, mate. Cocooned suddenly, with a shared topic of conversation to reach these strangers and, most importantly, to share our sadness, we got closer than we ever had that evening or indeed ever would again. I still didn't catch any names.

Wall of Arms charted better than *Colour It In*, at 13, a few months later. Markus Dravs, whom we would talk about every day since our time together, doing impressions of him and sending false demos to his website while he spent the next few years producing Arcade Fire, Mumford & Sons and Coldplay, had promised us that our dressing room was going to be full "when he'd finished with us". It was a phrase he coined, while getting us to do his washing, to which we conjured pictures of arena dressing rooms full of record-label executives, famous people from whichever city we were in and radio DJs with handheld recording equipment wrestling to get an impromptu interview with us. I invested in this vision and imagined it too.

He was right *in a way*: when the touring started, the dressing room was full. It's just, it was full of brass players. I'd been reluctant about the brass aspect of the record at first, worrying it would somehow degrade my importance on the stage. But I now welcomed it. It felt easier to punch the air to brass players playing my guitar lines, and it helped to have some relative strangers forever as company to diffuse the small tensions creeping into the over-familiarity between the five of us. The brass players, being effectively employed by the band, we realised fairly quickly, would not only play what we asked them to, but would wear what we asked, too. The tours were spent in search of dinner-lady outfits, or masks that we cut holes out of so they could come up for air occasionally. I took to playing shows in a suit, bought from the mod shop in the Lanes in Brighton, screaming and punching the air and doing the odd unconvincing jump, then coming off stage looking as if I had swum across the Thames in it, wringing it out of sweat in the evening, hanging it across the bus bunks that we half-slept in over speed-bumps and motorways through the night onto the next venue. I repeated this for every show. I had introduced tiny bits to my stage set-up too like, wait for it, a reverb pedal, a revelation to us all, which we treated with a we-are-not-worthy awe.

I had tried to pick up a few more tricks than just the down-stroked, manic, race-to-the-end guitar work that had made up *Colour It In*, and my playing began to incorporate some extra facets: an interpretation of what guitar picking was, an assimilation of something closer to guitar solos with the odd bended note, and a technique I'd just happened across playing to myself where I would play a phrase on the low end of the neck, then slide all the way to the higher to repeat it, an octave up, and back and repeat, giving the guitar lines a woozy, overexcited air that sounded more impressive than it actually was to play. We had all begun to be taken by acts of accomplished class and grace, diving back into Martin Scorsese's *The Last Waltz*, in which The Band play their last show, which explained the suit, and Richard Hawley's new records, and we had started to re-enact our own versions of what we imagined those things to be about, putting them inside the only way we knew how to play: very fast, very unimprovised, very rehearsed and very tight.

Slowly evolving musically exactly as we did in popularity, a fortunate coincidence not afforded most bands, The
Maccabees were getting bigger in England. That year, before
the Ashes came, we played Glastonbury Festival on the Other
Stage in the middle of the afternoon, looking out onto a crowd
of people that stretched in the tens and tens of thousands out
towards the horizon. It looked as close to the *There and Then*
cover as I'd ever experienced, though my legs knew it too, and
let me down, shaking for the duration of the show and forcing
me to occasionally stretch them wide in a vague rock-star
cliché, but for no other reason than it was the best way to keep
me upright. It didn't *feel* how Noel looked. We were a bit of an
earnest and flustered, if charming to some, mess, in those huge
situations and when we messed up the beginning of "Precious
Time", stopping the song and restarting it, there was a little
burst of relief in which everyone there, ourselves included,
accepted we probably weren't quite The Clash or The Band
yet, and could just enjoy the remainder being exactly who we
were. At that moment, the sun came out – relieving the until-
then rained-out festival – and I looked across the stage feeling
an even more exaggerated, blissed-out affection for my band,
if in a heightened state of stage fright, and noticed as I did
that we'd all begun to move at exactly the same time to our
music as we played. One step forwards, pause. Two steps back.
Swivel. Self-conscious pause. Step to the left. It would have
been impossible to rehearse it so synchronised.

The press photos we had done that year, the only ones we
had liked, were images taken separately, then pieced together
as if we were ghosts, blurring into one another. I dreamed that,
like the photo, I might sort of disappear into the group and that
we all might genuinely become a physical part of each other.
I don't think the others necessarily did. They certainly didn't
seem as keen to play cricket at the festivals with the stumps and
bats and balls I'd made sure were lugged in with our gear at all
times, just in case. The video for "Can You Give It", the album's

second single, a document of the Cooper's Hill Cheese-Rolling competition (where every year the village raced down a hill in Gloucestershire, at great physical danger, to catch a wheel of cheese), was released in time for the festival season and, coupled with the cricket backstage, must have made us seem like a kind of unknowing Monty Python sketch, where bands from America or The View, from Scotland, would momentarily pass a burned-grass area we'd turned into a match and quizzically stop and stare for a while, before shrugging their shoulders and asking where the free alcohol was.

Ironically, the more popular we became in England, the less we played there, each show needing six months' build-up to sell the larger venues we were booked in. So, we spent most of the summer back and forth through Europe, playing small club shows and festivals. Our festival billing usually landed us first on the main stage. Sometimes we were on at 11am. It was a slightly odd experience, walking on stage to a festival that was just waking up, looking out onto huge fields with sparsely scattered people across it, some looking at us, others over us, some through us. It was like charity fundraising, trying to get people to pay attention when they clearly had something else in mind and looked at you as a mild inconvenience. I used this attitude at those shows, an odd confrontational niceness, while half imploding occasionally with the localised joy of just playing music, in front of their bewildered faces. Playing in bright sunlight, without the safety of walls, meant that, despite the early billings, we still needed to feel the same level of drunk we did at our own shows. This would mean starting to drink at 9am. When we got off stage, filled with a feeling of half embarrassment and half buzz, the Ashes were on.

It was a hot, unrelenting summer spent on buses with broken air-conditioning, the windows of the sleeper bus all wound down to open their maximum few inches, craning our necks to try and feel the slight rush of air as we moved from European field to European field. Arriving in festivals at this temperature, with no shorts or summer clothes of any description, I would lurch myself every morning bleary-eyed from the bus across the dried, brown grass that seemed to determine all communal backstage areas.

Our homes-from-home inside these communal areas were small makeshift dressing rooms that, as a general standard, would come with a fridge, waist height, about 3 feet in width and depth, in which all the alcohol and ice was kept. I liked to try and get to the dressing room first, sweaty and searching for any kind of shelter from the heat. There was only one thing to do. I removed half the beer and half the ice, half expecting it to have never-ending choc ices exactly as my grandparents had, piling the contents along the remaining width of the otherwise empty room, and climbed into the fridge. It was the only place to stop the disturbing heat. I watched the 2009 Ashes mainly from these fridges, my suit wrung out to dry on the wall opposite.

The fridge was undeniably the most challenging of all the adaptations of the sad cricket cave. It was less easy these days to reaccess the teenage version of myself that could phase the background out and reach into the television, shape-shifting into one of the England cricket team. Instead, between the laptop showing Sky Sports and the fridge where I sat, there was constant movement and hustle in between, all of it non-cricket related. "Was your guitar out of tune?", one of the first questions asked by anyone to anyone else after stage, as I climbed in. Whoever was asked this, the answer was, without pause, always, "No, definitely not." "Does anyone have the drinks tokens?" "What time is bus call?" "Can I get these people backstage?" The ongoing questions, the absolute chaos of ten men in their twenties, plus a brass section, in a tiny room in blistering heat, inhabiting an ever-changing space that was also exactly the same.

The evenings between these unearthly-hour shows would often entail crossing the sea on huge car ferries. Most of the others would take sleeping pills and sleep throughout the journeys on board the bus, on the bottom floor of the ferry. I tried this once and woke up in the middle of the crossing, literally underneath the sea, car alarms going off everywhere, set off in response to the choppiness of the water, in entirely pitch black. Holding onto each side of my bunk, and praying that it wasn't the one time the ferry sank, I decided that from now on I would spend these journeys awake through the night, on the deck, next to a fruit machine. It was safer there at least. On this particular night, clutching a pillow and disembarking the bus on arrival, I ran to the television. There was no-one there. Phew. I had missed the last day of the first Test and, in a less internet-dependent world, I had managed to avoid finding out the score. It only took a question to the Dutch woman behind the cafe desk, me pointing at the television and in as simple an English accent as I could muster, saying, "Sky Sports?", followed by a gesture upwards with my palms and an inquisitive, hopeful look. "You have it?" She nodded. They had it! I prayed, as she switched it over, that it would be showing the last day of the Test. I had to double-take when it did, landing on the safest of safe sights I knew, the cricket highlights.

*

As I settle, the boat is beginning to wooze up and down, making it difficult for a second to focus on the score. England, I have to remind myself, are batting to save the Test match. It can't say seven wickets already, can it? The wicket was flat. I move close to the screen, to check. It does. On my way towards the television, holding onto various seats and pillars to avoid rocking with the boat to get there, I just miss Stuart Broad, who is walking away from me, back to the pavilion, LBW to the new nothing-like-Warne spinner Nathan Hauritz. Graeme Swann joins Paul Collingwood at the crease. Australia need three wickets. Collingwood flicks the ball through mid-wicket to bring up his 50. He waves his bat, not vertically but horizontally, giving the impression that the milestone will mean little if England lose. The body language tells me all I need to know from the two sessions of play I have missed – that this has been hard, and this is a fight England are likely to lose. Crucially, England still require 79 to make Australia bat again and Australia have a couple of hours to bowl England out. A warm surge of backs-to-the-wall futility moves through me, the tension filling me with a nostalgic sickness. That, though, could easily be the ferry which, as I occasionally recognise during the advert breaks, is rocking us up and down semi-ferociously.

Graeme Swann has batted for just over an hour, condensed into ten minutes of blocks and leaves and counter-punching swishes on the highlights. Collingwood, at the other end, is a vision of English obduracy and has batted for over five hours. Then, it snaps. Swann is out LBW to Ben Hilfenhaus, and the Australians, chewing-gum showing, are reeling away in celebration, cackling at the inevitable. It is only minutes later, in the highlights anyway, that I too must concede the inevitable. Collingwood, not particularly fancying Jimmy Anderson's chances of surviving at the other end, slightly changes his focus and begins to attack, dragging England towards a score of parity to make Australia bat again. It's his downfall. He loosely drives at a tempting wide half-volley from Peter Siddle, and is caught by Mike Hussey at gully. He is paused for a minute, both hands on his knees, looking at the floor, the Australian celebration in his ears, as if wondering whether he can take it back. He can't.

As Monty Panesar walks to the crease, the boat has started to feel like a bizarre simulation craft, as if it is reinterpreting for me the feeling of what it might be like to be Monty. Sick, giddy, clinging onto whatever lifelines there might be. Monty, even in the highlights, feels as if he takes an age to get to

Jimmy, waiting for him in the middle. Jimmy is, worryingly, now the most qualified batter to take England to safety. "I don't care if you get hit," says Jimmy when Monty eventually arrives, "just don't get out." Monty gulps. I hold on to the chairs, rattling in the storm, the windows outside nothing but pitch black and the occasional rising wave. Jimmy, inverted from the leave-it-to-me focus when he bowls, has his brows turned inwards, perennially concerned when he bats. It's a concern that I imagine him trying to airbrush from his appearance, the same way his obviously shy disposition has been counterbalanced over time by success. Monty, well, Monty bats like the deer I can't banish from my mind in Bible-Belt America a couple of years before. He is standing there, just waiting to be hit.

Peter Siddle, beaded necklace showing, jagged teeth, is ready to bowl his first ball at Monty. The highlights now, appreciating the brevity of all the gaps between the action, are playing it out in real time, exactly as it happened. Siddle is in. It's fierce and quick, a perfect in-between length. Monty plays a defensive shot, showing the face of his non-sponsored bat. The ball misses it and whistles through to Brad Haddin. He's survived the first one. David Lloyd, once the England coach, is on the commentary and can do nothing but just say his name, "Monty Panesar", leaving a gap then repeating, "Monty Panesar". Nathan Hauritz, at the other end, is spinning the ball alarmingly. He rips it past Jimmy's bat. The Australians appeal. It's not out. Jimmy looks more concerned than he's ever been, as if he's witnessing it from outside himself, hiding behind a sofa. Later the same over, the ball spins back in, hitting Jimmy on the pads. The Australians, The Nasty Boys Mark 3, are all up again, asking for it to be given out. It isn't. As time winds down, every ball is ritualistically followed by a complete stillness, a silence that even the boat seems to adhere to, and then when the ball is survived, a cheer from the television, as I briefly zone back out and feel the ocean throwing the boat around. The runs required to make Australia bat again are ticking down all the time. Eight, six, four, three. Siddle is now reaching 90 miles an hour, hurling the ball as if leaving a part of himself on it, towards Anderson. The next ball is desperate, fast but wide and outside off stump. Jimmy closes his bat on it, in a motion as if he is chopping wood. The ball careers off his bat and to the boundary. The crowd is suddenly up, cheering, the boat rocking with them. Every ball becomes enraptured by a fuzz of relief, runs starting to flow and Anderson and Panesar beginning to look around slightly sheepishly, both trying to hide small grins. They survive. The first Test is drawn. When I get back to the bus, there must be 30 car alarms going off in unison, triggered by the sea. It feels, to my deeply tripped-out, insomniac brain, as if they are celebrating with Monty, Jimmy and me.

The series woozes with the same back and forth, viewed from my prism of fridges and rocking ferries, to set up a perfect finale at The Oval, the sides tied 1-1. As it does, we are reaching our own festival conclusion, playing our customary early-morning set at Belgium's Pukkelpop. Pukkelpop is set up perfectly as a backstage area for fun, all the dressing-room cabins tightly packed together, encircling a free bar. It is a disaster waiting to happen for Sam, who has been drinking since nine in the morning to "prepare" for stage and, worn by the heat and the alcohol and the early-morning excitement, has passed out in the middle of the loungers in the communal, free-bar area.

He is wearing a Led Zeppelin t-shirt I gave him the previous Christmas. During his slumber, the Test is playing out in the background and, with Jonathan Trott looking alarmingly at ease for his debut Test match, Sam becomes a bit of a tourist attraction. At first, it is the small things. Using his head, tilted asleep on his shoulder but still just upright enough, to dispose of the shells from pistachio nuts. That is until the special guests for that evening's show turn up: Them Crooked

Vultures, the supergroup featuring Dave Grohl (Nirvana/Foo Fighters), Josh Homme (Queens of the Stone Age) and John Paul Jones (Led Zeppelin). With a gloaming feel in the afternoon, there is a huge deal of anticipation for these rock'n'roll giants suddenly populating the backstage area. Watching them arrive and serendipitously gather around Sam, sleeping in a Led Zeppelin t-shirt, completely unaware, it strikes me what I need to do. What I *must* do. Sam needs his photo taken with Dave Grohl. I hop out of the fridge. England have bowled out Australia for 160, well in charge, and Jonathan Trott is batting still with an unusual ease, a beacon of calm in a hostile situation. As it infiltrates me with a confidence of my own, I walk straight over to Dave Grohl and, borderline brazenly, tap him on the back of the shoulder. "Excuse me, Dave, but my friend over there is a massive fan and he says he wants a photo with you." I point at Sam, fast asleep on the lounger. It couldn't be more in his remit. Dave Grohl poses as I photograph him, tongue out in Sam's unconscious ear.

The vim with which Grohl responded to this request sparks a buzz of activity. Suddenly, there are photos with everyone. Dizzee Rascal. Maxïmo Park. All the bands I can find, European and Australian, lots of bands I have no idea who they are, all coming up and asking of their own accord. They are all posing with Sam, as I order a queue and make sure everyone gets their photo. Eventually, checking back in briefly on the cricket to see Trott still at the crease, I strike up enough courage for the vital one. John Paul Jones cuts quite an unassuming character, small in stature and not the kind you imagine would be particularly enamoured of prank photos. Nevertheless, I need to know. In the same way I had with Grohl, I approach him. "Excuse me," I explain, "but my friend is asleep in a Led Zeppelin t-shirt and I really think it would be a huge deal to him if you took your photo with him." He looks suspiciously at our sleeping drummer and, registering the left-field nature of the request, is plainly already finding a way to say no politely. Just before he does, Dave Grohl arrives, putting his arm around me and saying to Jones, "Oh, you should do that, that's hilarious." Moments later, we have a photo of Sam, fast asleep, in a Led Zeppelin t-shirt, with John Paul Jones of Led Zeppelin leaning next to him, grinning. When I get back to the dressing room, in a manic joy at what we've just made happen, Trott has a hundred. I get back in the fridge. Sam doesn't know he has met his hero.

The next day we watch the last of the Ashes, hungover in a Belgian hotel on a blessed day off, recounting how out of hand the evening got. As we do, England are bowling at Australia for the last time. As it always tends to, it suddenly happens very quickly. They are all hallmark wickets – belonging to Harmison, Swann and Broad – and as I roll over laughing about the night, England, as if it was nothing, have won the Ashes back. Easy.

Sam meets his heroes.

27

Hug Politics

The European run has ended and we have a month off, with time to do with as we like, away from The Maccabees. It is a disturbing prospect for me, with Laura-Mary away. Blood Red Shoes tours never seem to coincide with ours and mean she and I are beginning to spend months at a time apart. Any day with nothing to do leaves me feeling hopeless or alone, or both, and my head, reaching for something to fill it, refocuses on an old idea. I think back to sitting up with Franky for nights during the making of *Wall of Arms*, talking about Roots Manuva's *Awfully Deep* and *Run Come Save Me*. They are brilliant English hip-hop records, with rugged synth bass lines, funny, twisted and endlessly dark. I decide, in part because Franky would love it and possibly more because I need to kill time, that I'll try to get Rodney Smith (Roots Manuva) to do a new vocal to "No Kind Words". Franky, after all, had pointed out the song had something Manuva in the essence of it before we had, in turn, layered it with a bed of synths like those in Notorious B.I.G.'s "Things Done Changed". I can't get hold of Rodney at first, unsurprisingly, so it catches me unawares when, back at my dad's house, rarely daring to walk into that room at all anymore, an unknown number calls me.

"Felix, it's Rodney," the voice says in an unmistakable low pitch. "Tell me about this 'Bag of Bones', then." It is not "Bag of Bones" I want to be vocalled, I explain, but

"No Kind Words". Rodney's phone call begins a process whereby, with some back and forth, he sends me his vocal, sharp, succinct and undeniably him, and we patchwork the new song together. He eventually comes to the studio, literally wheeling in through the door on his bike. His vocal is incredible. We slightly shift the arrangement of the original song, taking out the drums in the middle section so "If you've got no kind words to say, you should say nothing more at all" sits in murky atmosphere before the song snaps into its original guitar duelling. The first thing I do when the mix is finished, in slight disbelief that it has come true, is send it to Markus and Franky, together on one email. The subject: "It happened!"

Markus phones me back immediately. "Are you sitting down?" I could be, I tell him, finding a bench walking through East London. Franky has been on holiday in Greece and caught swine flu. Swine flu has been in the press, but it isn't something I've conceived of being real. He is on life support. Two days later, Land takes a call in the same rehearsal room Rodney had wheeled himself into. It is Markus. Land repeats two words: "Franky died." It takes a while for the words to settle into the room. We all sit there, each by our own pedal board or equipment, in silence. I look around and every Maccabee has his head bowed, a couple of yards from each other. Some are crying. Some are not. Nobody touches anyone. Nobody asks if the other is OK. We just leave the room, each to our own homes. Franky was 29.

There is a trip to the funeral in Paris. The service, in which people spill out into the back of the church without seats, is carried out in French and we sit, dressed up, very still, through each speech from his friends and his parents, in a language indecipherable to us. I feel I am a comparative expert in the grief we are all experiencing anew and decide it is my duty not to get upset at all, which I manage until we leave for the Eurostar, recognising Franky's face in his mother's as we move to say goodbye, deciding at the last minute not to hand her the note I've written about how much I'd loved him.

*

I was heartbroken that Franky would never hear the Manuva collaboration, entitled "Empty Vessels", and the same way I had felt about Ben Hollioake, I began to feel about Franky, tripping into never-ending heaviness, a perpetual desire to do nothing but sleep. It, in turn, thawed the complete denial that my mum's death meant nothing to me, leaving me feeling lost and alone, like the time I had left Jess's house for the last time and found myself at Lana's gravestone, with KFC, sitting beside it, the cricket on the radio so we could both listen. I spoke to the slab of horizontal stone, telling it how well The Maccabees were doing, before running out of things to say and lying back next to it, staring at the sky and the tree that we used to see from the window. I would have lain there forever if I'd been allowed.

I still couldn't sleep without weed and still made sure, no matter how little, that there was always a pinch of it left so as not to invoke panic. Like the rehearsals or the activities or having the cricket on constantly, it kept my mind from wandering off piste to where some foreign hurt was, a devilish little bug that would dive into the deep well all my denial had been digging for it.

Unlike the highly *unanticipated* European dates, the UK home run came about at the back of the year. With no-one watching but ourselves, the rehearsals took on a fervent focus and a different sort of commitment to our usual rehearsal etiquette. Though we could barely talk about Franky's death, in the weeks building up to the tour, playing the songs that we'd recorded with and in front of him, watching him purse his lips and pinch his fingers together with how in love with them he was, we found a way to communicate it. The songs were Franky's too and every time we played them he was there somewhere, in the muscle memory of the song. When we left, suddenly feeling the reassuring sense that it wasn't only me that wanted to play forever, I would find that on the way home, picking up something from a shop or ordering something from a café, every woman who worked there, in her mid-fifties, who very casually said "Thanks, my love" or "There you go, darling" as I left, rendered me momentarily static. Each remark, an insignificant gesture when handing change over, perhaps without eye contact even, suddenly took on a bizarre currency. I would feel unnaturally comforted by the words that had been said and look for another excuse to stay in the shop, so they might say it again. Maybe I'd forgotten something. Maybe I needed another coffee. It was like lying next to the gravestone with the KFC and the cricket and the weed. It helped for a second.

When we headlined Brixton Academy in October that year, it was perfect. We had developed together just enough to hold big rooms, finessing the show to accommodate people at the back who might not be able to see us and yet still holding an essence of racing each other to the finish line, so the shows bubbled just on the edge of collapse, but never quite did. We had the whole thing down. Every stop in between the songs. The length of pauses required. Land, too, had begun to stretch his capacity for singing, adopting a croon and a quiver which showcased his ability beyond the bands to whom we had previously been compared. We played fast and tight and with purpose, just the right alchemy of being unsure and being committed, and turned the rooms into dens of flying bodies for an hour. There were hands as far as you could see and, tilting my head to the seated balcony area, I could see the whole place was standing there too. I felt time slow again, my monitors so loud that they encased me inside them and, noticing my shadow, silhouetted across the entire venue by chance of the light, I thought to myself, if I can just stay here, in this exact moment, everything will always be fine. I didn't notice that the backdrop behind us, which we had instructed to be a clean, old-fashioned drape to project hazy colours on as if we were in the 1960s, looked like a dirty and crinkled bed sheet. It was still a learning game.

Over the course of the touring just past and the time in dressing rooms, we had all learned various basic home-recording techniques and we decided that, instead of spending every day rehearsing, writing face to face as was all we had known, we would approach our next album by individually layering and bringing the music, already semi-realised, in for the group to critique/add to. I was very against this at first, resistant to any sort of change that might intimate something coming to an end. I thought of the hidden jealous pinch I had become familiar with in myself in rehearsals; when someone wanted to play some music to me and, despite my head bouncing around with how fantastic this music that my friend or brother had just made was, I'd swallow the pride and very fractionally nod and shrug, "Yeah, it's good. I guess." You know, so they didn't get carried away with themselves. I imagined this feeling, this jealous pinch, essentially based in the fear that if they could do that, did they need me at all, and I catastrophised that, when each of us was working alone, someone would be delivering music of such higher quality than me that it would become clear I was not a real musician, I still couldn't jam in B flat if asked and I would be cast aside as a fraud who had got away with it for too long.

To my surprise, and despite my early protestations, making the music away from each other and with autonomy over my own piece, really worked for me. I went to Denmark Street and, without knowing what a huge amount of them did, bought about 15 different guitar pedals. I stuck them in a plastic bag and carried them back to Brick Lane, my new home with Joel Porter and Jessie Ware, where they spent a year splayed out on my bedroom floor, connected to a tiny amp and a laptop. Sam and I developed a routine where he would come over, usually still up from a night before and, after I had given him the silent treatment for it for about half an hour, we'd set to making music. I took Joel's bass, upright in his room, and played it upside down alongside chord patterns I wrote on a fake piano. I felt newly unburdened by writing on an upside-down bass and keyboard and, where writing on guitar had buried in me too many precedents to try and beat, the music came far quicker and without anywhere near as much of the worry. Once it was in place, I would then play guitar, working out parts on top. I found I was capable of setting up atmospheres that I really liked. I'd send the instrumental music and then wait, clicking refresh on my emails, to see what the rest of the band made of it. Sometimes responses never came. The band didn't like all of it, but I'd learned that from cricket. Failure is the most common pattern. On occasions Land would phone me, raving about what he'd heard and with vocal ideas. That was the best feeling in the world: when something he had merged with something I did and we put it together. Strange songs that weren't limited to a band being in a room began to evolve.

We eventually moved into the rehearsal room at Terminal in London Bridge, which had the fresh ghosts of Roots Manuva on his bike and Franky's death moving through it every time we wheeled in our amps and put the songs together in person. I'd count the songs that I had contributed in my own head on the bus home, becoming hell-bent on music that I had started making the cut. Things began to work. "Glimmer", "Heave", "Forever I've Known", "Go" and "Unknow" came together piece by piece. I loved layering guitars back on the other songs the boys had too, the method of sharing giving me a private grace to not let my jealousy show to their faces. There were songs that came as cobbled bits of lots of different parts, like album opener "Child" where I played the fastest guitar solo I could think of at the end, just because I *almost* could now, and

"Feel To Follow", which I heard the beginnings of and felt a little guitar run, almost exactly as it stayed, just fall out of my fingers. Hugo brought in a song he'd imagined as "sounding like the Jackson Five", called "Grew Up at Midnight". Land slowed it down and added a new part, while I layered the end, to make it the future set closer. And crucially, while I was becoming nervous that all the songs were quite conceptual and not as direct as we needed (Fiction Records heard the first batch of demos and said that maybe this was "a concept record we needed to get out of our systems"), Land and Sam had worked on a simple, upbeat piece of pop music. They were excited about it and wanted to play it to us in person. I listened in the room, forcing my instinctive jealousy back down my throat, policing myself to try not to shrug and say, "Yeah, whatever", but to speak the truth, that I liked it, and help with the song. I did in the end, chiming in and helping it grow, working out parts for the chorus and singing harmony, and eventually it was too good for me to even try to hide. We called the song "Pelican". For some reason I didn't have the vocabulary to tell them how proud of us all I was. But God, I loved those songs. I loved the songs I'd made for the way that I'd forced them out of myself, and I loved the songs the others had made for all the beauty and imagination they sparked that I felt beyond me.

When we moved to Rockfield Studios in Wales to record the album, the same place Oasis had recorded *Definitely Maybe* and (*What's the Story*) *Morning Glory?*, we sat in the live room all day, hundreds of pedals all over the floor, making different atmospheric textures, noises we weren't sure how we'd even made them and then shouting back into the control room, "Record this now! *Record it now!!*" We didn't see Hugo for a couple of days and found him in his room, dialling his new toy, a drone commander, in and out of frequency. He hadn't realised how long he'd spent in there. They had Sky Sports in the residential room, where the cricket was always playing and Strauss's and Flower's own collision of personalities with a sense of purpose was being consolidated by the day, approaching the Ashes with a glowing, strutting "what if?" like never before.

When the England team reached the shores of Australia in November 2010, they were in unprecedented shape, with an unparalleled sense of preparation. They hadn't won an Ashes in Australia for 24 years and, with our album parked among some final aborted recording sessions, I watched through the night, ready to be fed the inevitable disappointment. You know, the preordained story to play out over a sleepless winter. It seemed intact when Andrew Strauss burst a pocket of anticipation by hitting the third ball of the series in the air straight to Mike Hussey. He walked off with his batless hand on his head, wedding ring showing around his neck.

*

At the second Test in Adelaide, however, things are different. The Australians are batting first. In the first over, without score, Shane Watson nudges the ball towards Simon Katich, batting at the other end. Katich, unprepared, finds the ball reaching Jonathan Trott at square leg more quickly than he imagined and, Trott striking the stumps with a direct hit, is run out without facing a ball. He's replaced by Ricky Ponting who, alarmed at what he has just seen, edges Jimmy Anderson's very next ball to Graeme Swann in the slips. There is a tiny moment when Swann noticeably keeps the ball to himself, as if the moment is precious, time slowing for him as he realises he has kept it safely in his hands, before the celebrations burst around him. Anderson takes four in the Australians' first effort, Swann five in their second and Pietersen breaks them with an imperious 227. It is an innings of such obvious superiority, of such brutal ease and panache, that it is almost embarrassing. Alastair

Cook at the other end, in his own way dismissive of the Australians' threat, scores 148.

The Maccabees are spending that week on a small one-off tour around the north of England and I am watching Pietersen's and Cook's innings through the night in a hotel bar in Leeds. On the table next to me are a group of men, cricket types, who cheer every run. They are exorcising the 24 years of hurt understandably boisterously, laughing at shots of Ricky Ponting, scar somehow more prominent than ever on cheek, scratching his head. They shout, "Yeah, fuck you, Aussies" at him, with every boundary. I begin to feel an unfamiliar rage inside me towards these men. I have rarely ever felt anger. Displacement and sadness and unrest, yes. But never anger. Though it sits unnaturally within me, as Pietersen cuts and pulls and drives and my companions cheer each stroke with smug satisfaction, I begin to silently fume at the cricket on the screen, at the teams in front of me. Do they not know we have an understanding here? England are supposed to lose in Australia, and that is where we share our hurt. I turn back to these men, revelling in all this winning as if it is something *they* deserve credit for, and I froth more and more at every small celebration.

Eventually, I snap. I turn to look directly at them, long enough to transmit my disgust. "You think this is good cricket, do you?" I sneer. There is a brief pause. "I'm sorry?" I raise my voice a little louder, even more serious. "*I said*, do you think this is good cricket?" "Well," the leader of their pack says, nudging his mates, "that depends if you're Australian." They laugh and clink drinks. I remain unmoved. "I'm not Australian, and I don't think this is good cricket. It's boring." They are obviously quite perplexed by this, unsure whether I am starting a fight or asking a genuine question. "You don't know what you're talking about," I say. "I'm sorry, what did you say?" their unappointed spokesman responds. The rep for the gig, a cricket fan who, until now, has happily sat with me and watched the game, has seen enough. He walks over to the men, says something that looks a lot like an apology on my behalf, worryingly like "He's in a band" with a raise of the eyebrows, and at that pulls me up by my arms, ushering me out of the hotel bar. I stand in the lift with him, escorted back to my room, disgusted at the dickheads I have left behind me, while he nods on all the right cues, making sure I walk all the way down the hall and into my room.

I wake up very embarrassed the next morning and, coming across the same men in the breakfast hall, I trade looks from across the café, sheepishly pouring myself coffee. I gesture to apologise. The man has not calmed down his end. "Yeah, what the fuck was that about?" he spits, and turns his back on me. I feel like tapping him on the shoulder and explaining that I have a deal with cricket that England lose a lot, and through that I can feel pain, and them winning in Australia has robbed me of that and I resent them for that, and anyone else who enjoyed it, because that distasteful, ugly *winning*, is not what cricket is about. I want to tell him I watched my mum die and I was never allowed to be angry about it, always mindful not to disturb the situation any more than it already was, and that cricket owed it to me that I could be sad with it as compensation. I could have said that, but I chose not to. Still, where there had been denial, at least now there was anger. I would be told later that, in grief, that counts as progress.

Processing all this disturbing winning, I move into a new place, a mews in South East London with Maccabees merch guy/general hype man Jake Farey and Nick Buxton, drummer with our local heroes La Shark. The mews is slightly set back from the main road, relatively secluded, making it perfect for parties. In the first one, that New Year's Eve, I take the party, growing numbers way out of control, up to the top of Telegraph Hill, just up the road, to watch the fireworks and, with everyone coming back down into the house, trampling the mud into the carpets, find Jake's door and my door are broken. As morning breaks on the New Year, Laura-Mary and I scrub the entire house, covered in dirt and sick, with one sponge, England having beaten Australia in the Boxing Day Test in the most unthinkably comprehensive of defeats. The 90,000 Australians had left the MCG vacated before the close of play on day one, Australia bowled out for 98 and England 157-0, their ritual Boxing Day pom-bashing ruined. I was still cleaning the house two days later, when the teams met for the final Test in Sydney, England winning by an innings amid scenes of times-of-our-lives joy. I was conflicted, semi-proud and yet strangely possessive, and hungover. They won the series 3-1 and haven't won there since, which is probably just as well.

28

Bob

By 2011, The Maccabees have stumbled across our first, and only, personal studio. In an almost hidden car park in Elephant and Castle on Walworth Road, around the back of the McDonald's, it is advertised as office space – three narrow floors, eventually ending up at a few rooms at the top. In a strange serendipity, unbeknown to the agent as he takes us up the stairs the first time, it is an abandoned recording studio. There is an old live room, a playback room and a vocal booth. One piano is left as a clue to its past life, in the corner of the biggest room. The space has been used, the agent says, as a gospel pop-up church, then later as a squat. We can't believe what we have found, all of us doing bad impressions of people not willing to pay anything at any price for the unloved space he is shrugging us around. It is on borrowed time, he continues, with the buildings being lined up to be torn down and built back up as redeveloped flats, but we can rent it until then. He doesn't tell us that The Jesus and Mary Chain had called the place home for years, christening it the Drugstore and making *Honey's Dead* and *Stoned & Dethroned* in there before vacating it.

As we set about our studio in a slew of amateur DIY, I am beginning to wonder whether the productive tension that I have told everyone about is spinning treacherously close to an opposite kind. It is a respectful sort of cleaning job that we do very tenderly, as if not wanting to disturb any resting magic The Jesus and Mary Chain have left behind. As we do, though, when the five of us are in the room together, cleaning the walls with industrial cleaner, it feels as if, rather than an otherworldly, alternative, goth-rock presence, a strange fog of familiarity has begun to squeeze the room for air. There isn't anything we can agree on. The colour of the carpets. Whether the bathroom should be painted. Where the chairs go in the live room. What the control desk should have on it. Even the things we do agree on are loaded with a sort of passive aggressiveness that sinks itself into all band decisions. At my best, even when trying to stand down and keep the peace, I find myself loading unhelpful prefixes onto my statements, things like, "OK, sure, if *you* think so, let's do that," while pulling an unhelpful face. Every time I go to open a door, knowing the others are on the other side, I brace myself for it, conscious that my world is going to feel suddenly tense and taut and cold, as if I've just jumped into freezing water. I pause, hand on the handle, taking a deep breath, before going in. I know everyone else must be doing the same. It is a terrifying feeling – the band is facilitating every aspect of my life I hold dear: all the childlike dreams being slowly realised, a family, a daily purpose, regular validation and iron-clad self-identity. I can feel the impending difficulty of keeping the thing moving, of keeping each person together and on the same side, while trying to usher us to our next stage. As always, I never stop to consider whether it is what the others want too. I just assume we are going to be REM or The Smiths or Blur or Pulp or our own version of any of them one day, with VH1 classic-album documentaries made about our "difficult times" and everyone will probably thank me in the end.

Our new studio becomes a permanent home where our gear is always set up and we can come and go at any time we want, each with a thick industrial key for the triple-bolt locked door. The last person to leave has to turn off the power in a little "smoking area" storage space behind the control room. There is a big handle attached to a machine that looks as if it might belong on a Second World War submarine and that, when you turn it from upright to horizontal, plunges the entire studio into darkness. I am often the last one in the studio, reluctant to leave, turning the lights off and scaling the half-painted stairs, expecting one of The Jesus and Mary Chain to leap out from the walls.

The session at Rockfield has not been a complete success. We are back with nowhere near the amount of finished music we thought we would have and, with our budget entirely blown, it is decided that we will "rescue" our third album by recording ourselves in the Drugstore. Hugo, always the most organised of mind for recording activities, is handed the responsibility of producer. It is hard to control what the essence of the album is, with a lot of the home demos being kept – all of us having grown too attached to unrepeatable lo-fi sounds or half-mistakes we'd made at home – and the Rockfield recording, in part, meshes with rerecording ourselves for the first time to a click track, and layering and layering with no-one there to tell us when to stop.

As ever, there is a lot of waiting around and, whenever I sense a dead end in the minefield of piecing the record together, during lunches, without telling anyone, I walk 15 minutes down the road, with my membership card, and watch Surrey play county cricket at The Oval. The pitch, which I once ran across towards Chris Lewis, has become a sort of spiritual escapist expanse, like looking out at the sea. It is a miracle that this exists, I think to myself, in the middle of all the tension and the racing and the calamity of the world outside that leads back towards the studio. Nobody knows I am here, only the handful of old men with packed lunches, keeping themselves very much to themselves. They are all little islands, every day further and further adrift from one another as the season moves on, slightly more irritated with no-one knows what. I time my visits so that I only have to watch for 15 minutes before lunch is called and, with a smaller section of the old men, like pigeons, we walk across the pitch, up to the cordoned-off square, and imagine what it must be like to play there, none of us in conversation with the other.

*

On that same expanse later that summer, Rahul Dravid, as usual looking entirely upright in anything he was doing, bats in a Test for the last time in England. I watched from the suddenly full stands, still perturbed by the chatter that surrounded Test matches as the sun, moving through the stands, produced shards of light across the pitch by late afternoon. As it began to set, a patchwork of shadow into light back into shadow again was painted across the Oval outfield, where I had stood alone with those irritable men and where Dravid now stood, waving his bat, even in defeat. He front-foot pulled. He stopped the ball stone dead under his eyes in defence. He drove with heartbreakingly defiant grace. How typical of cricket that, eight years later, England's modus operandi of reaching number one remained less memorable than a totally futile, endlessly beautiful expression of singular application. It was a fleeting moment when, for those who were willing to receive it, an art form rendered a sporting result obsolete. This was the thing about cricket. In reversal to the famous sporting cliché, we *do* remember second best. We remember them *most*.

I was buoyed by the image of Dravid, standing among the wreckage unbowed, and took it back into the mixing of the record, which we finished at the end of that summer, finally naming it *Given to the Wild*. On our way back from mixing engineer Cenzo Townshend's studio in Suffolk, we listened together at last to our finished third album, crammed into the car, drinking, smoking and high-fiving each other. After all the growing tension and creeping infighting, it really sounded *good*, like something new and something none of us had individually been pitching for to begin with. It was more than worth it, the process suddenly disappearing as if it were an intangible dream.

Given to the Wild came out in the second week of January 2012 and was by far our best-received record to date. The songs that had begun as "conceptual" and intentionally experimental were, by and large, received as a sort of statement record. People heard Talk Talk and Spiritualized, bands we loved and had aimed for, but they also, less intentionally on our part, heard stadium groups like U2, and it landed us, for the first time, as a vaguely front-running UK band. I felt it, the future I had forced to come true through not allowing any other image to pop into my head, become slightly more real.

With this, I felt myself step further into the world I'd been desperate to interact with as a child. The *NME* asked if I would like to speak to Mick Jones from The Clash for a feature. I very much would. Fulham Football Club asked if I'd like to play in a team of my former heroes at Craven Cottage at a charity match. I definitely would. We were asked to record in Abbey Road, where The Beatles had made so many of their records. We definitely would. Would I like to go on Jimmy Anderson and Graeme Swann's show to talk about cricket with them? I absolutely, 100 per cent would. My brother Will joined the band, too, replacing an entire brass section and meaning the touring of the record housed us three as half of the entire band, living out each and every one of our *Top of the Pops*-propelled, impromptu-performance fantasies.

The songs from *Given to the Wild* were, for the most part, much more down tempo and far more atmospheric. It made the early tours for it an odd identity-wrestling match, with the bigger halls and spaces often filled towards the back with older people who had come to listen to the band they had just found out about and imagined as being a version of (we hoped) Talk Talk, *Low*-era Bowie or (probably) Coldplay. The front half was usually full of the diehards from the previous years, ready to pogo to the high-energy songs they had grown up with. It was hard to leave the old us, because the songs would invoke a sort of mass sing-along and crowd-surfing that would make good gigs very quantifiable. The more stuff going on, the more bodies through the air and flying shoes, the better it was. Playing the *Given to the Wild* songs, meanwhile, meant that the venue would still and people would listen and applaud much more respectfully afterwards. It was disconcerting for a while, and I felt desperate for us to play an old song that I could feel a visible connection from. To be sure that people were enjoying themselves.

My diaries, very messily, document everything. We go to Australia where I occasionally recite survival advice handed out if you are lost at sea: "Always swim parallel to shore to avoid rips – rips are deceptively calm parts of the sea that suck you away from land." These strange nuggets of information merge ominously with other fragments copied studiously from galleries; for example, "Louise Hearman... Untitled 472... her dark and mysterious paintings create an atmosphere of disquiet where the unexpected looms large and threatening." It all reads, the dissecting of each gig and various Polaroids of band members sleeping on floors, like a subconscious grappling with the fear of losing it all, reaching for survival advice at every corner. After a Japanese tour, it is littered with pages upon pages of fan art, handed to me before, after and sometimes during gigs, in which Japanese kids could all somehow do stunning hand-drawn manga cartoons of us. I'm not sure what they imagined I'd do with all the drawings of me. I rolled my eyes towards the band as if I'd throw them away immediately, giving the impression, "You'd have to be some sort of ego maniac to keep these", when in fact I Pritt-sticked them down in my book to keep forever. After the last song of every show, looking out onto the crowd staring back at me, clapping and cheering, each time *slightly* more like I had imagined Noel might have felt at Maine Road, I took

278

There and Then-ish.

out my Polaroid camera and took an image of them, looking back at me, as if they were moments I could maybe keep. The problem was, with a lack of light in the smoke-filled rooms, the environments were never remotely conducive to Polaroid photography and, minutes after the show, I waited by the developing photos, my adrenaline rattling around my body, hoping that this time it would have captured somehow how it felt, but each time the image slowly revealed itself as a memory of nothing but the first few rows and then mist.

It was only because it was such a good time. Colluding with this fever dream, we were booked on a moving Australian festival for the first time. On Australian tours, the distance between each city means that 1) there are a lot of days off and 2) all the bands travel together. This meant that, in a moving circus of sorts and by the luck of the festival booking, we were ferried around on planes and buses and cars with my new heroes, Public Enemy. It only then struck me, queuing for another domestic flight to another far-out place in Australia that none of us had ever heard of, watching Flavor Flav take off the huge famous clock that hung around his neck to put it in the tray that comes with security, that I really, really must have made it.

Beginning to see very little daylight, playing every evening and moving to the next town, I continued in my natural fix of hyper-friendliness. I had found my regular way of greeting anyone, young or old, male or female, by darting up to them and hugging them. The boys did not all feel as comfortable with this as I did. If I walked into a radio studio first, hugging each of the five strangers, whoever they might be, it provoked a decidedly awkward chain reaction in which, in order to meet the precedent, the other members of the band would have to reluctantly hug the other five strangers too. It was a lot of hugs to get through. Walking in first and hugging, I was told, was banned. I was to walk in last, and if I still wanted to hug, I could, but only once all the other handshakes or gentle nods had been carried out. Initially I felt robbed of my liberty to hug who and what I liked, but I accepted it as a time-saving necessity if nothing else.

By the time we reached New York, further sanctions had been enforced. I was no longer allowed to walk around the dressing room 40 minutes before stage, meeting each band member's eye and asking if they were "up for this one, yeah?" I'd begun to imagine us as a unit like Flower's England. Everyone needed to be pulling together. Keeping going was the key to everything. There was no time to stop.

But with all the semi-comical intra-band politics, each one turning us further into an unwitting Spinal Tap deleted scene, we merged with continued purpose at every show. Especially during the big ones where – our entire crew woven together with a shared sense of pride and commitment – for an hour I felt us slowly becoming the band I had always dreamed we might be. By that, in essence, I mean a popular one. We worked out all the dynamics of moving between the new and the old versions of ourselves immaculately and headlined the second stage at Reading and Leeds that summer, pulling a crowd spilling far out of the tent. I had introduced a part to the set that involved me insisting the crowd jump up and down when a song kicked in. It wasn't particularly cool, and whenever I did it I could feel the band half-squirm, desperate for me to not blow everyone's aloof. I could never help it, though. It was too suffocating a feeling, to ask something of a sea of people and see it delivered back in unison. I was choosing my battles and, if there was no hugging or pep talks, I knew that at least there could be jumping.

It was with that buoyant energy, jumping bit still in the set, that we moved to Spain some weeks later, to play Benicàssim. At Spanish festivals, then at least, the headline act would play at 11 at night with the group that were technically supporting them playing half an hour after they had finished. This year we had been booked to immediately follow the headliner – the actual, real-life Bob Dylan. Needless to say, it was a huge event for us all. So much so, Dad made the journey to Spain to see it.

*

Five minutes from his stage time, Bob appears, straight off his bus, which has been parked there all day, and straight onto the stage. We watch in the distance as, flanked by security, he is shepherded up the stairs. It is an odd booking for him, given that Benicàssim's main clientele are late-teens, early-twenties Brits, prone to taking their tops off and drinking themselves to oblivion across the tarmacked festival site. They have little, if any, reference for Bob, who conducts the set with no cameras allowed on his face, rolling out reincarnations of his life's work in unrecognisable new versions. At first, we watch with our dad, with defiant pride, squinting with our ears to make out what song he is playing. It was sometimes three minutes in before we realised it is, say, "Like a Rolling Stone" – completely alienating and completely brilliant.

Towards the end of his set, I have an epiphany that, being the next band on, we might be able to stand side of stage to watch the end, if we pretend to be setting up or to have some important business to attend to with our showtime. Once we explain who we are and when we were playing, we are allowed on and stand there, yards from Bob and his band as he plays "Forever Young". The band are very close together, each within touching distance and, from the closest vantage point imaginable, you can make out something that you wouldn't have imagined from the crowd: Bob is smiling. It is a very powerful feeling, to be standing there in front of Bob, all those years since the tapes in the car, watching with my dad and my brothers. It is as if – just like the wind that had knocked on my door and held the house for a second – everything feels, silently and implicitly, like it is all for a reason and it was all OK.

We never meet Bob but, wide-eyed and bouncing with the realness of what is happening, I walk onto the same stage half an hour later to an audience that, unlike Bob, do have reference for us, and sing every word as if it is the only night of their lives. We have everything down. The dynamic in and out of every section. The balance between instinct and repetition. The band even seem encouraging when I do my bit about "everyone in this fucking place jump when I count you in", all of us looking back and out onto the outreaching land, as far as we can see left and right and into the distance, every single person bouncing up and down as if they are in one, completely unified state.

That evening, walking off stage, I can feel my body fizzing like I have not felt it before. I am not ill, or sick, or dying, but completely a seen part of the world. I have never had more confirmation of it than standing on that stage, the same one Bob fucking Dylan has just been on, watching the horizon sway in unison. It has been absolutely wild. So wild, that I don't need to drink any more or smoke myself to sleep as I normally do, but for the first time simply slip into my bunk, as we move to the next festival in Portugal, and stare at the roof of it, inches from my nose as we rattle down the motorway. My only diary entry that evening is "No wonder proper rock stars have egos."

I must have sunk into a deep sleep for a couple of hours, because the next thing I know, I am waking up to find my body taking flight in the thin air between the mattress and the ceiling. I look out through the curtains and there are different members of the band and crew, holding on, or being flung across it, as we rock back and forth. Nobody says anything, we just hold on. After one last wave, the most aggressive of them all, the bus feels as if it is tilted completely for a second on one set of wheels, deciding whether it will roll over or

Dylan on stage, smiling.

come to earth, before landing again, bouncing us around in our bunks and coming to a still. We all slowly tiptoe down the stairs, as if the crash has been so dramatic that we might walk downstairs to find ourselves in some other dimension. The driver, it appears, had fallen asleep at the wheel. Our mobile home, where a road intersected, has careered at full speed into the break in the roads. We are stranded, somewhere in Spain, for the entire day as emergency services eventually take the bus, completely written off, away. It only takes looking at the road we have crashed into to realise how lucky we have been. Nothing can save you from a bus crash, or getting ill, not even standing on the same stage as Bob.

29

Half-celebrating

I don't know whether there is a unified sequence of events that connects all groups of people tied together by purpose, but certainly, then as ever, the England cricket team contrived to forebode something in my own life. Inside Flower's England camp, there was little place else to take the side once they had achieved number one in the world, other than to keep going faster and harder and with less relent. With it, the members of the team, once so complementary to one another and drilled perfectly in sync, began to wilt internally. The unit, so habitually fostering of success, began to squabble. Who was responsible for what? Who owed more to whom? Who could survive without the others? Kevin Pietersen, now sought after by all the high-earning T20 leagues around the world, was told he could not play in them because of his international obligations. Pietersen flexed his frustration at this, while the team continued across the summer winning in a strangely joyless fashion. What, after all, was there left to do other than win some more, feeling slightly reduced emotional returns each time? They all *looked* the same. It was almost exactly the same team that had beaten Australia so convincingly only 18 months previously. It's just that, this summer, there was a small disquiet in the way they held themselves.

*

At Headingley, Kevin Pietersen walks to the crease. He looks over the head of his partner at the other end, the young James "Titch" Taylor, who appears barely taller than the stumps. Something is stirring inside him. The South African fast bowlers, Dale Steyn and Morne Morkel, perhaps the most feared in the world, look so harmless in his wake, it is as if they are throwing beach balls at him. He pulls and baseball-hits them, completely unorthodox cricket shots with no element of risk, and stands still and swats the ball to every corner of the ground. It is an explosive sulk of an innings, a brilliant counter-punching 149 that pops out of the television as I watch and forces me into gawped giggles. In the post-match conference, in a Shakespearean twist, Pietersen takes to the press muted and glum, simply saying, "Being me, in that dressing room, it's hard." His next match could be his last for England, he says.

Andrew Strauss, it later transpires, has been the subject of text messages from Pietersen to the South African dressing room, allegedly telling them how to get him out. To the England players, this is tantamount to betrayal and Pietersen, despite his innings the week earlier, is dropped for Strauss's last game. England lose the final Test at Lord's, which Strauss, years since his career started in shock at his run-out on debut from Nasser Hussain, ends with his face in a similar hurt, a greyish pallor, obviously distracted. It is the first series England have lost in eight and, with that, the subtle tension that was written into the players' body language before Pietersen's innings bursts into a public soap opera.

As we left again for the road for an uninterrupted eight-week stretch, alongside the flight tickets for the outbound journey, wedged in among the pages in an ongoing attempt to keep absolutely everything, I had stuck a cutting from a newspaper bought at the airport to read on the flight. The headline reads "England in disarray over Pietersen". The fallout it described wasn't that of a cricket team, but the same story I'd read across the history of rock music, as if it were taken from the pages of the *NME* I had also determinedly kept hold of from years before. A group unravelling. Time distancing each one from the others. Success breeding contempt. I pored over the details, looking for clues to the pitfalls and ways they might be avoided, desperate to not be part of the same story myself. In smaller writing, on the same page, I have written that *Given to the Wild* has been nominated for the Mercury Music Prize.

Tripping into a vague expression of a rock band across the different continents, eventually affording ourselves the luxury of walking around wearing cowboy hats in foreign towns, living every day in a dreamy repetition, we return exhausted. Laura-Mary and I have almost completely lost sight of each other, Blood Red Shoes tours taking her to different parts of the world at the same time as me, and that Christmas, returning from each tour with different in-jokes and best friends and takes on each city, we split. We can't hold on to the sort of enforced, distanced loneliness our relationship has morphed into and, with me spending the months unable to give any kind of straight answer to her about anything at all, I let the whole thing slip semi-knowingly into oblivion. When we do Christmas *Top of the Pops* that year, I don't stop to think that we are inside the television, me and my brothers, the way I dreamed I might be when booing all the non-guitar acts 15 years earlier. I am too tired.

*

Home, rather than a tangible place I could picture anymore, had become a nondescript feeling which, by now, I was only receiving on stage or briefly on the bus, being rocked to sleep down the motorway. Even the thoughtless evenings that smoking provided gave no sense of belonging anymore, the habit having somehow been jolted out of me by the Bob Dylan experience. And so, with everyone exhausted, I insisted we keep going, to America. Back to find that little safe moment on stage. Despite our beginnings of success elsewhere, we were still at a very low level of popularity in the US. That was still to do, so let's do that. So, now with a vaguer sense of collective purpose, off we packed ourselves and our elevated sense of what the band was down into small, half-empty bars across the American continent.

*

Given to the Wild and its bigger spaces mean that we no longer fill the stage naturally with all the sound coming directly from it, but use in-ear monitors. With these plugged into your ears like headphones, you can hear yourself sing better and the sound can be controlled for live engineers out front, helping to keep tempos steady and consistent, everything designed more meticulously, so that, in effect, we are only capable of, at best, recreating the exact same gig again and again. Playing this way without the safety of distance and big stages, we find the half-full clubs watch us nonplussed.

When we last played clubs we used the time to unselfconsciously kiss each other on the cheek, share mics, put the stands on each other's shoulders, rolling our sleeves further and further up our arms in a friendship-based frenzy; now we return to them in little pockets of our own, looking straight forwards, listening to our own ears, recycling the music without eye contact. The experience accentuates the isolation in each of us and breeds in me, rather than the desire to be completely blurred into the group as a non-individual, a more solitary mindset. How much of all of this am I responsible for? Is it quite a lot? Is it nothing at all? These sickly little thoughts become part of my daily contemplation. I am unable to decide whether I am pulling a reluctant dead weight or I am the one being pulled. It is hard to tell with my guitar playing, too, which is now so full of reverb and delays that it is as if it itself is doing its best to paper over all cracks.

Confusingly, back in Europe, while we haven't even been

there, it is going better than it ever has. Our songs are on repeat on the radio. *Given to the Wild* wins Best Album at the *NME* awards. We can't get back in time to receive it, stranded by cancelled flights off the back of an American tour that has left us even less popular than we were at the start of our mere-mortal in-ear-monitor slogging across its unsympathetic club circuit. Florence Welch picks up our award for us and, by the time we arrive six hours late, driving straight to the after-party looking as if we have sailed home by boat, it is broken, the famous middle finger chopped in half. I have kept in conversation with Florence since touring with her earlier in the year, the blissed-out tours with the cowboy hats, and our communication has escalated into a near-constant text dialogue, my days slowly tripping into staring into my phone, watching the three dots appear then disappear as she types her response to me, then doing the same, followed by sickening periods of waiting for her to text back.

I don't usually have to wait long. Maybe it is all part of being a global pop star, but with Florence nothing is subtle. She appears, to my complete shock and borderline panic, very keen on talking to me at almost all times. It is like a force field, part filling me up with everything I have been chasing down and part filling me with infinite dread. She is the only musician I have ever met who lives in an actual house to herself, right behind the gasworks at The Oval that Nasser Hussain had stared through in 1999, and she herself is landing from a few years in which she has turned round to find herself a world-famous singer. There is nothing off limits for Florence. Drugs can be ordered at any time. A pub will stay open just because she is in it. Tables at restaurants are cleared immediately if she is outside. Drivers wait to take her from wherever to wherever next. And soon, through my commitment-phobic indecision, we are painfully entangled.

Almost every weekend, nights are spent becoming mornings, then nights again, eventually going through her wardrobes, full of Janis Joplin-style jackets, trying them on and taking photos, wearing high heels and wide-brimmed hats and jackets that make me look like an extra from the *The Lion, the Witch and the Wardrobe*. The next morning, spun out and the house littered with strangers or the debris of the day before, we both know we will probably break up dramatically. I just don't know, I will say. It is too soon. I am too confused. She will be in tears. A few hours later we will be staring back into the little disappearing and reappearing dots on our phones, waiting to begin the entire thing again.

When the season comes round, this little rhythm of high stress, comically up and down, together then not, then back together again then not coincides with a rare gig-less summer. I spend the vacant days the only way I know how to spend uncomfortable and dead time, watching county cricket at Surrey. It is, as always, just me and the 40 old men and a couple of local photographers. Post-fall-out, Florence knows where I will be, staring into the strange green field populated with men in white clothes and often, the consolation that linked that weekend's break-up with that weekend's make-up, is done at The Oval. It will only take ten minutes usually, sitting in the near-empty stand, before I realise the photographers aren't taking photos of the cricket anymore. They are taking photos of Florence. I am generally just out of shot. Then at lunch, spilling out onto the expanse with the usual wordless suspects to look at the pitch, she walks around it, spreads her arms in all the space, while the players, off for the interval, lean back out of their dressing-room window, staring back at her. I feel as if maybe the county cricketers now recognise *me*, the speck in the distance walking around with Florence, as someone sort of subtly special too. That summer, me still insisting I don't want a relationship and yet in contact with her almost every waking second, she tells me that she will marry me, which I pretend not to hear, before – without being asked – she climbs onto the stage at the pub in front of the house band, does a shot of sambuca, then flings the glass behind her, towards the drummer, at a rate. He ducks and keeps playing "I Heard It Through the Grapevine".

When we are walking down the road together, too, people from a distance away notice her walking towards them. Is that? Oh my God, I think it is, you know. Yes it is. Shall I? Florence has already developed, through the fame that encompasses her life by now, a technique of walking straight past any kind of attention as an act of self-preservation, and we march past, me haplessly in tow. It stirs a horribly familiar feeling which I later identify as what I used to feel when walking with Lana in a wheelchair: people notice and then, their faces changing, decide to either pretend they haven't seen or stare as we pass. It is the *exact* same sensation, as if somehow, by some unconscious and uncomfortable familiarity, I have chosen it again. I begin to feel myself once more like a child, helpless, at the same time tied to and separate from the person receiving the glare.

Florence at The Oval.

During our summer off, The Maccabees continue to win awards and inside the excitement and validation, momentarily denying the exhaustion that we are no doubt all suffering from, the decision is made. It's the same decision we have made at every stage. Rather than taking any more time off, we will go straight back into the Drugstore, with its half-painted bathroom and unresolved DIY issues – each an image of the challenges involved in democratic decision-making – and make our next record. To begin with, it goes well, too. We set upon the studio imagining the album as a kind of *Given to the Wild* Mark 2: an image of its predecessor with music that sounds as muscular as *GTTW*'s songs have grown on the road, becoming big and direct where they need to be rather than lush and wandering. There is a song called "Something Like Happiness", a beautiful lyric from Land, for which Hugo has pieced the chords together and I finish with high guitar parts that all meet each other at the end and come to fruition like a sort of cinematic credits roll.

With visions of the last journey back to London from Suffolk, where it had all been worth it and we'd sat in the car celebrating, we are back there to mix "Something Like Happiness", our benchmark for our next record, on 10 July, when the Ashes begin again. England are strong favourites, despite last year's defeat to South Africa, having reinstalled Kevin Pietersen under Alastair Cook's new leadership.

With England being so favoured, it causes an inner conflict that clearly I *like* a lot of the Australian side. I like Ashton Agar, a 19-year-old picked to bowl lovely, loopy left-arm spin and bat 11, receiving his cap on the first morning in front of his family, his younger brother, watching the baggy green being handed over, following it until it lands snug on Ashton's head, his face lighting up as if he is looking at someone completely new. I *like* Chris Rogers, the new opening bat, who lacks any kind of force-fed Australian machismo and, compressing his body crab-like when about to receive the ball, is suddenly squeezing a Test career out of his unlikely attributes. I *like* Shane Watson, too, who can't help but get out LBW, his face a pained image of "Oh no, I've not done it again, have I?" every time it happens. I *like* Ryan Harris, for his modest economy and humble disposition, despite regularly proving himself one of the world's most potent fast bowlers. I also *really like* Phil Hughes. He is typically Australian in many ways, Hughes – when on top he dominates bowling attacks with flashes of pure Australian cuts and back-foot drives. He swaggers too, softly. Yet, in his everyday, in his bustling and trying, there is a vulnerability as well. It all comes together to make them slightly, well, more English propositions.

We are back at Decoy Studios in Suffolk, and the laptop with the cricket by now is always with me. I have worked out a way of keeping it just inside my peripheries while being out of the way enough not to obstruct the general conversation about the mix of a song. As a rule, mixing is a bit stressful for all concerned. Once it is done, that is it. The song is finished. There is no more "Imagine this, though, when it's done" or "Once that's got reverb on it it'll sound great, trust me." All the bargaining techniques we use for each other when arguing our points, and our collective ones when presenting to the label, management, friends, then worst of all, the world, are no longer applicable. It's also, importantly for each member, the last moment you have to make sure your parts are loud enough. It sets off a bizarre game of poker in which we all listen back and succinctly nod, making vague general points before taking the chair next to Cenzo, who has already taken himself outside to count to ten twice today, and gently suggest, for no other reason than the greater good, that our own part "comes up a touch". The problem is, once your guitar is "up a touch", the bass needs to be turned up a fraction, which means the drums need to be louder, and the whole thing is constantly on the brink of exploding. The

Ashes are a useful escapist point for this where, while Cenzo is outside counting to ten, I can zone back in. England, with a young Joe Root opening the batting, have been bowled out for 215. It seems like a low score until Australia bat. They look a mess. Steve Smith, to whom we were introduced as a leg spinner years before, is now batting in the top order. He looks all at sea, as if he is way out of his depth at Test level, in my expert opinion.* He somehow makes 53 ugly runs, but he is out and, with Cenzo back in the room, amid an occasional raising of hands and band members asking whether there is any way that it can all be a bit "crispier" or "punchier" or "sort of make it sound an off green" and other phrases for things for which there are no actual musical equivalents, Australia are 117-9. Phil Hughes, batting at six, is still not out and he is joined by a sad and startled-looking Ashton Agar. "That's a shame," I think to myself, "The Ashes won't be that interesting this year, if Australia are this bad."

I'm staring at the back of Cenzo's head, waiting for my moment to tell him, when the boys aren't looking, that my guitar should be a little louder and that everything needs more reverb on it. I must be getting slightly anxious about it because I've spent slightly more time than usual turned away from the screen, my private sad cricket corner. When I look back, expecting to see a between-innings analysis of Australia's collapse, they're still playing. Jimmy Anderson, whose figures were 5-14 when I last checked, as serene a bowling-as-art replication as cricket has seen, has been doing his usual thing: running up quickly and rhythmically, his body coiled with no aspect of the momentum disturbed, then unleashing the ball as if it were a continuation of himself, always in roughly the same place, sometimes swinging late and persuading outside edges and at others not, leaving even

---

* Turns out to be one of the most gifted and successful batters in the history of Test cricket.

the world's best leaving their bats there and hoping for the best. Except, he hasn't got Agar out yet.

It's the first time we've seen Ashton Agar in England and, as a debutant left-arm spinner batting at 11, I am expecting the wincing, the deer in the lights or the Tufnell/Panesar back leg moving away. He isn't doing any of that. In fact, he looks like Ben Hollioake, tall and at ease, hitting the ball further than he is gesturing to do. Anderson runs in to bowl and lands the ball on his perfect length. Agar punches it, without complication, for four. Graeme Swann, a comforting clockwork routine of all his familiar actions, chewing gum and drying his hand on the sawdust on the floor before bowling, is in. Agar paddles him for four to the recently moved fielder. I lose attention and, anxious not to miss my guitar being turned up, move back to the desk. By the time I come back, the song suitably reverbed, Agar and Hughes are still going. It's 162-9 and they only trail by 50 now. Steve Finn has been pulled by Agar for four and I lean my head towards the computer just enough to hear Ian Botham say, "It's almost embarrassing, to be quite frank." The prospect of a competition begins to stir inside my silent bones, feeling them strobing again with that energy of an Ashes contest, while pretending to the rest of the world I'm not.

Agar has 50 by now, flashing a charmed grin. Then it starts to get silly. He is down the pitch to Swann, two steps then lifting the ball over long-on for six – a shot completely reserved for the young. Meanwhile, Phil Hughes is ushering him like a proud older brother, respecting him enough to allow him to continue, a steadying and encouraging influence. Stuart Broad has no more answers than anyone else and is clipped away to cow corner. I'm back in the fog of a mix, refocusing for a second to see Anderson run in and, perplexingly to the entire ground, Agar flick his back leg out like a flamingo and caress the ball for another four. As Agar nears his hundred, I've made a call for myself. I care slightly more about witnessing Agar reach this debut century than I do that my guitar is loud enough in the mix of "Something Like Happiness". The rest of the band are huddled around the desk and I have grabbed a pair of listening headphones, a decent foil to make it seem as if I need to listen in isolation, leaning forwards towards the screen with my hands around my eyes like blinkers. Agar's mum and two brothers are doing the same as me: the camera keeps cutting to them. He has 98 and England are getting desperate. Broad bowls a short ball and Agar, as he has for the last couple of hours, leans back in nothing-to-lose instinct. Except for the first time, there *is* something to lose. It's as if he remembers this just at the crucial moment and checks his shot, pulling out slightly. The ball is in the air for a second, his mum on her feet, only for it to die halfway through its ascent and find Graeme Swann, who gratefully takes the catch. Ashton Agar's debut Test innings as number 11 ends two short of a hundred. He smiles and shrugs as he walks off. I can't believe the levels of hurt I have just experienced on behalf of an Australian cricketer. The whole of Trent Bridge stands to applaud him.

And I am back to the mix, pushing all the feelings back into my stomach and reapproaching the desk as if I've been deep in musical thought, ready to offer my thoughts from my headphone listen. "Only thing is," I choose to offer, "I think my guitar could be just a *touch* louder." After all, if I had been listening, that's probably what I would think.

We love "Something Like Happiness" but, reasoning that our next move can't just be a kind of steroid-enhanced version of our last record, we go back to the drawing board in the Drugstore. The Ashes series, as we start from scratch, continues to play out in the background. England can't stop winning. It's a defensive sort of victory, though. Jonathan Trott begins to struggle for runs and, though they land at The Oval 3-0 up with the series won, there's no particular sense of national celebration as there might have been in years past. With my love for cricket taking on a very small sort of fascination in music circles, radio DJ Gordon Smart asks me if I will be his Radio X show's "cricket correspondent". I take to this task with an earnest enthusiasm, imagining myself as selling the game to unwitting casual indie-rock listeners. It's only when, just before the third Test, Gordon asks me if I "spend time at the crease", I realise he hasn't been taking it as seriously as me. I blush and grow more sullen from that point on in my weekly updates, eventually saying in as purposefully unde-tailed language as I can for him on the series situation, "It's about 8-0 to England, Gordon." And that's my first cricket correspondent's job done.

England choose to blood a couple more new players at The Oval. Firstly, there's Chris Woakes, a young, polite, hand-some all-rounder and, more to my interest, a new left-arm spinner, Simon Kerrigan. We are writing songs down the road when the Test begins. I have tickets for days four and five when I will wander down and watch the series conclude.

I, like many, haven't seen the 57 wickets Simon Kerrigan has taken in county cricket and the way he earned his inter-national call-up. Kerrigan, from the laptop, which I've now completely mastered having just in the corner of my view, on at all times, carried with me from room to room, looks slightly off colour. He is called on to bowl early, with Australia off to a positive start despite Jimmy Anderson's usual early breakthrough. Something doesn't look right. The first ball is wide, outside off stump, but fine, and hit away for a few. But it gets worse. The next over, his arm stops completing the action, sort of staying suspended in the air after it's delivered the ball, paralysed. There are long hops and short balls. I have a guitar in my hand, recording, but am watching Kerrigan and experiencing a kind of gag reflex of *that* feeling, of how humiliating cricket is. In between overs, Graeme Swann walks over to him. He's struggling to know what to say. He just pats him on the back and Kerrigan is off again, completely alone. Shane Watson this time hits an array of balls scattered across the pitch for 18 off the over. Kerrigan is taken off and doesn't bowl again for the duration of the five days. I'm too slain by this by the time England are chasing an improbable fourth win in fading light on the final evening to concentrate properly. Even as they just fail to do so, and the team line up in front of the stands to raise the urn, it's Kerrigan I'm watching, there in presence but his head somewhere else, half-celebrating.

30

Simon Kerrigan and the
Unmarked Run-up

"People used to tell me that left-arm spinners get the yips. It just wasn't the case for me. It never happened," says Simon Kerrigan, who did not take to cricket by having it handed down through generations, or as part of his school's tradition. "My school was a state school which had no cricket at all and my dad didn't play, but it was on television at the time, and I used to occasionally catch a glimpse of it over his shoulder." Although it didn't provoke a gut response as such, the game did leave a marked enough imprint on his imagination that when he next saw mention of it, he couldn't resist. "I just saw it on my primary-school window, on the cloakroom, 'Players wanted for Grimsargh Cricket Club'." Soon, at the age of ten, Kerrigan was playing for the Grimsargh Under 13s. It was the youngest age group they had and playing with boys all older than him gave him an immediate sense of small belonging. "I don't know if anyone else has told you this, but cricket is the sport you choose if you're not that good at anything else."

Hooked on cricket from thereon in, playing for the local club, he would go and watch the famous Lancashire sides of Atherton, Akram and Co., while spending most of the time in the car park, not learning to smoke as I had, but playing cricket all day, remembering what he had seen from the professionals, taking it back to the car-park games and then his club as he moved up the age ranges. "I was just a left-arm seamer at first, playing for the club second team sometimes. As I grew up, I got slightly quicker, but as I did, I stopped swinging the ball, which was a bit of a problem against the older blokes, who just began seeing it a mile off and whacking me everywhere." Kerrigan would end practices, knackered from running in then chasing the ball that had occasionally been smashed past him, bowling spin, because it was less effort. "I just suddenly realised that all these players who were once hitting me everywhere were getting out every ball." Finding his captain one practice, he announced, "I bowl spin now" and was promptly dropped to the third team.

Before he knew it, developing a method like a "Duracell bunny", where he would race through his overs without pause for contemplation, rushing the batters for time, he had been so successful that he was the leading bowler in the first team. "It was really mad and fast. I used to go to the Lancashire trials and never get in, but suddenly, turning up bowling spin, I was straight in." He went from the academy to signing a pro contract just as quickly. "I had never been taught by anyone how to do it or anything, I didn't even ever mark my run-up. It was just like bowling left-arm spin was somehow my natural thing to do."

Awakening this dormant skill of bowling lovely, loopy stuff, if hyperactively, soon he was looking around during training and finding himself alongside players he had deemed heroes off in the distance through the car park only a few years earlier. "I was training with Muttiah Muralitharan, Stuart Law, Jimmy Anderson, Freddie Flintoff. I suddenly thought, bloody hell, it's achievable, this." At times he himself was startled at how smooth each progression had been, spending the evenings before full of anxiety, but then taking the ball without marking his run-up, bowling each one as similarly to the last as possible, making the step up with relative ease.

Rocketed straight into the Lancashire first team, Kerrigan

began to put in game-winning performances, pulling crucial Championship matches in Lancashire's favour. He took 9-51 against Hampshire in the penultimate game of the 2011 season, capturing the final wicket with four minutes left, which led to Lancashire becoming champions. Eventually, with his reputation coming before him, he was brought in to play for England where, as I looked on from the studio down the road, a crumbling wicket looked as if it required another slow option for the last Test of the Ashes. "It was the same thing as always, when I was lying in bed the night before, with all the anxiety and lots of doubt, but that's how it had always been and in the past it had gone well." Unbeknown to the selectors, the call-up had come just when Kerrigan was experiencing a first slight dip in form. "A couple of games before the England game, I'd bowled a couple of beamers." Kerrigan had never let the ball go without bouncing before, not even in the nets at Grimsargh. All of a sudden, with these tiny incidents lacing themselves into his burgeoning paranoia, he began to imagine doing it on television, on the biggest stage of them all.

"It was the perfect storm, really, where I just couldn't stop replaying what I'd do if this went wrong or that went wrong. I would never advise anyone to spend their entire evening before a big game worrying about every little thing that could go wrong." Kerrigan walked out onto the field, alongside the already crowned Ashes winners, with "six or seven different thoughts and all different random bits of advice floating around my head". It was the opposite to every part of his career up to that point and, suddenly finding it odd that he didn't even have a run-up to mark out, he felt himself suffer an unconscionable dip of belief, right at the moment he was asked to bowl.

"I still battle a lot with what happened. It's amazing how quickly you are on the outside looking in." That single game for England led to a stark decline in his form at Lancashire, too, where he found himself working harder and harder and slowly becoming more and more frustrated with not being able to do what had once been second nature to him. It got so bad that he left Lancashire in 2018, dropping out of the tier of professional cricketers only five years after making an England Test appearance. "It got to the point where trying wasn't helping me. I absolutely thought I was never going to play first-class cricket again."

With his enforced break from bowling, the first time he had not bowled since seeing that poster in the cloakroom, his body suddenly, as if leading him itself, wouldn't let him stop. "I just found myself sneaking down to the nets and not telling anyone, like it was a secret." Learning to simply trust what his body was telling him to do, he rediscovered a love for bowling at non-professional level and, as we speak, has just signed a first-class contract, jumping back into the game at 30, with Northants. "I can see myself bowling into my fifties and sixties, just because I enjoy doing it really. That's what is important, I've realised. I guess I've accepted that I'm always going to be a proper cricket badger." Me too, I say.

Simon Kerrigan – "Cricket is the sport you choose if you're not that good at anything else."

31

The End of the World As
We Know It

Only a few months divide the English Ashes series from the next Australian one, in 2013-14. Even from the outside, it has the taste of cricketing ennui, a sense of the cricket world being sucked into a tiny vacuum in which the only series with a sort of constant commercial clout is being squeezed for all its worth. It's hard to look forward to another Ashes overseas, with England having retained the tiny urn, with the same boyish "what if?" or any real sense of escape. I now await it out of a, maybe misplaced, sense of duty.

When the Ashes turn up, however, despite the lack of "what if?" and the series ennui, I'm semi-grateful. We don't know what music we have made or where it's headed – we are almost past being able to know. There are no songs we agree on. I am completely flipped out by my relationship with a global pop star. Nobody has told me to stop making music and have a break, or at least if they have, I haven't listened, and yet, every day, I am scrapping for some kind of inspiration, playing the same thing on the guitar around and around, hoping it will eventually turn itself into a universal smash hit by divine intervention, every day less connected with my bandmates. It is, then, a disarming shock to find the England team, on arrival in Australia, not themselves at all either. Something has snapped. They are all the same personnel who have made winning look like a mechanical right: Graeme Swann, Matt Prior, Joe Root, Steve Finn, Jonathan Trott. Yet they all look slightly drained. Trott, once the embodiment of belonging, whom I watched from the upturned fridges of European dressing rooms, goes out to bat in the first Test, looking slightly lost.

Mitchell Johnson, who was so roundly mocked by the travelling support the previous series, is back in the Australian side. This time he has come with a moustache. It's a cartoonish moustache that invokes a memory of Merv Hughes 20 years earlier, running in to terrified batsmen. It's not clear if it is the moustache per se, but he is clearly in a new rhythm with undeniable purpose. Alastair Cook, so belligerent and unfussed in the last tour, is dismissed early and Trott, walking to the crease, slowly and ill at ease, is pelted. Johnson runs in over the wicket, creating an extremely awkward angle where the ball is reaching Trott at lethal speeds anywhere between his ribcage and his head. Short ball after short ball. Trott is flinching, trying to look his usual self in between each one, but something has given way. As the camera half zooms towards him inspecting the field, it looks for a second, to the middle-of-the-night eye, as if a tear is rolling down his cheek. His wicket, an inevitable poke down the leg side to one of a series of Mitchell Johnson short balls, is the catalyst for England to be bowled out for 136. The game is over before too long, England beaten.

Jonathan Trott had felt out of form for a while, shielded for a second under the guise of a winning England side. Something, he began to sense, wasn't OK. The simplest things, things he would usually do as part of a natural process, began to elude him. Just work harder, he thought to himself. Just keep going. It will get better. He did and it didn't.

The day after the Test, to the surprise of everyone, he leaves the tour. He has undergone sleepless nights, crying as he eats his cornflakes in the morning, cap shielding his eyes from his teammates, before going to the ground. In the morning of the game, he has walked past Stuart Broad and Jimmy Anderson, on the physio desk, in tears still. His reasons for leaving are given as a "stress-related illness". With that, him being the symbol for the side's reliability, the whole deck of cards comes down. England lose the series inside three remarkably one-sided Tests, crumbling as a unit in front of everybody's eyes. Mitchell Johnson continues to bowl so ferociously that the fear begins to be palpable from the television, each English batter an image of myself or Tufnell or Monty or the deer, suddenly looking to be forcing themselves to even stand in the way.

After the third Test, Graeme Swann leaves the tour too, retiring with immediate effect, saying he can't bowl anymore. Steve Finn has forgotten, it seems, to bowl at all. Only in the last Test, when a young redhead by the name of Ben Stokes is airlifted in, fronting up to Mitchell Johnson and talking back to him, scoring a counterattacking hundred, do England even look as if they are ready to play any kind of competitive cricket at all.

That January, Andy Flower quits and, watching these cricketers, each wondering who they were without cricket and whether the whole thing was worth the cost in the first place, I tell Florence I can't do it anymore. It is too much, the back and forth. I am clearly incapable of making any sort of decision, and that is a decision in itself.

32

Andy Flower and the Laws
of Impermanence

"It's a complicated process, travelling with a squad of 30 people, all with their own individual issues and spotlight and pressure to perform," Andy Flower tells me, seven years after I watched through the television as his England side were dealt their final rites in the early hours of winter mornings. It's only that, as he does, I find that I am not picturing Trott, Prior, Finn, Anderson et al., but for some reason all the bands whose stories, burned into my mind like Grimm's fairy tales, are variations on the exact same theme – The Band, Fleetwood Mac, Public Enemy, The Clash, Sleater-Kinney, The Slits.

"I think there is a misunderstanding that successful teams need to have everyone getting on really well together," Flower continues, "but whenever a group of human beings are trying to create something under pressure, you are going to get a range of reactions to that situation. There is actually, in lots of really successful units, discomfort and a kind of productive tension; sometimes you don't get people pushing themselves and each other to greater heights without that." It's as if I want to carry this information back to the band then and re-present it, imagining myself with a chart in front of the other Maccabees. In the daydream they are yawning at me as I show them a graph with an arrow pointing towards the sky, reading 'discomfort = growth = record sales!' What reactions are the specifically English ones, I suddenly am desperate to know, as if I might also be able to send that advice back in time to the old me, attempting to usher my band into a sense of cohesive purpose. Flower thinks on it for a second, his every sentence typically delivered with clear consideration. "Well, in my experience, I would say that in an English dressing room you are more likely to get passive aggressiveness. Where an Australian dressing room might say, 'What you talking about, mate?', an English one might be more of a sideways glance." Now I am thinking about Pink Floyd and Genesis and The Kinks, all the English groups who seemed to fall out without even telling one another. "Two or three players will be looking at each other," Flower says, with me now picturing David Gilmour and Roger Waters in whites, "and you know what they are thinking, but they won't say anything." As he finishes the sentence, it is myself I'm imagining, locked in some perpetual state of 'It's fine, it's fine, keep going' on that tour bus, rattling down the motorway to the next gig, concocting ways that the band can keep progressing while continuing to get along with each other, still years from acknowledging that, rather than for some undisclosed greater good, it was probably for my own benefit and distraction.

"I think, as one of the leading figures in that group, I missed some of the big-picture stuff," Flower says, as I airbrush all the bands out of my mind and re-focus on him and his team. "My mistake was probably setting up being number one in the world as the ultimate and contributing to a misunderstanding when there were more important things at play." You *did* get to number one, though, I say, reeling off the team's unprecedented achievements. "Yes, we did, and for a long time it was actually a very productive unit and an enjoyable place to be. One of the difficult things about cricket, though, is that the elation of winning is fairly fleeting. For whatever reason, when you lose, it stays with you far longer. That might be why people fear failure so much. It really does stay with you." With a team who had in time, almost unknowingly, bent themselves towards a *need* to win, contentedly or otherwise, the natural law of the universe had forced its teeth inside it in that last series in Australia. "There is sometimes, with successful teams, an element of fighting the impossible by trying to achieve some kind of a permanent state. It was very sad to see Trotty in tears in Brisbane in the dressing room. I'd always had great affection for him and he had kept those mental and emotional issues at bay for so long. It was a big thing for the team to see him like that."

"I do still think about it," he says of the series, "maybe because it coincided with a very tumultuous period in my personal life too." Just as life tends to concoct, he tells me, in the immediate aftermath of his resignation, he got divorced too, suddenly adrift from both the job that had informed all waking hours and his wife and three children. "There have always been two major stresses in my life that really affect me personally: regretting things that I've done and people that I've hurt, and then not being sure about what the future holds." Flower, understandably, felt that both were being tested. As he tells me this, I sense a twinge of acknowledgement as if, with distance and on this acknowledgement, I can suddenly pinpoint exactly why the break-up of this team was so alarming to me from the other side of the world – it was there, somehow written on all of their faces, their purpose suddenly popped, each of them staring into his own new beginning away from the pack, the fear of a winless unknown only just dawning on them.

Flower, in his previous life a Zimbabwean cricketer of profound repute, is considered the greatest batter his country has ever produced. He was a member of the first Test team Zimbabwe ever fielded, against India in 1992, and saw out the next decade of his playing career forever outpunching the odds against sides with infrastructure and resources vastly outweighing his. During the 2003 World Cup across Africa, he wore a black armband to protest the "death of democracy" in Zimbabwe under the rule of Robert Mugabe and, in essence exiled as a result, he left the country never to represent them again. "The feeling of discombobulation of leaving all my friends and, to a large extent, my family," he says of the following year spent largely alone in Australia and then England, "made it a very difficult time for me. I feel I did the right thing, absolutely. But there were some personal consequences. For people who haven't experienced that sort of loneliness, I think it's hard to understand how it can affect you." Cricket is littered with the names of players who have left everything to continue their careers in different formats, morphing to a different nationality, chasing down their ambitions in wildly unknown surroundings. "I felt distinctly uncomfortable and less confident," Flower remembers.

The slow rebuilding of his life, the shifting with his new environment and forging of a new path, leading him eventually to his position as the England team head coach and three Ashes victories, then that winter of having to start over again, have undeniably shaped the man I am speaking to now. "I've had very close personal experience of associating your career and your results with who you are. I can tell you, if your self-esteem is tied up too closely with your results, you are going to give yourself an extremely hard time with your life." As he says this, I am back in my imagination to The Maccabees, scrubbing out the linear line on my graph of how we make it. "The main thing that has helped me rationalise the events in my life is the firm belief I now have in impermanence and that we are always in a state of transition, and just accepting that," he says. "Doing your best at the moment in time you are in, understanding that all you can ever do is accept your situation and react to it, I think that is a much more comforting way to live." Flower has spent recent years practising the art of meditation, which he believes he is only just starting to get underneath the skin of: "I think understanding yourself is important, and that's a big part of meditation, getting to know yourself."

How does his ongoing relationship with cricket sit against this, I ask, since he is still an extremely high-level coach, juggling numerous different teams in different formats? "I probably am more fascinated by the individuals involved and how they are thinking or feeling. My philosophy these days is that people's emotional health is the most important thing and teams should embark on a joyfulness that comes with sport rather than the ruthlessness that is dominated by chasing winning." And the England side of that winter? "I think, like anything, a strength that is overdone can bring about cracks. But I will say, the thing with cricket …" – yes, go on, I say hopefully – "is that it still surprises me every day. I still am struck by some miraculous situation where a team wins from an unwinnable situation. There's always something extraordinary to witness." There really is, I tell him. I've noticed that too.

Andy Flower – "I think, like anything, a strength that is overdone can bring about cracks."

33

Finding Ways to Say It

We still weren't done. I hadn't felt like Noel on *There and Then* or Freddie at Edgbaston. It couldn't snap before I climbed through God-knows-what door I was imagining into the realm of the safe and the loved. If I wasn't in this band, I began to think, what would I be? *Who* would I be? I tried to consider it, but like the swelling in my throat which I would force back down but didn't name, I couldn't even see a person. Onwards. Just keep going.

Every day I took the same route through Elephant and Castle and along Walworth Road in which we'd all grown to be on nodding and waving terms with the cafes and the tailor and the kebab shops, and it became clear how much the area was changing. The Heygate estate, a maze of council homes which took prominence over the eyeline, was to be knocked down; thousands of people being rehoused. We'd turn up to the studio and find hundreds of Italians camped out on the road, in sleeping bags, their squat having been evacuated, leaving them with nowhere to go. It left a distinct feeling of transience, of life being slowly squeezed out; the general malaise of incoming gentrification, which we berated but I felt in some way responsible for too, being middle class and now calling the area home.

Trying to invigorate the writing process for the album, we had decided, spurred by Land's initiative, to make a film of the record, too. We brought in James Caddick and James

Cronin, who had made our cheese-rolling video years before. They would document this outside change, living with the communities who were still hanging on, the music we were making occasionally soundtracking it, one of the stories being us making our record. They found a host of characters, all within a stone's throw of the studio: the vicar down the road, the guerrilla gardener who took it upon himself to look after the rural parts of the area, the Peckham basketball team, the pie and mash shop, the tailor and Natty Bo, the Charlie Chaplin-enthusiast singer. It was a healthy diversion tactic in which we'd wait for the Jameses to come and distract us from our stifling counterproductivity and ask them about each of the stories and how the film was moving. As we were buoyed by the stories of the outside world that we hoped might float ours, I didn't realise that at the centre of the transience, and the people clinging on, our very world might be moving on too, the documenting of a band's last effort together in a studio; a group of people, once cohesive and in love, becoming very passively dysfunctional.

With an image of Jimmy Anderson and Moeen Ali, unsure how to console each other as they lost a decisive Test against Sri Lanka in the final over, phased into my head, my own daily life was now in a rented shared house in Peckham Hill Street. People were always coming and then going out; parties back at ours on a Wednesday night after the pubs shut, waking up with the collateral damage of the evening and various people in the living room and starting again. I buzzed off it, the constant activity, the unbelievable privilege of having countless close friendships. At the same time, I seemed to be incapable of simple emotional boundaries or the word no, ending up in a slew of half-relationships with girls I genuinely liked, but couldn't find a way of voicing any kind of feeling towards, beginning with a rush of emotion and possibility before becoming half-mute, trying to work out how I could get out of it without them disliking me too much. It was hard for me to accept love, but also hard to turn anything down. All options needed to be available at all times. I began to freeze over at the sight of couples on the street kissing each other on the lips, even just a routine peck to say goodbye, as if the very sight of it sent a physical shock through my body. Unnerved, I tried my best, whether it was on television or on a train or tube, not to have to witness it again.

We had really got into our stride with our parties by my thirtieth birthday and the celebration, beginning at a Camberwell pub, turned into a sprawled-out event through the night into the next day, with me insisting "Buddy Holly" by Weezer and nothing else be played in a particularly hazy period between 4 and 5am. The next morning, finding myself in the foetal position in the garden among the rubble of cigarettes and beer, the house completely ruined, we went straight back to the pub.

After that, it was back to the studio. The way for The Maccabees to progress, we were told, was to be writing up-tempo hits that fit on the radio. That was all anyone from outside asked. Are there hits? Which one is the single? I really tried to do this, to show the way towards some sort of creative clarity by presenting this to the band, but it didn't happen. The music I was making was more wistful and wandering than ever. "Kamakura", written years earlier about the most peaceful day walking around Japan, was finally twinned with a Land lyric that made it click. The others I had, guitar-picking things, eventually came together: "Ribbon Road", "Dawn Chorus", "Pioneering Systems". I loved them, seeing my musical ability evolve, but they were all so, well, sad. It wasn't until Laurie Latham, a calming presence whom we had met a couple of times at John Reid's Christmas parties, came in to help that the album began to take shape. Laurie had made the Ian Dury and the Blockheads records and Echo and the Bunnymen's "Bring on the Dancing Horses", which I had played to death for years before we'd met him. We were heartened that Laurie described both those processes as a nightmare, with the bands not in communication with each other while they did it. It herded us into a sort of nostalgic togetherness, each of us too fond of Laurie to do the passive-aggressive thing in front of him. There, it started to take shape, the music being wrapped up with a discomfort that helped the songs burst into life and suddenly, in the room, in front of Laurie, we realised what our record was going to sound like: a response to the synthetic, layered atmosphere on the album before and a real band-in-a-room recording.

Despite all the trying and failing, when we found that split second when it worked, it *really* worked. We might still be the sort of musicians that lived in constant fear of someone shouting, "It's in B flat..." and being found out, freezing and looking at our instruments as if they were completely foreign objects, but, better than ever at each of our roles, we were very good at being *The Maccabees*. The album was going to be called *Marks to Prove It*, an off-the-cuff lyric Land had written to the opening track, a palate-cleansing, tempo-shifting, frenetic release of a song that we had hashed out towards the end of the process. I liked the title a lot. It made a lot of sense.

In the fog of the record now gathering momentum, and a completely frantic spin of all the half-relationships I'd half walked out of, I became, during this period, very committed to buying vinyl records. During a trip through record shops, leafing through racks, forgetting what I'd come in for and leaving without it but with six other records, I looked up and noticed them – perusing the aisles, aside from me, were all men of a certain age, alone. I flashbacked to the county grounds and pictured myself there, too, alone, 30 years younger than and completely separate from all the other old men, themselves separate from each other too. Cricket asked for nothing but to watch it. Music asked for nothing but to be heard. I looked down and noticed myself entirely dressed in blue, like an eight-year-old child. I didn't want this to be it, projecting an entire life alone, in my perpetual sad cricket cave. Armed with the building dam that I had plugged in my throat and had forced back down so often, I decided, on recommendation and after some half-hearted resistance, to go to therapy.

*

Lisa Jacob's room is relatively small, with shelves of books adorning the back wall and a chair sitting in front of them. Next to the chair are a box of tissues and a small, open bin. Opposite me, she sits down. I look down for a second, at the bin by the tissues, and notice a few discarded used ones. Someone has been here before, crying. That's not me, I think. This will be pretty brief. I explain my situation, that I am struggling to have close relationships without feeling the need to run away, and that I've just turned 30 and I don't want to end up in record shops or at the cricket, alone, at 70, not remembering what happened with the rest of my life. I am in a pretty big band, you see, I try to drop in humbly.

"What is the worst thing you can imagine in your life?" she asks. I don't even pause for thought. My band breaking up is the worst thing I can ever imagine happening. It isn't until the end of the first session that she asks about my past. "My mum died when I was 17," I say. "But that was a long time ago." I don't really want to go into that.

In the following months, I return every week to Lisa's. There are all kinds of theories we work through. The memory of my mum smiling through the suffering not enabling me to vent any kind of suffering of my own, for what could be worse than her illness or, maybe worse still, it stopping me from allowing anyone else close to me to voice any suffering at all. The need for me to be "special" in the eyes of absolutely everyone, alive in all their minds, no option or possibility ever closed: after all, the one person that I was truly special to was

317

gone. That I had replaced intimate relationships, in which there was a chance of loss, with hundreds of tiny, controlled interactions. That the disease that had held the house in every day, and the silence we had all met it with in dutiful concession, was provoking a silence in taking up any space anywhere else since, too. That we were brothers who never fought or squabbled as there was always something bigger happening, leaving me with a repressed child still inside somewhere. That I had been starved of touch from a young age from my mum, unable to hug or kiss or hold me, and that, in turn, might be informing my body's sudden dislike for any real, sober, intimate contact with another woman. That my identity might have been completely dependent on being a "good boy", attentive and passive, never disturbing any peace or adding any burden to anyone. That in some way the discomfort in the room when The Maccabees rehearsed was familiar enough for me to somehow seek it and need it. That I might be holding on to adolescence because leaving it would mean leaving her. That I might possibly have a more manipulative side, so that I could knowingly use people for my own gain. That I could do this with my eyes and my attentiveness and my engagement. That I didn't really know how *I* felt about anything, it turned out. I knew how other people felt about things, and I knew how to agree with them. And finally, that the feeling surging through my throat, threatening to pour out, was unprocessed grief.

Every week I leave Lisa's almost giggling, as if some knot has been undone. It is a mammoth relief to have a place to at least explore all of these things without the fear of something disappearing, away from judgement, to play with them and then use or dismiss each theory. It occurs to me eventually that, bizarre as it might sound and much as I know cerebrally that it is impossible, I still expect that my mum might just come back soon and that I'll be able to show her all the stuff I have done.

I hope cricket, of course, through this upheaval of the mind, will serve as some kind of understanding friend, and between the studio and Lisa's and the chaos in Peckham Hill Street, I am just desperate to find it to watch anywhere. I spend most nights half sleepless, aimlessly checking my phone for scores.

It's a horrible habit, picking up and putting down your phone through a late evening. I am checking and checking again when it pops up, "Phil Hughes suffers serious head injury in Sheffield Shield match." I stop for a moment. That can't be real, can it? I put the phone down and pick it up again. The news alert is still sitting there. I cannot help it. I'm immediately searching the internet, looking for the incident. I find it. I wish I hadn't, but I find it. Hughes, not even two years since he ushered Ashton Agar through the highest ever tenth-wicket partnership stand, an effervescence of both youth and oddly lovable Australianness, is facing fast bowler Sean Abbott at the SCG. He is 63 not out and in timely form given that he is about to take Michael Clarke's place in the upcoming Test match. He's in a red helmet, the red of South Australia. The footage is slightly blurry, as if it has been in some way doctored and what I'm about to see is censored. The ball is short and Hughes motions to pull it, but it gets steep quite quickly on him and by the time it reaches him, he's missed it and turned his head slightly on it. It hits his neck. There's a moment when he stutters, putting both hands on his knees, as if catching a breath and then, with the opposition – many his Australian teammates – moving towards him to see if he's OK, he falls forwards onto his chest. His arms don't break his fall. Two days later, again in a sleepless daze, but this time knowing why I'm checking my phone, it comes in. Phillip Hughes has died in hospital. He is three days short of 26 and still 63 not out.

A cricket ball had never actually killed anyone before, let alone one of the masters. Phil Hughes and all the cricketers that I watched every day, they were supposed to be invulnerable. It was hard to explain, to anyone outside of the cricketing world, why you could feel so moved and so heart-broken for someone you had never met or, indeed, even see speak. It was difficult to explain that by watching him bat, in a certain sense, you really *did* know him – that spending your time watching a cricketer cemented some kind of bond between you and the unsuspecting performer that wasn't messy or complicated, but somehow pure. Cricket fans left their bats outside their front doors that evening. It was hard to know what else to do.

*

We finish the recording of *Marks to Prove It* in February. Despite the stress it has caused, we have wrestled it into a neatly focused record which eventually contains a different element of each album before, almost acting as an encapsula-tion of every process. It is, we feel as it's signed off, a sort of definitive Maccabees record. We have always been search-ing for what *we* sounded like, or what we should sound like next. This just feels undeniably like us and, though of course wearing all our current and long-served influences openly, us alone. Hugo has written a song for it, which sits right in the middle of the album, with the words "I understand that it never ends, she's waiting round every corner, round every bend, when you're scared and lost, don't let it all build up, break the silence." I know what it is about. Nobody needs to say. It is a beautiful song – a short, succinct articulation of everything I've ever tried to say, from my acoustic strum-mings through to the bathed-in-glory stage rants, to the odd insistence that the band never ever stopped. We have never spoken about it. I only hear, when watching the cut of the film for approval, that he has been in therapy himself and the song is about the process. In his song, and his interview, I recognise it as being easier to tell a camera and complete strangers in a song than the people closest to you, or even easier to feel grief on behalf of someone you never knew than someone you loved. That, in some ways, it turned out, was what we were using music for. Will had been doing it for years, writing great songs far more developed and fully formed than the earnest strum-alongs I had forced out when I was his age, full of lines of his own experience and littered with references to the house. It didn't occur to me either that, when I eventually finished album-closer "Dawn Chorus", a constantly unfolding chord progression on picking guitar that I had been studiously working on, hoping a band member would eventually walk past and say, "What's that beautiful piece of music, surely *you* didn't write that?" (they never did), when Land sang, in one take, the lyric, "Break it up to make it better", over it, he might be referring to us.

All of these routes within all of us, trying to say things without being able to say them, peppered themselves through my life now, as I also tried to force my own words out of somewhere.

34

What Kind of Man

We are *all* lost to our phones now in the studio. There is rarely a moment in the space when someone isn't checked out, looking down at some device, half in the room and half out of it. I silently cast aspersions on the others for it, without noticing that I am doing exactly the same thing, probably more than anyone else. I wonder often what they are looking at, what is taking up all of their time. Since Phil Hughes, mine has been a mindless sort of scrolling, through daily cricket updates, for fear of some tragedy popping up again on the screen, or through all the music websites. I still tell people that I don't check the music news. It's as if, somewhere unwritten, there's a guide to things you say as a musician. One of them, it occurs to me, is to give the impression you don't read anything ever written about you; that you exist above and beyond on some in-it-for-the-art-only plane. I am never sure if you are supposed to say you don't read it, but then read it anyway, or say you don't read it, then actually not do it. I can't imagine anyone doing the latter. I try to affect this schtick – "Oh, what, reviews? Press? It doesn't matter to me" – before leaning back into my phone and searching my name and The Maccabees, and reading absolutely everything, before finding the criticism, as if I've been looking for it, and staying there for a while, hovering over it.

It's mid-February, a week since the anniversary, which, given I've put so much dramatic zest into my thirtieth birthday, passes with relatively few pinches of sadness or impulses to eat fast food by the grave. Studio time has finished, everyone leaving at six, which now happens as a kind of race, each Maccabee watching their clock as if they're in an office job, and then bolting out the door at the exact moment the clock turns, as a kind of expression of the life that they have to live now outside of the band. I stay. I always stay. I write down pedal settings or go back to the picking-guitar things I have been playing on repeat all year.

I go to my computer for the music news. The headline news, everywhere, is "Florence and the Machine releases new single with dramatic video". I gulp. *Dramatic video?* The song is called "What Kind of Man". I gulp again. I can feel my eyebrows turning inwards. The studio phases out and suddenly, at the rate of seconds, shrinks. It's just me and the glare of the screen now, the room tight around me. I fear that I might be exactly the kind of man she's talking about. I fear I might be *literally* the man she is talking about. My finger hovers for a second over the screen again. Click. Play. Oh for fuck's sake, there's a bloody opening sequence.

Florence is in a car with her partner, driving through rural England. They are in conversation. She turns to him: "So, you think that people that suffer together are more connected than people that are content?" He turns: "Yeah, I do." That guy can't be me, I think. He's driving. I can't drive. It can't be me, I tell myself, his body is too well defined. She goes on: "What if you've gone through a disaster, like a storm or something, together, but the people are creating the disaster within themselves?" It then cuts to what, terrifyingly, looks like her actual home. Shit. It *is* her actual home. The same one I spent a year partying in then breaking up in on repeat. And then to a series of dramatic re-enactments of things my memory sort of remembers. One of the break-ups, her sitting on one side of the bed, me on the other, turned away from each other. There's a short flash of a sex scene. There's another conversation in a cab, one that looks quite familiar. Suddenly I'm thinking, this is going to get *really bad*. The song hasn't even started yet.

She is clearly very angry at this man and they are locked in a tangle of sequenced dance, the man becoming broken and bruised even before the second verse comes in. "You're a holy fool, all coloured blue, red feet upon the floor," she sings. I look down at my outfit, all blue, and my red socks against the mangled rehearsal carpet, then lift my head back up in time for the chorus, as she continues, "What kind of man loves like this?" and repeats it again and again.

I can't believe what I've just seen. I want to check it again with anyone in the room, but they've all left. For a second, I have visions of myself, eating Pot Noodles, my life disintegrated, watching this video on repeat, not being able to leave the house for hearing it or seeing the video while Florence gallivants around the world bathed in an against-the-odds break-up-story victory. It is, after all, a really good song. That's the worst part. I really like the song.

I don't sleep all night, watching the video over and over, and the next day, in a sort of mock bleakness, begin the studio session by wordlessly opening the computer, searching the video, getting everyone's attention as if I have very sombre news to announce and pressing play. "I don't think this is necessarily you, you know, you can't drive..." they say at first. I say nothing, simply nodding back to the screen to insist they continue. They navigate their way through the lyrics, just as I had done, and then begin to wince, one by one, before collectively eventually turning to me, when the penny has dropped, and saying, "Well, *in a way*, it's a compliment." I'm not sure I am seeing it that way yet, I tell them, while catastrophising that she is going to call me out on David Letterman or Ellen or Jay Leno, when they ask, "So, Florence, what kind of man *exactly* loves like this?" That day, Phil Walker, editor of *Wisden Cricket Monthly*, phones me and says he likes the cricket article I've sent and the "sooner I stop messing around with rock'n'roll the better". I'm beginning to think that might be a good idea myself.

I am completely wrung out by the entire process and, what with the "What Kind of Man" living nightmare – the song, much as I had worried, *does* follow me around, in restaurants, on TV, in tube-station adverts, prompting me to respond by sticking my tongue out, dead-eyed, like a sick child as I walk past them all day, every day. My subconscious knows where to take me. I need to get to the sad cricket cave. And quick. The only thing is, the only cricket on at the moment is the 2015 World Cup, co-hosted by Australia and New Zealand. England have started nostalgically badly and are in very serious danger of being eliminated from the tournament. They follow it by being beaten by New Zealand in their joint heaviest one-day defeat in history. Geoffrey Boycott, on commentary, calls it a "murderous assault", which I not only memorise but write in my diary. That is exactly the kind of lack of perspective I am after at the moment.

New Zealand are absolutely fantastic, a modernised version of the side that beat Nasser Hussain's England back in 1999. They bowl England out for 123 and, almost beyond the realms of possibility, chase it down within a mere 13 overs. Brendon McCullum, the New Zealand captain, is in brutally dismissive form. His every shot is a full swipe of the bat, the ball flying off it to each corner of the ground, reaching his 50 off only 18 balls. It's the fastest 50 in a World Cup ever. He continues, in a fix of confidence, further still, adding galloping to his stroke play, sauntering down the pitch to the English fast bowlers and crashing the ball everywhere. England are run ragged and the winning runs, appropriately, are four wides bowled by Stuart Broad. My brain twitches perversely. I need to be where this is happening. It's all done hastily. I know a friend of a friend who has a place to stay. I can get a flight to Melbourne. Maybe I can get a ticket off Jimmy Anderson, I think. I give it a day after the "murderous assault". Of course I can have a ticket to the quarter-final at the MCG, he says, if they qualify. I take it as a half joke. I know it's going badly, but there's no way we'll not get to the quarter-final. We'll have to lose the last game to Bangladesh for that to be the case. I thank him, pack my bags and, with two weeks between the record finishing and the rehearsing for live shows beginning in earnest, I head to Australia.

England *are* beaten by Bangladesh. The next morning, as I am flying out to watch them in the World Cup, the team themselves fly in the opposite direction, home. It's a low for new captain Eoin Morgan and his side, who are in the worst shape an English one-day side have been in in living, or for that non-living, memory. I, however, now have a ticket for Bangladesh vs India. I'm flying to the other side of the world to watch one game of cricket between two teams in which I have no vested interest whatsoever.

*

Melbourne is a handy place for someone without a particu-larly explorative spirit or any sense of direction who wants to feel as if they are exploring. Its grid system is especially helpful for me and gives me the impression that my new soli-tary mission has embedded me with an inbuilt compass I never knew I had. It hasn't, I learn each time my phone with the map runs out. Everyone, obviously, speaks English, too. So I can feel smug about being on the other side of the world without ever feeling really, actually, truly lost. The friend of a friend's apartment I've been told I can stay in is, when I arrive, a home unlike any I've ever known, basically a garage with the big sliding shutter down on arrival. I lift it up, squeez-ing my head below it. "I'm Felix," I say. They have no idea what that means or what I'm doing there. A phone call later, I'm reluctantly shown into an abandoned room. I leave, go to the pub, drinking alone and writing a song on my teeth, wired with the feeling of being alone on the other side of the world. I tiptoe into the garage that evening, then straight out of it the next morning, instead finding a tiny Airbnb that I share with an Australian couple and an American traveller. I turn up to the MCG, feeling a rush through me on walking through the opening, swarmed with noise and celebration. The Oval on a Wednesday this is not. The ground is huge, four times the size of the patch in South East London. I am sitting next to a Bangladeshi fan who holds a baby while his daughter prods her younger brother's face, an Englishwoman behind me tells me how good-looking Imran Khan was, an Australian man on the other side, with strap-on binoculars, argues about the attendance with his daughter, whether it is 70,000 or 80,000, counting the empty seats, while trying to avoid the long white hairs that spring from the ears of their neighbour in the South Africa shirt. India win, Rohit Sharma scoring a hundred, as I sit there with no thoughts of anything but cricket in my head, bathing in the celebration with which it is received.

My trip is spun out into an adventure, meeting new friends and a girl I'd half kept in touch with from our last Australian tour, Laura, who is seeing a 40-year-old businessman with two kids; we walk the streets all day talking about the way our lives are headed and what we wish was different, and I am asked to DJ at a club courtesy of Anglophile music head Jonny O'Hara, accidentally muting a Jamie T song halfway through and causing the club to boo, before driving to Great Ocean Road with them both and ducking bats and asking a million questions about all the animals that look border-line like dinosaurs to me. I gaze at the clouds over Manly Wharf. I take 400 photos of trees that all seem so spectacular and colourful. My spirit of adventure, bolstered by the grid system in Melbourne and adrenaline pumped by the atmos-phere at the MCG, is enhanced. I stay for the semi-final in

Sydney, Taz, a friend from the Australian Maccabees tour, putting me up on her sofa. I end up on a boat across Sydney to pick up tickets that Kevin Pietersen has left me through a friend of a friend of a friend. I watch Australia beat India in the semi-final, where a South African man befriends me and tells me for six hours that Barry Richards would have scored quicker than any of the modern cricketers and that I can stay at his next time I come to Australia for cricket.

Then, finally, to the final, with Joe, a political journalist who takes me for dumplings and, strangers bonded by cricket, we spend a day talking about nothing but the game unfolding in front of us: a fucking World Cup final. Brendon McCullum's New Zealand, so lovable and so attack-at-all-costs, have just beaten South Africa in a thriller that I watched in a Melbourne pub, but are sucked into inhibition by the occasion. Australia win it at a canter. As I watch them receive the World Cup, while a long-retired Shane Warne interviews them on the pitch and asks, for the four-hundredth time, how many beers they'll all be drinking that night, I briefly notice that it doesn't actually mean that much to me. I am just lucky to be alive, I realise. All the problems from home, the ones I have been so broken and confused by, I suddenly realise, too, are all privileges of existence, all of them just proof of living, not necessarily of any failure at all.

My grandfather Harry has been ill back home and, his memory failing him, he is beginning to forget who we are. On my last night in Australia, on Joe's sofa, I dream that I am with Lana and my grandpa. He is dying, and she is in the red fleece she would wear when I was young, before I had heard of multiple sclerosis. She is looking after him. I gesture to her to open the door and ask her if she will come with me. She can't, she says. But I can tell her what I find out there.

I return home to The Maccabees to rehearse for the first tour for our fourth album. The London show is at the Coronet, two minutes from the studio, the gig creating a snaking queue through Elephant and Castle in the streets we've been making our records in for years. *How Big, How Blue, How Beautiful*, Florence's album, is released. It's full of words from texts we have sent to each other and incidents from the two years we have spent in and out of each other's lives and produced by Markus Dravs. I pretend that I haven't listened to it much. I listen to it every day. I start to feel that the way she talks about this relationship, the *idea* of me in these songs, is the way I feel about cricket, and if I hadn't been so distracted by the game, watching Test matches through the night and going to sit alone at county cricket during the days, I might not have to be listening to records about how shit I am, everywhere I go.

35

Florence and the Ground That
Cheered On a Heartbreak

"When you had the cricket on, there was just this glow about you. It's the happiest I ever saw you, which was quite hard to compete with." I feel myself half blush as Florence tells me this, partly because, even if the glow she is talking about might be the reflected glare of the television, I know that there is some truth in it. I'm semi-braced for a tirade about misplaced priorities, but instead she is saying it softly, as if it's an old gentle fascination she is reciting from long ago. "Cricket, I found actually, was like having a boyfriend babysitter. It was really good for me, because I'm very daydreamy and distracted and if you had the cricket on, I didn't feel pressure to pay attention to you, because you'd be so absorbed. I knew you were well taken care of with the cricket."

This set-up she is describing, though, of me watching the cricket while she darted in and out of the room, clearly having a conversation with herself as if an idea for a song had suddenly flashed into her head, wasn't always a particularly harmonious relationship triangle, she is sure to point out. "I think the level of dedication that you could commit to cricket, compared to the amount of commitment you could give a real person, seemed really baffling to me." I know, I tell her. I know. "There was this different consistency and

331

commitment and devotion to all these people you didn't know." That *is* strange, I think, as my mind flashes for a second to the Battersea Dogs Home for Cricketers I've built in my imagination, full of people I have never met, heartbroken by Test-match failures. This dedication, she continues, in the light of my complete indecision, was understandably confusing, because "I'd think, well, he does *seem* like he can be very committed to *something,* so you never know..." She stops to consider herself, then. "Maybe it was me being attracted to the unavailability in you. You've always been someone who has passions and you've never put having a relationship at the front of your life, which I have, so I think you were just really interesting to me. I think most of all, I found it sort of endearing, how much you loved things that weren't having a girlfriend, especially cricket and sport in general.

"I found it fascinating because, to me, you were quite a cool guy in one of my favourite bands, and you chose to spend all your weekends with these old men with scorecards and packed lunches." You didn't worry that I was going to become one of those old men? With the scorecards and the packed lunch? "No! You had really long hair and a leather jacket. It felt quite sort of subversive being there. It was just so different to all the other 'rock' dudes, you just sat there on your own among all these old men. It was sort of intriguing." It's quite a losing battle to remember ourselves then, to remember the sense of gravitational pull that was drawing me to the cricket and somehow Florence to me at the cricket, but without the confused mania that my head spun itself into at the time, perennially concerned and unsure, I have some delayed affection for him and, always, for her too. It's as if Florence does as well. "I do think at that time in my life, I was careering to the edge of self-destruction. I think you represented some kind of stability and goodness and the cricket made sense, because it was consistent and cosy, and just behind my house. So it felt safe to me."

It's for some reason important to me that cricket might have made some sort of positive impression on her, what with the amount of time she spent with it on next to her, or on through the radio in the night, that at least she might now have an inadvertent yet solid understanding of the game. Can she explain the rules to me? She changes her tone of voice, as if by speaking in a manner of authority she will mind-wash me into accepting her explanation of the rules as verbatim truth. "So people shout LBW a lot and you get called out if someone thinks it was going to be a leg before wicket, so you would have got out, but your leg was in the wicket." Weirdly, I do sort of know what she means. What about the metric, the scoring system, I press on. "You hit the ball with the bat, then the teams swap, so sometimes you have to bat and sometimes you have to bowl." Right, I say, less convinced now, but still kind of knowing what she means. "Not all batters are good at bowling and not all bowlers are good at batting and you can have issues with that sometimes. I know that Jimmy is a very good bowler but not very good at batting."

I nod, recognising the words as a sort of jumbled-up reinterpretation of something I had tried to explain to her years ago. But what about the actual scoring? How do you score runs? She adopts the tone again. "Right," she begins, as if she's explained this to me a million times before, "so you hit the ball with the bat and if it gets out of the green bit that is instantly a lot of points." How many instant points? "Ten." I don't correct her. "If you hit it to the edge of the green thing, that's also good points, maybe not as many as hitting outside of the stadium, but still, it's good points." Her tone, the convincing voice of authority, is now breaking, and she is laughing as she visibly rummages her head for more cricket rules. "Basically you have to start running back and forth between the stumps, and then if someone catches the ball when it's in the air, you're out. But if they get it back to your base, you keep running." That's that solved, then.

After the break-up, Florence felt occasionally taunted by The Oval, almost overlooking her house, that spent the summer producing sounds of general collective happiness that carried over into her garden. She would stand there, shouting "Shuuutt uuuppp" back at it. "It felt like people were cheering on my heartbreak." She spent that summer giving up drinking and drugs entirely – "I tried to rope you into all that too, but you'd never come as far into it as I would" – while writing her third album. I tell her about the night alone in the studio, watching the notifications spring up everywhere like little incessant devils about her new single and watching "What Kind of Man" until the line about blue clothes and red socks, then, in a state of complete shock and trauma, ending up unable to do anything but rewatch it again and again, imagining my life as not worth living from this point on. She laughs. "I knew that would get you!", then she softens, turning into the serious songwriter interview voice. "I liked putting in our private jokes. I think sometimes, when I'm writing songs, it's not about wanting to hurt someone, but it's about preserving a memory that will be lost otherwise. It's sort of saving something. I also like feeling uncomfortable, so the fact that I knew you'd feel uncomfortable when you heard that almost made me a bit nauseous and like I was flirting close to the edge of the boundaries. That's when I feel like I'm doing something right."

The yin-yang with Florence, where she will be saying something incredibly serious, that makes a lot of sense, and then when you are completely locked in, snap it in half with a joke, is triggered, just as I am refinding that little part of me that was proud to be in that song. "Also, I just thought it was funny."

On that subject, I pick up, how does she reflect on it now, because at the time, between us, it *really* wasn't very funny at all. She laughs again, louder than she did even when she was explaining the rules of cricket. "I hope you're going to make clear that we are laughing when we did this." Then,

334

again, she is suddenly serious. "Unfortunately, I think you got caught in the storm of my self-destruction and you were the life-raft that I wanted to grab onto." I think of her clinging to me, like a cartoon, and then me clinging to the entirety of cricket, all three of us being pulled under the surface. "You were, understandably, saying 'I don't really fancy this.' In your indecisive way, though, you did think about it for about a year. It was long enough for me to have gone completely mad." That is true. She stops, and smiles, looking straight at me. "But, I do think making a whole album and a film about it might have been a bit of an overreaction."

It was maybe an overreaction, I gladly agree, but not one I am at all unhappy about anymore, instead proud of and nostalgic for with the pain removed. After all, it wasn't about me, really, was it? "I think what you represented was a re-imagining of myself. Things would get dark in one relationship and I'd just jump to the next thing and think, 'Oh, I'll be different here.' I'd usually use people to become someone else and with you, I felt you were such a decent person that I thought if I could be with you then I would be a decent person too. You were the first person that didn't want to really dive straight in. But I think it was actually problems with drugs and drinking and not liking myself at all, and, really, *that* was what that record was about."

"Love Triangle" by Florence Welch.

36

Five Wickets in 19 Balls and
the Number One Record

Cricketers' hands are big. When you shake them, your hand tends to be inside theirs. I don't really know this until I am invited to join *Test Match Special* in the late May of 2015. *Marks to Prove It*, finished and worth the sweat, is beginning its cycle and, a certain personal litmus test in my own mind that the band are becoming bigger than ever, I am asked to be the guest at the tea break of the Lord's Test. New Zealand come as heroes to everyone, even Moeen Ali in his own admission, after their World Cup exploits. The last time I saw them is fresh in my mind, beaten at the MCG, cowed by the occasion when it really mattered. I know how they feel now. Lord's is too big. It makes me feel stuffy and mute. *Test Match Special*, as an experience, is too much for me. What's more, *they're* too big for me, the voices and the characters that pepper my every solitary moment, all crammed into a press box in real life in front of me. I've spent so much time preparing for what I might say if I was ever on *Test Match Special* that, now I am, I have nothing to say at all. I feel my face swelling red, presented with Boycott and Tufnell and Agnew and, with the interview turning into a slightly manic episode in my head where everyone speaks too quickly and too loudly and appears three times bigger than they actually are, I half-answer vague questions about rock music while feeling the pores of my skin swell up, all screaming at me to *say something interesting*. I have nothing. I am relieved when the cricketers finally take to the field, meaning our interview is over, when I'm showered with texts, mainly saying things like "Are you OK?" and "Bit nervous?"

When I take my seat again, blending back into the Lord's hum, suddenly welcoming the chatter and the distraction as protection from the cruel exposure of the commentary box, England are batting. Joining Alastair Cook at the crease is 23-year-old Ben Stokes, who has already struck up some momentum just before the break. He is, still, an unproven part of the England set-up; the last time he played at this ground, he failed to score in either innings and was swiftly dropped. Here, with the game in the balance against an if-in-doubt-attack New Zealand side, he decides that he'll do the attacking here, thank you very much. His back-lift at the crease, from my vantage point of just above the bowler's arm, is unlike any I've seen in an England player. He settles himself, as if every part of him is engaged, at once light on his feet and domineering in physique and then his bat triggers, as the bowler is about to deliver the ball, backwards and forwards, first slowly and then, a second time, lightning quick, relatively loose in his hands. It's like watching an animal in the wild, stalking slowly, instincts alone engaged, before pouncing. Today, there is not an area of the ground that isn't available to him. Tim Southee, succinct and seldom off target, is driven down the ground; Stokes simply stands and watches the ball. He forces Southee to stray further to the off side, and hits him through gully. He clips Trent Boult through mid-wicket for four before blocking him next ball. The *block* goes for four. Boult bowls him a yorker. He blocks it again, turning it into a shot of positivity out of sheer insistence, and it's four again.

Stokes's shirt collar is now visibly pulled up. Southee is hit for two sixes, neither out of the middle of the bat, both flying into the stands over mid-wicket. Everybody is at the whim of Ben Stokes. We all know he is going to do something bionic every ball. With each delivery, the hum I've blended back into hushes; it's an intentional quiet, everyone just wants to hear the purity of the ball being hit hard by his bat. The New Zealand attack can do nothing but smile and continue as each silence is followed by a pure thwack and a roar. It feels as if he has only been in an hour, when he half-middles one through mid-wicket to bring up his hundred. It's the fastest Test century ever scored at Lord's. He is out moments later, trying to hit off-spinner Mark Craig to South London, and the whole crowd, myself included, stand to applaud him leaving. It feels important, like a tiny moment in time, and yet no-one in the ground knows it will not be the most special of his innings, by some distance. That would take some imagination. As always, I find the *Test Match Special* highlights that evening, for the end-of-day review, to relive the innings and, more privately, my 15 minutes of cricketing fame on the radio, hoping it wasn't as bad as I remembered. I notice that they have decided, unusually, not to provide a link to listen back to the interview after the fact today. I am silently humiliated and, with it, relieved.

There's no time to pause, though. The Maccabees PR machine, which I am very keen on organising, volunteering to receive all band emails and designate them to each member of the band if and when necessary, is starting up. It's to alleviate everyone's stress, to make sure everyone is happy, to keep the thing moving. Of course, I don't acknowledge, even to myself, that it's a form of control too. Maybe this way everyone will live happily ever after and we will tour on and on and on and become bigger and bigger and then it will all be fine.

We play Glastonbury, just as the sun goes down on The Other Stage. Florence has headlined the festival the night before, I know because en route to the festival we all watched footage of about one billion people singing, "What kind of man loves like this?" She is at the side of the stage for our show the next day – the first person I see when I walk on. I want to go up to her and ask what the car crash is all about, but she looks happy, and I feel happy that she looks happy. It is absolutely magic on that stage and yet I still feel nothing like Noel on the cover of *There and Then*. My legs are shaking and Florence is staring at me and I don't have the time to appreciate it for a manic kind of hopscotch through my pedals, occasionally looking up and thinking, "Fucking hell, that's way too many people."

When *Marks to Prove It* is released, off the back of some good reviews, which I've said I haven't read but of course I have, as well as a decade-plus of gradually gathered good-will, it is in a chart battle for number one in the country. It's exciting for everyone, but for me and Hugo it takes on a life-or-death importance. I'm not sure what I imagine will happen the other side of it if we are number one or, more pertinently, if we are not number one, and I don't ask him why he needs it so much either, but we take to a last-week album campaign with fervour. Last-minute acoustic in-stores are organised across the country, radio shows are booked, we fly back from a festival in Scotland on a private jet to do Channel 4's *Sunday Brunch*. There is no stone unturned and nothing we are unwilling to do.

Thursday 6 August 2015 is the last day of the campaign. We are up early for a hastily arranged morning show in Kingston, one that we have booked the day before, cramming another hundred people into independent store Banquet to sell a handful more records. After that, we are driving to Brighton, then to Manchester, then back to London, for more of the same. It coincides with the first day of the fourth Ashes Test. England are leading 2-1 with two to play and this is the pivotal moment in the series. My head is so frantic, trying to juggle this sudden obsession with having the number-one-selling record in England, full of coffee and urgency, that I won't be able to focus on the cricket properly. As we walk on stage just as play starts, I ask Tom Clues, our guitar tech, who knows absolutely nothing about cricket, if he can keep an eye on the score for me and tell me if anything important happens. England are bowling. We are playing acoustic versions that have snowballed and now aren't acoustic at all, but require amps and pianos and guitar changes and, confronted with the strangely exhilarating prospect of playing the songs quietly in front of a morning shop crowd, I'm enjoying myself. Two minutes into the first song, Tom mouths the numbers four and one to me. I twitch my head to the side, half inquisitively, still playing the guitar, then half frown at him. He must mean four from one over. It strikes me then that Tom doesn't understand the scoring system in cricket at all. He must be just reading out whatever numbers he sees on the screen. After the second song his eyes are open, searching for my attention. I meet them eventually, after tuning my guitar, and he very slowly mouths the numbers "ten" and "two". "Oh, brilliant," I'm thinking to myself, "he's just telling me the runs scored after every over." Minutes later, "fifteen" and "three". Yeah, I got it, Tom, thanks. A minute later, "fifteen" and "four". Right, cheers for telling me about the maiden over, Tom. It's a short set, only a few songs, in order to get up and down the country on the campaign trail, but there's time during our last song for him to catch my eye one more time and to very purposefully mime, with great importance now, "tweeeenty-oooone" and "fiiiiive". I've switched off from his updates by now, though, and, sweating buckets by 11am, I walk off stage to have a quick fourth coffee of the morning, ready to sign the records before the van pulls up, like a Led Zeppelin band getaway arranged by Del Boy and Rodney Trotter, for us to dive into and take us to Brighton.

"Apparently that's good," says Tom with a shrug, as I get in the van. "Twenty-one for five?" "Sorry, what?" I say. "Australia are twenty-one for five?" "Yes," he says, shrugging again. "Well, why didn't you tell me!?" I'm scrambling suddenly across the seats, gesturing for the radio to be turned on, shouting, "909 or 693 medium wave, 909 or 693!!" The station is finally dialled in and the *TMS* box, the one so dauntingly big in real life, my hands so small in all of theirs, is talking at the same rate as my head is running. "My word," says Jonathan Agnew, "I've seen some things in this game, but I'm not sure I've seen anything like that, what a catch that is from Ben Stokes." For the fifth wicket, in what I had mistaken for an eventless over, Ben Stokes has dived full stretch to his right, to catch Adam Voges. The ball, they are reaching for the words in order to explain, was behind Ben Stokes and travelling "at a rate", when he plucked it out of the air. Stuart Broad, apparently, it being his fourth wicket, is in such a state of euphoric disbelief that, eyes out of his sockets, he puts both hands to his mouth, running towards his teammates, in dream-like shock. Broad, just as they are describing the manic half-hour, takes his fifth wicket. He's taken them in 19 balls and, like the spell that won the Ashes while I watched from fridges and ferries years ago, he has somehow found something even more remarkable. Australia are bowled out for 60.

The next morning we are at Heathrow, awaiting the final week's album charts, before flying to Poland. I'm in WHSmith, whiling away time until the flight. Hugo, to my right, looks down at his phone. His eyes are suddenly huge. Quietly he says, "Yes ...", then slightly louder, "Yes...", then bigger still, "YES!" It can only mean one thing. I turn to him. "We did it?" We did it. I'm suddenly full of a surreal rushing joy and, just as I experience my body flush with it, I look across at the newspaper racks. The front page of every single one has Stuart Broad, hands over his mouth, his eyes wide, running. I need to phone Dad. I do and, as the words pass through my mouth, that we did it and we're number one in the whole of England, it suddenly occurs to me how sad I feel. I feel that rush that usually I stop at my throat, the one I now name grief, but off guard slightly, it catches me and moves through the top of my throat and, unable to form words, I am trying not to cry. The conversation is swift. I know we are both thinking the same thing. There is someone who can't see it. For a second, it dawns on me that I had felt being number one might be some form of bargaining in which, like a computer game, I might get my mum back as a trade-off. She's definitely not coming back, I suddenly realise. Then, I push it back down and, spotting the band the other side of the airport, run towards them, tears in my eyes, hands to my mouth, looking as if I've just taken five Australian wickets in 19 balls.

37

The Meeting

For a month, it's brilliant. We are *that* band. The number-one band in England. A surge of nostalgia sweeps through us all and, as if it all might have been for *this*, we buzz along in buses and on stage with a sense of how it all started, all connected with a pride for what we have done and who we are. I feel as if some storm has been weathered and we have reached a conclusion of sorts where, in my mind, we will stay; living happily ever after inside all the documentaries I've seen about the bands that finally made it. This feeling, however, is quickly jolted by returning to America to find they clearly do not care for our number-one record, as we tour the continent realising we are *even less* popular than we ever have been. I stay a week longer than the band when it ends regardless, to walk around New York watching baseball – which I have fallen for as if I am an eight-year-old child with cricket again – in bars.

*

The first thing I receive on my phone, turning it on slightly before you are supposed to as the plane bounces off the tarmac and skids to its stop under the relief of grey skies at London Heathrow, is a message from John. There will be a meeting tomorrow, I'm told. It's unusually vague. Normally I am the first to know about the meetings. I'm generally the one who is arranging them. Jetlagged and caught completely unawares, I turn up the next day.

I have been preparing myself for it for a decade, evading its possibility every day and yet, when it arrives, it is still a complete shock. He's tried and tried, Land says, herding us into a ring, but he can't do it anymore. He's really unhappy. He has been for a long time. He's tried everything. He wants to leave The Maccabees. There is not enough time for me to process that I recognise what he is saying to be true – that I have known this and attempted to keep the whole thing going by taking on more and more and just praying it resolves itself, because I can't do it without him. There's still more to be done though, surely? We're not there yet. We're not on the cover of *There and Then*. I haven't *felt* that yet. I am so upset that I don't register that I am upset at all and, watching the words fall from his mouth, ordered and sure, his eyes to the floor, I occasionally look up to the other members of the band and see us just as we had been with François, each processing this loss on his own, together yet suddenly alone, short sentences being separated by huge vacant emptiness. It is not clear to me or anyone there whether the meeting lasts ten minutes or three hours and as it rolls out, time envelops itself so much that it is as if it was not fifteen years ago, but yesterday that I walked into Land's room asking for Rizla, him a teenager contemplating what he might do with his life and me looking for someone to invest in the idea of a band, leaving the room with a song. Suddenly all the quiet guitar rehearsals with my brother are recent history too, stitching together who we were going to be, then each moment of undulating joy on those stages getting incrementally bigger and bigger, covered in sweat looking across the stage towards Ru, Sam and Rob, around every corner of the world. The sheer amount we squeezed into time, once endless and without boundaries, is suddenly tightly packed into a sequence of events racing through my head chronologically as I sit, staring into a space just over all their heads, as they simultaneously sit with their own thoughts.

Eventually, the way I have learned a death is followed by functionality, the meeting rolls out with a startled and impromptu practicality: with a whole year of touring, a contractual commitment to complete, we decide that, in order not to turn the whole thing into a strange public funeral march, we will not make an announcement until the last shows a year away, our first, and only, headline sets at Latitude and Benicàssim festivals.

The next year triggers a horrendous familiarity in me, as I recognise that resurgent feeling that I have learned to call grief, played out in real time, this time not numbed or blissed out, but nonetheless with us all strangely muted from expressing it. Everywhere we go, we are the biggest and most popular we have ever been. People want to know how it feels to have finally made it. "Really great," I tell them all, wincing. The shows are intense and purposeful and completely connected, not just within ourselves but seemingly with everyone else in the rooms too. Through the genuine but transient joy and the smiling and the answering questions about how we finally made it, how we are finally a complete version of everything we wanted to be, I harbour the realisation that it is all going to be over very soon. I begin to have visions of my mum dying, smiling through the pain, and me knowing the end was near and yet going into school a bounding teenager. We still reach places we have never been, playing Moscow with PJ Harvey before we tour Australia one last time, where I watch Ben Stokes score 258 against South Africa through the window of a television store.

The cricket is everywhere in Australia. With a few days off in Melbourne, I'm invited to the commentary box to watch Australia vs West Indies, where Brett Lee takes me onto the outfield. I feel as if he wants to meet a rock star. I'm not that, I want to tell him. I'm not who you think I am. We come back and tour the UK, the most anticipated and three-dimensional shows we have ever put on, little masterworks of rock'n'roll performance where I scream into the air with every moment I have and, slipping in and out of panic attacks, wave back at crowds, knowing what they don't: we are saying goodbye. We win Best Band at the *NME* awards. I accept it, grinning, lifting it in the air exactly as I imagined I might do one day, feeling myself the person I imagined as a child, any second about to disappear. I'm drinking quite a lot – enough at least to make me constantly either foggy or sad or distracted. The enforced silence the band have tied ourselves to while this all plays out, I'm hoping, will morph itself into reality and the impending end will simply not ever come. Or maybe, the touring will be so good, the decision will be changed.

Through every visit I make to his now permanent old people's home, Harry has become more and more vacant. He still asks often where Lana or Abla are, each time having it explained to him that they are dead, which he hardly registers, before asking it again half an hour later. When we visit just before we leave for another unspoken farewell tour, he doesn't know who I am. Andrew, trying to rustle connection, says, "Felix was on *Test Match Special* the other day, Harry." "Oh, I know a Felix, too," he says. The Felix he knows is still six, playing cricket in his garden, bowling at the green stumps behind him while he blocks the ball in a perfect forward defensive. Then, turning to me as if to a stranger, eyes slightly widened, he asks, "Have you been to any good Test matches lately?" I have, I tell him. Loads. It is the last time I see him.

*

As the touring duties, loaded with this secret loss, continue to play out, it becomes clearer and clearer – however much I wrestle with it internally – that The Maccabees are undeniably coming to an end. Land, since the meeting a year earlier, has been clear that he would happily publicly announce his decision as he had done in the room, or would equally announce the break-up however which way the rest of the band want to play it. The four of us, in dressing rooms after shows where we have waved back to audiences in each town for the last time, move every day closer to the end, trying to find a way to navigate the parting of the five of us, juggling each option: playing on ourselves and somehow morphing the band into a new entity, announcing that Land was leaving and splitting, or delivering a mutual break-up and all moving on, the band behind us. It is a desperately hard thing to decide, no option feeling satisfactory, every day the feelings see-sawing between one and the other until, like all the decisions The Maccabees have stalled on before eventually making, since the very beginning – when we shared one tuner around the band to disinterested pubs full of yawning regulars – we decide that we will do what we have always done and announce it as a shared split. Each has their own take on a way they have been silenced and why and how our band is ending, and we just concede that – as we had learned through the years of searching for what our band actually stood for – maybe there is no way to really express how five people with such a deep history see one shared thing with any sense of coherence at all. It is best, we conclude, to go out as we began: slightly ramshackle, but nonetheless together, and grateful for each other.

I've written the press release. It's been sent around the band, a few amendments made. Then it's out. A few days after we stand waving back at people in the distance at Benicàssim, this time as headliners, on the same stage I had watched Bob Dylan do the same, smiling under his hat, the statement is sent out and it's all over. It only hits me then, how lost I am. I'm completely stranded. It's like the call from Jack ending Jack's Basement and the break-up with Jess and then Laura-Mary and then Florence, and François and Phil Hughes and all the other losses, personal or otherwise, that I have clearly carried unresolved grief into; the debt of a numbness coming back to do its thing. I don't want to speak to anyone. I just want to go out and drink. With the sensation of someone who has stepped off a train only to realise that they have left their bag on it as it pulls away, I feel light and confused, staring out into a suddenly empty stretch of time.

There is only one place I can spend my time where I don't feel dizzy or on some level ashamed of myself, like a mask has been pulled off my face and the world can see me for what I am. It's The Oval. The saddest cricket cave ever. Kumar Sangakkara is enjoying his twilight years at Surrey, having just retired from international cricket and, with a whole life of cricket behind him, he is unbearably beautiful to watch in his batting. Every element of his run scoring is of a man who *knows* himself, a life lived, completely calm, driving the ball with such beauty that, sitting alone among the old men I am now sure I am destined to decay with, my heart aches every time he does it. It is as if, when he bats, there is no competitive element to the cricket at all and the game is turned into a kind of museum piece. It's only on the other side of this, my brain momentarily airbrushed by the beauty that has passed in front of my eyes, that I forget the hunched-over, suddenly light existence that I am now living. It was all so recently, I think, that everything was exactly as it should be, as I leave the gates of the expanse that I once ran across to catch Chris Lewis, that has become an excuse for not thinking, back into London, wet and dark and layered and mean.

38

Kumar Sangakkara and the
Singular Expression

"It was a *feeling* more than a memory, just the sensation that everything had worked and there was this instantaneous reaction in all my muscle memory. Instinctively my brain knew it was as close to perfect as I could get. It's very hard to recall the events of each shot, but the feeling, I always remember."

Kumar Sangakkara is in Colombo, allowing himself for a second to trip back to 2017 at The Oval, where runs flowed without cognitive thought. I tell him about the context in which I watched him play these shots, now recollected only in the fibres of his body; how each shot looked so breathtaking, it was as if the purpose of them must have been to please and to ease, for artistic validation as much as competition. He laughs, barraged in praise. "Actually, I've never wanted to play a beautiful shot. I just wanted to play an effective shot. But I did come to understand that cricket is a game of aesthetics and that there is a rhythm to how doing it right feels."

Growing up in Sri Lanka, Sangakkara's coaching was very similar, at first, to a structured English colonised style. The emphasis was all on the orthodox. His father, every morning, would throw him hundreds of balls, critiquing every stroke, leaving Sangakkara with a habit of holding the pose for a second when he had done it absolutely right, as if to print it under his skin. He moves through the process, every aspect of the motion emphasised: "The high elbow, the back lift, the movement back and across, the head position, the finish position, holding the pose, then completely ridding it from my mind and focusing on the next."

As his father threw him these countless balls every morning, Sri Lanka was facing a brutal, 25-year civil war. It began in 1983, when Kumar was six. His house was suddenly full of friends. They would play cricket all day, before being ushered indoors, his parents telling different friends to wait in different cupboards. It was a nuisance to the rhythm of their matches. Years later he realised that all the friends invited round were from a Tamil background and his mother and father, of a social standing to evade too many inspections, had agreed to take them in to try and keep them safe. As he grew, different versions of this war invading life, the Sri Lankan cricket team lost regularly, and lost gracefully, a product of the English schools set-up that had reared it.

It wasn't until Arjuna Ranatunga took control of the Sri Lankan side in 1988 that it started to change. Tired of losing in the same, restrained, learned manner, their style of cricket not their own, Ranatunga searched the country for unorthodoxy, for players who could do unusual things, a Sri Lankan team that played cricket *Sri Lankan style*. He gradually found cricketers from all different backgrounds, not just from the elite English system, each with a natural technique that set them apart. Among them were Sanath Jayasuriya, from a humble background with supernatural hand-eye coordination and innate timing with the bat. Muttiah Muralitharan, a Tamil with an elbow deformity that meant he delivered the ball with his arm slightly crooked, spinning it wildly in every direction at will. Aravinda de Silva, a blessed talent exemplifying the hardened shell of Sri Lankan existence with a gift of being able to hit the cricket ball wherever he desired.

It was with this team that Ranatunga began to make some progress, teaching his side not to accept defeat as a foregone conclusion and to embrace all the things that set them apart. Muralitharan, with his unusual action, was called for "throwing" the ball in an illegal fashion by an Australian umpire in 1995. Rather than accept it, Ranatunga defended Murali. The entire Sri Lankan side, made up of all the different types of backgrounds that were engaged in civil war back home, stood together as one in defence of their bowler. "Suddenly, the whole country is defending this Tamil player, without thinking about ethnicity or anything. He was just one of us." A unified people, in line with Ranatunga's side, stood by Murali. "That really set the tone. The team was a micro-representation of how Sri Lankan society should be. Their access to being in that team was not about their wealth or their race. Their identity was that they were these wonderful talented athletes, who had this ability to thrill. They performed magic, as one, to provide ultimate escapism from the war at home."

Sri Lanka won the World Cup in 1996, still the greatest upset in the history of the tournament, and the game burst across the country as not only a viable option, but *the* one true form of expression. Sangakkara, fresh from watching de Silva and Jayasuriya bat with grace and technique, idiosyncratically Sri Lankan, made his debut for the Test team in 2000. His own generation contained an influx inspired by the World Cup winners of 1996, with all sorts of players capable of previously unknown talents: Tillakaratne Dilshan, who would get on one knee to the fast bowlers and scoop the ball back over his head; Lasith Malinga, who bowled unplayable yorkers, letting the ball go with his arm at an almost horizontal angle; Mahela Jayawardene, a childhood prodigy teammate of Kumar's with whom he would spend the rest of his career in friendly competition.

In 2009, a flicker of a news story in my memory, the

Sri Lankan team, on tour in Pakistan, were on their way to the ground in Lahore when the bus was ambushed and attacked. Under the gunfire, diving under their seats, Sangakkara moved his head and felt a bullet whistle past his ear, just where his head had been, and yet "our main thought was that we had been through a few minutes of what people go through every day. Why would it not be us? What makes us so special that we wouldn't get attacked too?" The sentiment speaks in some way of the message delivered through his bat on those grey days at The Oval: a man who knew that cricket was simultaneously very important and completely trivial.

It is only on speaking to him that I can finally articulate and examine why and how watching Sangakkara hold the pose of his achingly beautiful cover drives momentarily voiced a healing in the days at The Oval. In it was not just a vehicle for four runs, but somehow voiced through it too there was his dad, throwing cricket balls at him constantly, the residue of a 25-year civil war, all the names of greats that paved the way for him, and a near-death experience under gunfire on a team bus. It was all, silently, in the shot: the gentle articulation that life can be long and hard, that every person you share your life with influences it in some way and then, in a simple expression behind your conscious will, they are somehow there with you too, accumulating into what makes you you. Sometimes the shot didn't need to go for any runs at all, and it was still possible to feel all of that.

I am too rushed, too aware I'm speaking to Kumar Sangakkara to neatly describe this revelation that has occurred to me, the reason why watching him bat felt like art, and how that was helpful to me, but instead, racing inside my head to find an indirect way to say the same thing, I ask whether he ever felt as if the life he had lived was present in his batting towards the end of his career. He pauses for a second before telling me, "I was always

354

brought up by my father to say change was inevitable, and you must change to survive."

If it feels to me like going to a moving art piece, watching him and feeling that the world is a beautiful place, what, in turn, gives Sangakkara that feeling? In essence, I'm asking Kumar Sangakkara, what's *your* Kumar Sangakkara? He pauses again for a second longer than the cricket questions, another a little off the beaten track. "For me, that place, that feeling, is home. Whatever happened in cricket, when I walked home and my wife and kids were there, everything just faded almost into insignificance. But I'm glad you felt that way. That was my job, to give a sense of joy, what you described for yourself. As cricketers, our job is basically to give that to as many people as possible, to inspire passion in others. The game is not real life, but it's built on the values of real life. It's a beautiful, stunning game." And with that, like at The Oval, preparing to leave again, I have never been more convinced that sport can be art too.

Kumar Sangakkara – "It was a feeling more than a memory."

There's one last thing while I'm here, I say. Did I hallucinate seeing him at a Bob Dylan concert a few years ago, or
was that really him? "Yes! I'm a Dylan fan. Although, I have
to say, at that particular concert, he rearranged his music so
much that I spent the whole time going, 'What's this one?
I *think* I know this?' I found it hard." With that, I want to
take him back to the Benicàssim, to the side of that stage, to
repeat to him what I have just considered internally, about
a life lived somehow adding up somewhere until it is stored
inside you in your every action, and to see if it would change
his mind once he saw Bob smiling under his hat.

39

There and Then

The Maccabees decide, in time, that there will be some farewell shows. We will play a handful of warm-ups before two nights at Manchester Apollo and three nights at Alexandra Palace. The shows sell out instantly, far quicker than we have ever sold any tickets before and, now able to speak it out loud, it's a kind of alien buzz, the same way that death, I have learned, brings its own adrenaline that is somehow enjoyable. I busy myself for months collating every photo of The Maccabees that has ever been taken, phoning photographers, asking every person who has worked with us and anyone who has ever spent any time with the band to send everything they have. It's for the end-of-tour programme – hours and hours every day of scanning our own faces, watching us grow up and change, different cut-outs of us kissing each other on the cheeks, all the set lists and gig tickets and wristbands I've kept. There's endless stuff. As I'm doing it, the abandoned house in Purley, past the waving woman, soundtracked by Van Morrison putting a name to aspirational pain, into the "no milk today" routine and out into the garden towards the green-painted stumps and the twirly whirly and the long-forgotten tree house, is sold. We go, one last time, to trawl through Harry's things. There are, too, oceans of our grandparents' letters and papers. No-one has any idea what any of it is; it's all going to get thrown away. I look at it all, the remains of a life that nobody has any context for. Then it's back to The Maccabees stuff. At least we can make sense of this death, I think. You know, get all the papers in order so people can understand the story.

It's sort of worth it, the programme, if, I realise, a little excessive as I present it to the band when we turn up for rehearsals. The book is too big for anyone to fit in their pockets. I've been distracted and desperate to create some kind of perfect funeral for the band, to be present at the death, to own the situation and, like Alan Wells, to take off my helmet and let those rooms see me and say, "Look, I'm still here." The truth, though, is I am cut in half and throughout the last shows I am completely bereft, not sleeping, hardly eating, sitting in hotel lobbies just staring into space. How can I have nothing, I think to myself, on loop. I've tried so hard to avoid exactly that.

The Maccabees – live for the last time.

The end of the band and outpouring of goodbyes, however, have inspired a confidence in us that, throughout this last tour, we are unquestionably the best we've ever been. We sound like all of our favourite groups and yet, somehow, completely like ourselves. We are just The Maccabees and The Maccabees are an indefinable thing when the five of us play. The final shows at Alexandra Palace are beyond anything I've ever felt. The poetic sadness at the whole thing being cut short when at its peak has inspired an emotional response not only in us, but in what feels like everyone at the shows. Here's a place, we decide, to say goodbye, and say goodbye properly, in celebration. Every person in the room, bringing their own loaded loss or goodbye they never quite got right or had the opportunity to say, brings it into the space and we exorcise it together. It's an exorcism I can feel in the walls, almost a solidified object that leaves the room as we do. We present a completely unified front and during every show I have moments where I stop and can *feel* every single person in the room completely united and living together, inside the same moment. It's an almost supernatural sensation, and at its strongest for small windows of the set's peaks, which we symbiotically build and explode into, born out of years of constant communication that stretch back to our teenage selves. I feel myself and all my band lifted and wrapped by it, in exactly the same way I had been by the storm the night Lana died.

After we play the final notes of "Pelican", we all stop, taking our instruments off carefully, laying them down and looking out over Alexandra Palace. People won't leave. Every single one of them is staring back at us, their arms in the air, clapping and clapping and clapping. We don't leave either. I don't want to. I want to look out into that crowd forever. We stand there for minutes, encouraging wave after wave of noise from the crowd before standing still to look back and, just before it's finally time to exit, time to crawl out of this skin and into one completely unknown, I raise both my arms, exactly like the cover of *There and Then* and I see myself from outside my body, in front of a sea of undivided attention, alive in the minds of everyone. A guitar *did* get me there.

There and Then: Noel Gallagher – Maine Road, 27 April 1996.

Waving goodbye: Me – Alexandra Palace, 1 July 2017.

40

The Healing Game

I t is possible, I am told, to grieve at any stage after a
death. For some, it requires the life you have built since
to crumble away, in order for you to register the first loss
you are trying to escape. There is no dodging it or slipping
away. It will get you eventually.

*

In time, caught between the fading memory of who I have
so recently been and sprung back to contend with delayed
teenage grief, I spend the next year surprisingly pleasurably
adrift. I do radio shows for John Kennedy, who I listened to
as a teenager, taping his album playbacks on *X-Posure* before
clambering over the alphabetised CDs to stare into those
trees, a show The Maccabees had later been a part of, trying
on all the band-type quotes for size. Being the host of his
show on occasion is a welcome distraction, where at first I
am disturbed by my inability to speak incredibly straightfor-
ward sentences under pressure; then I slip into a general state
of buzz with licence to talk as enthusiastically as I like about
records into the late hours of the night. I begin a record label,
Yala!, named after the repeated Arabic word Abla would
shout at me and Harry to stop our cricket in the sprawled-out
garden, beckoning us inside. We put out seven-inch records
with new artists just to see if we can get them some attention,

my co-founder Morad Khokar dragging me along with a new sense of optimism: *Yala* was a phrase his mother, from Morocco, had used at him too. We put on monthly nights at Jake's new club, Bermondsey Social Club, making big cut-out letters of "YALA!" that I spend all day sticking up on the walls, watching them fall down and resticking them with hundreds of bits of double-sided tape, while soundchecking new bands that I love and am in sudden awe of. I can't fathom how I had so recently done what they are doing.

Scurrying around in an extremely spit-and-sawdust type way, the nights become full-scale, into-the-small-hours parties and it is as if a switch clicks in my head late in the evenings. Full of relief and new responsibility as a sort of indie music club host, celebrating my birthday one year and receiving a cake, I decide to throw it across the club. I wake up, foggy and fulfilled, trying to work out who that person was. With Lisa, back in therapy, we discuss it and I choose to allow the teenager, who was starved of the petty squabbles that defined most of my friends' childhoods, to do what he needs to. Maybe I need consequence-free play, she says, and in the flux of pleasurably adrift unimportance, I let myself do just that, even if it means throwing cake across clubs in my thirties.

In the midst of experiencing my living self on the other side of my self-built purpose, I imagine all of the cricketers, too, on the other side of their own careers. Suddenly the Battersea Dogs Home for Cricketers in my mind is empty. The Marks and the Martins and Chris Read and the rest of them probably aren't there waiting, suspended in time, I realise. Who am I to quantify and project this sadness onto them? They might be better off without the cricket.

I try to limit, with inconsistent success, late-night private searching for old Maccabees gigs and interviews on the internet, gradually attempting to let that person go, and take to, as a sort of nicotine patch, staring at my face in the mirror for long periods, poking it and stretching out all the places that suddenly have deep-set lines that I hadn't noticed before. Tucking in where my chin appears to suddenly be slightly doubled, it feels as if age has been stealthily hiding for decades and has then suddenly attacked, while I try to find some relationship with the new person I am, who looks unusually weathered. I notice the very slight hints of my grandmother's Palestinian face, understanding suddenly how a face evolves, life marking itself across it, forcing out all the ugly parts that you've tried so hard to hide, and bringing out an essence of all the people you have known, until it becomes impossible to hide any of it.

I spend some time learning how to write, sent off on little missions by Phil Walker at *Wisden Cricket Monthly* to talk to people about their love of cricket. I tell Gary Neville that the Manchester United team were like the Australian team in my memory: horrible, horrible winners. He laughs and says that cricket toughened him up more than football, having to play with men twice his size from an early age. Musician Nadine Shah, sitting down the road from a snow-covered Oval, tells me that cricket helped her access her parents' Pakistani heritage, giving her a direct connection with their home that she otherwise struggled to find. The feature pieces that I am using as a rope to connect where my life is leading, through conversations solely and safely about how great cricket is, take me to the actor Toby Jones, writers Kamila Shamsie and Sebastian Faulks, Radiohead's Ed O'Brien, composer John Altman, politician Ed Miliband (who asks about The Maccabees split, gently consoling me before saying, "You should try losing a general election") and more until I am beginning to build a new picture of myself, a sort of roving reporter living the alternative life to the rock star that maybe – I can't really remember anymore – I actually was.

At times feeling unnervingly like the waving woman on that journey, happy because, well, why not, I am asked by

Radio 1 host Greg James, whose shows we used to appear on, if I want to do a BBC cricket podcast with him and Jimmy Anderson. It could maybe be called something like *Tailenders*, he says.

It takes me a second to square in my head that the actual Jimmy Anderson I've watched bowl for all those years is up for talking about cricket, or anything else, every week with me. Receiving a call from a listener on our third show, a Bristolian shoe salesman, Matt, who claims to be related to Sachin Tendulkar but dislikes cricket, our show is spun into an ongoing saga and little pockets of loosely cricket-based hilarity that I begin to look forward to every week; knowing I will leave with my endorphins kicked into being, struggling for breath from laughing so much, the newly christened "Mattchin Tendulkar" more of a cult cricketing icon with every passing week. Hugo and Sam, a little reluctantly at first, eventually become the show's "live band", chiming in on all things non-cricket related and glazing over otherwise. Between that, and the *Wisden* writing, I head back to Australia for the Ashes, this time as a cricket writer.

*

I open my laptop at the Melbourne Cricket Ground. New document. Open. I stare at the blank page, freshly entitled "MCG Day One". Behind it, there is the Melbourne Cricket Ground in all its glory, through a pane of glass, left open just a touch so that the sound of the 90,000 people in there for the famous Boxing Day Test match, the classic hum that I have been lost and disturbed by at times and saved and encircled in at others, can waft in. All the people who write all the words I inhale every day are here, all in physical proximity. Am I a cricket writer now? Like, a real-life one? I'm suddenly actually inside the world, a universe where I am far and away the last person imaginarily batting with a banana or whatever else I can find; here everyone is doing it, picking up pens and rehearsing forward-defensive shots, Michael Atherton spinning an apple, everyone picking up stationery or fruit and nudging or nurdling or ripping the ball, nibbling it off the seam.

There's a rhythm, too, which, being on the inside but feeling as if I'm from the outside, I can observe. The way the morning session of a Test match is treated as a kind of social, people firing chat across each other, restless in their chairs, the English writing staff repeating the word ominous as Australia build an opening partnership on a flat wicket. Then, the slow intensifying of the day, where you can sense each writer beginning to formulate what their unique take on the play is going to be, before, eventually, as the last session nears its conclusion, there is a total silence, as if everyone is sitting an examination, the tap, tap, tapping ruminating through the room while writers anxiously flit between their computer and the game; after all, the story of the day can still be completely changed by the last ball. When it is over, I come to from the information overload and look back at my laptop. "MCG Day One." The page is exactly as I left it. Distracted by the presence of all the people writing the articles I will be reading tomorrow, I have not written one word.

The cricket media, I find out in a hurry, drink a lot more than bands do, and the three-week trip, to watch England eventually beaten 4-0, mainly involves drinking. It's in the pubs and bars, sofa-surfing between bizarre Airbnb spots that have swingers' fancy-dress parties in the back garden, or a hanging Elmo costume suddenly appearing in darkened alleyways, watching writers finish pieces while they finish drinks, generally drifting along in a sun-kissed content, that I register a new truth. People absolutely *do not* respond to you the same way when you are in a band as, when introduced, you tell them you are a cricket writer. The platform with which I could perform my social "I'm just a normal, nice guy" schtick, with the safety of them knowing that I was *really* in a big band, so I was very special actually, is completely eroded when a stranger asks and I say, "I'm writing about cricket..." I watch face upon face upon face glaze over and sigh at myself in my head, me being just a cricket writer with a match report that is completely blank.

*

Eoin Morgan, meanwhile, some years on since the World Cup exit that I had flown out to meet them on as they flew back, has been building a new one-day side in his own image. Taking their lead from the New Zealand that had dealt them their "murderous assault" then, Morgan has set about finding new criteria for his team. Himself Irish, he has looked for an English side characteristically un-English, for cricketers who will set about their task, driven not by failure, but by belief, unafraid to innovate and invent, to stretch the game to places people didn't know it could go. Packing the team full of hitters of infinite variety, all of them capable of shots and feats far beyond any England team yet, they beat everyone in the world, harmonised with miserly bowlers who ask constant questions of opposition teams, calm and calculated.

As the one-day team builds a foreign anticipation into the cricketing public, I feel a strange sensation developing in my relationship with the game. Whereas I always used to feel like it was me pouring life into cricket, a void that didn't ask anything back, channelling loss on loss through these men who so publicly had to deal with it every day, I now begin to think of it as a conscious, living thing that has begun to symbiotically steady the course of my life, protect me and move me forwards. *Tailenders* is teaching me to bring a flippancy to my world, making me see that overthinking everything is not always necessary, and I start to go to nets and bowl again, re-accessing the child who I had decided to let play once more. With that, too, as if the game is picking each piece of my life back up and handing it to me, film director Barney Douglas contacts me asking whether I'd like to make the music for a film he is making called *The Edge*, about Andy Flower's England team. It is about the cost of greatness and the residual damage of what it took to play for England in the fallout, he says, and he thinks I might relate to it. I spend months watching scenes of Jonathan Trott discussing his confidence leaving him and, across beautifully cinematic scenes where Trott is submerged under water or stranded in a field, with an urban electric storm overlooking it, I make music to meet it.

It is my responsibility, I decide, to punctuate all the feelings I attached to cricket for so long, and to suggest them, subtly or otherwise, so that anyone might understand what they felt like to me: human stories about success and failure and our inevitable impermanence no matter who we are. I remember the ferry where I watched Monty and Jimmy save a Test and make woozy synth music to the same moment. Me and Sam, reconnected through having a project to work on, re-imagine Kevin Pietersen's innings against South Africa in the style of *The Jungle Book*, Sam performing a wild, unrestrained drum solo which we accompany with brass and string instrumentation through flashes of every shot. Andrew Strauss, at the end of the film, tells the audience, "In some ways, the things you hated the most are the things you miss the most; the pressure, the scrutiny, that's what you miss, because it makes you feel alive." When I see the scene, I play a guitar line: semi-hopeful and semi-sad, a motif emerging without instruction from my brain, that when I look back, my hands moving without being asked to and finishing the music, I recognise as a part of myself, saying goodbye reluctantly to a dream and hopeful of what is next.

At the film première, I pose in the team photo with the entire England squad, the world number-one side I had invested so much of my life in, just on the edge, smiling as if, for a second, to an unaware stranger, I might look as if I *was* actually in that England team.

England Ashes winners, from left to right: White, Swann, Douglas, Anderson, Collingwood, Panesar, Bresnan, Bell.

41

Acceptance

In the clearing of the new and as the hurt dissipates, it feels as if the time the multiple sclerosis had taken to bring about my mum's death has had to play out again in its entirety, before any of us could process it. Back from our long journeys back to the surface, we tentatively bring her up more regularly in conversation, not a lot, but enough that it is no longer a leaden heaviness in the room and these small moments of conversation, in turn, help erase part of the guilt I have forever been harbouring in my mind. My dad tells me that the evening I put my head around the corner, on 5 February after Oasis, just before she died – the visit I had hated myself for because it was so brief and so distracted – had for a moment cut through all the pain Lana was feeling. Her son enjoying life so much washed away any hurt in her, he says, and it was possibly the single most powerful thing he'd ever seen. He'd turned to her after I left the room, saying, "Do you remember the day he was born, Lana?" and she'd nodded, both of them brought back to the joy of the birth of their first child, that she had insisted was at home and not in hospital. With this knowledge, I let go of all the guilt that had persistently plagued me since being pulled away by music and cricket, reframing the moment as an altogether different experience: a gift back to my mother, who had taught me to go into the world and live in it properly, just as her strength and dignity in the face of the disease's last act was its own lesson then. I find an email from my dad years earlier, sent to us all as The Maccabees were on tour, and I now re-read it to myself, affording myself the space to understand it.

I just wanted to send you this image which may be difficult, but I do get a strangely beautiful connection from visiting Mum's grave. As I am sure you know, Friday is the 13th year of Mum's death. That day time really did seem to take on a different dimension and I always remember how strong you were – such a credit to yourselves and Lana. The most difficult issue for Lana was knowing she would not be able to be with you as you all grew up and entered adult life – Mum wanted to be with you more than anything. She loved you so much. She would be so proud of the way you have managed so well with all you have had to cope with and all you have achieved, you are all so creative and work so hard and are such good thoughtful young men – all Lana would have hoped for, she would have really enjoyed your music and your sense of fun. Lana is never far from my mind and am sure never far from yours – she gave us so much love and these things never leave us. I am also very proud of you all and hope my love also stays with you.

42

Jos Buttler, the World Cup
and All the Life Beyond

t the 2019 World Cup, against a backdrop of a politically divided England, it becomes clear that Eoin Morgan's team stand for more than just self-belief. The captain from Ireland, Jofra Archer from Barbados, Adil Rashid and Moeen Ali of Muslim faith from Pakistani heritage, Ben Stokes born in New Zealand, Jason Roy born in South Africa, Liam Plunkett with his American passport and Yorkshireman Jonny Bairstow in the mould of his father, a professional cricketer who struggled with depression after his retirement and was found hanging by the bannisters at home when Jonny was young. They are an assembly of back-stories from every type of background imaginable, all unified in one cricket team.

They reach the final, fittingly against New Zealand. It is a morning of prickly, close heat that is just on the border between summer and the change and is riddled with tense excitement. *Tailenders* records live in the hour before the game, just before *Test Match Special* takes over the airwaves for the day and, sitting looking over the outfield at Lord's before the actual World Cup final, we broadcast our show. How am I inside the frequency that has hummed at my constant existence, suddenly looking back at it from the inside out, I ask myself. We finish, I leave my guitar in the *TMS* studio and we take to the nursery out-ground where the game is on the big screen, to drink and watch New Zealand bat. England are smart and savvy, the pitch slightly sticky, and they restrict New Zealand to 241. It's just nine short of what Postman Pat's Greendale restricted their opposition to in what is quickly becoming the second most important cricket match in my life after the one in progress.

It is halfway through the run chase, with England stuttering at 86-4, Jos Buttler new to the crease, joining Ben Stokes, when I privately notice a joyful lightness. I am not secretly hoping that England lose. There is no harbouring of a silent desire that I need England to be beaten in order to feel unification with the world around me, all heads in our hands asking what we do with the England team. In fact, I desperately want us to win. It's as if I am suddenly filled with a bubbly simplicity, my inner feelings actually aligned with the words coming out of my mouth; I genuinely want this to happen. As I quietly acknowledge this epiphany, one not unlike Adam Hollioake realising that without Ben happiness could still come from simply recognising it, Lord's suddenly becomes very tense. Jos Buttler and Ben Stokes know that it will be down to them to chase the majority of the runs, and they set about it together.

A focus is harnessed everywhere and, as I had been with Atherton and Donald decades earlier, *everyone* in the ground is suddenly switching on and off, as if they themselves are preparing for each ball, with a bizarre sense that out of the gates, the rest of the country, the world even, is watching too. The game, for the first time since 2005, has been put on terrestrial television. On the big screen we can see that Trafalgar Square is full; households, cricket enthusiasts or otherwise, are all connected by this *event*. Unlike Chris Lewis's friends 24 years earlier, none of them even have to get up in the middle of the night. There can be nothing in the world more important than what is happening right now for anyone and, the same way I would stand by the stage and inhale the sound of everyone clashing together for one shared purpose, thousands of lives aligning to share in one feeling, it somehow is calming. There is no-one else to be than myself, here, genuinely wanting to win, inside this ground.

Ben Stokes drags England closer and closer. Every incident is barely believable, a game of unprecedented drama unfolding and, with the scores tied, a *super over* is in progress. Cricket is like *The White Album*: after all these years, somehow better than it ever was. It's come to one final moment. New Zealand need two off the final ball. Anything less and England have won the World Cup. I can feel tears swilling underneath my eyes, as if there is no life beyond this moment, no future or past, just a game of cricket which means everything to everyone. Over, just to our left, Archer runs in to bowl. My heart is pounding, pounding, pounding, forcing itself through my reddened eyes. He arrives at the crease. The ball is full, overpitched, and Martin Guptill forces it away on the leg side, towards Jason Roy. Time, for a moment, is so stretched that every motion Roy makes, every ripple in his kit against the wind as he goes to receive the ball, is thick in the air. He picks it up cleanly and throws it in. Jos Buttler is waiting behind the stumps, Guptill running for the second. The throw is not quite accurate and Buttler has to move a few feet to his right to retrieve it. Guptill, a few yards short of his crease and noticing how close the ball is to reaching Buttler's gloves, is now diving. The ball reaches Buttler and, as he takes it and stretches out to his left, the whole of the crowd, as one, move with him, motioning the ball to the stumps. Guptill, his bat outstretched, is still not in his ground. Buttler is outstretched too, gloves first, the ball inside them, breaking the bails.

Like an explosion of camera film, taut and then suddenly unwinding itself, Buttler is running away, throwing the ball

Jos Buttler – breaking the bails.

in the air, then his gloves into the sky as well. I catch him in my eyeline for a second, being submerged by his teammates, just before I feel myself going under too, becoming a mesh with bodies, of random hands around my face and different strangers' voices in my ear.

"I know it's easy to say after it's happened, but I think it was destiny, it just feels like it was always meant to happen," Jos Buttler says, recalling his iconic run-out. "I've never felt anything like it."

While the team are queuing on the outfield to pick up their medals, he tells me, just unmeshed from each other too, Jonny Bairstow is standing in front of him. Amid all the chaos, Jos notices that Jonny is separated slightly, inside this moment of reaching a pinnacle, in some way reflective and sad. "I could just sense that he was in his own little world, looking off into the distance." He stops for a moment. "I knew who he was thinking about." Jos, without predetermining it, feels himself turn to Jonny and says, "Jonny, your dad would be so proud of you."

Jos pauses now, reflecting on this two years later, as if it still surprises him, still unsure whether this moment of private grief should have been left to Jonny alone, unvoiced. Then he says, in a tone of gentle vindication, "But I'm glad I said it. It was a really proud, happy thing. I think it's good to normalise these things."

As he tells me this, it's as if I can relocate myself at that exact moment in time, the other side of the rope, somewhere slowly surfacing with – like every single other person surfacing too – my own loaded understanding of what this cricket match has just meant. In that tiny moment of complete liberation, it was as if nobody need ever again answer the question why cricket was important; it was all in that congregated feeling – a whole sport turned back to reward all those who had poured themselves endlessly into it. And all of us, as young as we ever would be, for a moment belonging to each other in a far deeper way than just strangers, suspended in bundles of escape before we remembered ourselves, silently acknowledging our own lists of people who we wish could have seen it too, re-entered London. The same London, dark and layered and mean, that slowly broke us apart again, our finality dissipating back into the streets, yet each of us rejoining with a sense that on the other side, the next part of all our lives would, this time, somehow be different.

The End.

Picture Acknowledgements

Courtesy of Felix White 3, 12, 20 above, 20 below, 33, 62, 121 above, 121 below, 121, 150, 260, 291; Courtesy of Florence Welch 335; Courtesy of Reuben Gotto 360 below; Sam Neill 358; Alamy Stock Photo PA Photos 73; Doc Foster Photography Tom Foster 198; Getty Images Patrick Eagar/Popperfoto 142, Samir Hussein 283, Andrew Benge/Redferns 279, Andy Kearns 374, Bob Thomas 41, Charlie Crowhurst 355, Clint Hughes 302, Clive Mason 117, Daily Mirror/Mirrorpix 16, Dave J Hogan for Noah X 368, David Munden/Popperfoto 15, David Munden/ Popperfoto 160, Gregory Warran/Photoshot 204, Hamish Blair 223, Laurence Griffiths 343, Patrick Eagar/Popperfoto 82, Philip Brown/Popperfoto 48, Tom Jenkins 185, Tom Shaw 401; Jill Furmanovsky 360 above; Shutterstock Prerna Saini 14, Robbie Stephenson/JMP 374.

Publisher's Acknowledgements

Page 325: Extracts of lyrics from "What Kind of Man" by Florence + the Machine reprinted with permission.

Author's acknowledgements

Firstly, a huge thank you to Trevor Davies, my editor at Octopus, and my agent, Nick Walters at David Luxton Associates. I'm very grateful for all the time they have both put into making this book what it is, ever since its conception, especially as it slowly morphed into something far bigger than I'd originally anticipated. During the process, I've been lucky to lean on a lot of people to help me make sense of what it was I was trying to say. First and foremost Barney Douglas, who read this book at least three times at different stages of completion – an incredible gesture – and became a consistent and inspiring confidant throughout. Phil Walker, the first person who persuaded me to write about cricket at all, did a huge preliminary edit followed by cricket fact-proofing at the end, and has also been a constant source of support, common sense and inspiration.

There is no chance that this book would have been written without all the Tailenders: Greg James, Jimmy Anderson, Mark 'Sharky' Sharman and Matt 'Mattchin Tendulkar' Horan. I'm forever grateful for the little show we dreamt up a few years ago and the life that it has miraculously been given in the world. There are a couple of brave souls and great friends who don't even like cricket and still read full drafts for me and helped immeasurably by doing so: thank you Lauren Glasgow and Margaux Katona. So many others have contributed in ways they may or may not realise by talking about ideas, reliving moments with me and/or reading bits and reassuring me I wasn't mad: Lisa Jacobs, Florence Welch, Frank Ryan, Jack Penate, Joel Porter, Rosie Skinner, Callum McLeod, Rachel Wilson,

Jessie Ware, ZeShaan Shamsi, Elliott Andrews, Jake Farey, Morad Khokar, Amy Khokar, Alice Walton, Laura Davidson, Laura Dockerill, Tara Postma, Pamela Jarvis, Gabriel Burne, David White, Lea Anderson, Matt Gray, Lizzie Marion-Davies, Jules Pearson, everyone at RLT, Tamzin Merchant, Katinka Byrn, Cat Hartland, Adam Collins, Vithusan Ehantharajah, Matt Thacker, Jack Leach, Bella Mackie, Barney Ronay, Daniel Rodea-Ryan, Clemmie Telford, George Sewell and Sarah Simmonds. Thanks also to Noel Gallagher, Clare Byrne, Ignition Management and Jill Furmanovsky for licensing the use of the precious 'There and Then' photo for the cover.

A huge thank you to all the people who have worked so diligently and patiently on the book itself: Alex Stetter and Caroline Taggart on the edit; David Eldridge at Two Associates, Juliette Norsworthy and Mark Harrison on the cover; Allison Gonsalves on the production; as well as Megan Brown and Karen Baker on the PR, on which note I'd also like to say thanks to everyone at Octopus as well as David and Rebecca at DLA. I'm proud to be part of this with you.

A massive heartfelt thank you to all the players in conversation in the pages of this book for their time and for being so open to it, all of whom had unknowingly contributed to my life in some way at some stage. Thank you to my uncle, Paul Odell, for his time and the excuse to catch up; to the The Maccabees – band members and extended family – for the best times and to the all-important people from different parts of my past for giving their blessing in being part of the story.

Most of all, thank you to my brothers Hugo and Will and to my dad, Andrew (who has been a huge part of the process throughout) for recognising that this was the way I have remembered all the experiences we have shared, and being so supportive in giving me license to speak about them this way. Finally, thank you to my grandparents Harry and Abla, and to Mum – Lana White – who I hope would have liked this.